Leading for Diversity

Leading for Diversity

How School Leaders Promote Positive Interethnic Relations

❖ Rosemary Henze ❖ Anne Katz ❖
Edmundo Norte ❖ Susan E. Sather
❖ Ernest Walker ❖

CORWIN PRESS, INC.
A Sage Publications Company
Thousand Oaks, California

For information:

Corwin Press, Inc.
A Sage Publications Company
2455 Teller Road
Thousand Oaks, California 91320
www.corwinpress.com

Sage Publications Ltd.
6 Bonhill Street
London EC2A 4PU
United Kingdom

Sage Publications India Pvt. Ltd.
M-32 Market
Greater Kailash I
New Delhi 110 048 India

Printed in the United States of America

Library of Congress Cataloging-in-Publication Data

Leading for diversity: How school leaders promote positive interethnic
relations / by Rosemary Henze . . . [et al.].
    p. cm.
Includes bibliographical references and index.
  ISBN 0-7619-7897-6 (c) — ISBN 0-7619-7898-4 (p)
  1. Multicultural education—United States. 2. Educational
leadership—United States. I. Henze, Rosemary C.
  LC1099.3 .L44 2002
    370.117—dc21
This book is printed on acid-free paper.

                              2002005181

02 03 04 05 06 07 7 6 5 4 3 2 1

Acquisitions Editor:	Robb Clouse
Editorial Assistant:	Erin Clow
Production Editor:	Olivia Weber
Typesetter/Designer:	C&M Digitals (P) Ltd., Chennai, India
Indexer:	Will Ragsdale
Cover Designer:	Michael Dubowe
Production Artist:	Michelle Lee
Cover Photographer:	Dana Freeman

Contents

Acknowledgments

This book as well as this project would not have been possible without collaboration and assistance from many people. Above all, we want to thank the school staff, students, parents, community members, and district administrators who agreed to participate in the study and share with us their practices and approaches toward making schools safe places where interethnic relations can flourish. We feel honored that people took the time to introduce us into their worlds and talk with us about the dilemmas they face as well as the successes they have had. We hope that we have been able to give something back to these school communities—by listening, by reflecting what we learned back to them, and by creating case studies about their schools. Through this book, we hope to share their wisdom with other schools (names of schools and people have been changed throughout the book).

We thank the funders—the Field Initiated Studies Program and the Center for Research on Education, Diversity, and Excellence—for deciding that this project was worthy of support, for the assistance and feedback they have provided, and for the reminders that helped us stay on track.

Many other people provided us with advice, perspective, and assistance along the way. We especially want to thank Tim Beard, Reynaldo Contreras, Fred Erickson, Michèle Foster, Delia Garcia, Ted Hamann, Margaretta Lin, Ray McDermott, Suzanne Peregoy, Judy Shulman, Beverly Tatum, Roland Tharp, Sau-Lim Tsang, Terry Wiley, and Hanh Cao Yu.

The staff at ARC Associates was, as always, supportive. Jeff Abramson, Honny Fong, Yolanda Hoover, JoAnne Kagiwada, and Peter Ting provided the infrastructure that enabled the project to stay within its budget, kept the computers and software running, answered incoming calls, and created an attractive format for our final report. We also want to thank the transcribers—Yvonne Price, Tina Palivos, Matt Kramer, Miles Kramer, and Sara Calderon. Last, but not least, Greg Paulos worked as an intern with the research team in the summer of 1999, providing much needed assistance in the cross case analysis.

In the process of moving from a research project to a book, we appreciate all the assistance from the editors, Robb Clouse, Kylee Liegl, and other staff at Corwin Press.

We have learned much from all of you and appreciate the collaborative spirit that has helped us accomplish our goals.

x HOW SCHOOL
LEADERS
PROMOTE
POSITIVE
INTERETHNIC
RELATIONS

The following reviewers are also gratefully acknowledged:

Susan M. Perlis
Assistant Professor of Education
Marywood University
Scranton, PA

Festus Obiakor
Professor
Department of Exceptional Education
University of Wisconsin–Milwaukee
Milwaukee, WI

Andy Thacker
Principal
John Motley Moorhead High School
Eden, NC

Scott Abrams
Alternative Education Teacher
Marshall Alternative High School
Bend, OR

Marty Krovetz
Professor
Department of Educational Administration and Higher Education
San Jose State University
San Jose, CA

About the Authors

Rosemary Henze, PhD, is an Associate Professor in the Department of Linguistics and Language Development at San Jose State University. She began her career as a teacher of English as a second language and, after receiving her doctorate, worked for 14 years at Art, Research, and Curriculum Associates in Oakland, California, where she assisted school districts in addressing issues of equity and conducted research and evaluation studies focused on bilingual programs, school change, and race relations. She also worked with Native Alaskan, Native Hawaiian, and California Indian groups on issues related to language maintenance, ethnic identity, and bilingual education. In all her work, she seeks to apply scholarly knowledge from anthropology and linguistics to address systemic educational problems.

Anne Katz, PhD, has worked for 20 years as a researcher and evaluator for projects connected with the education of linguistically and culturally diverse students. She served as the coprincipal investigator for the national study focused on successful leadership in diverse school settings that provided the empirical base for this book. As a teacher educator, she has provided and supported professional development in the United States, Brazil, and Egypt. She was instrumental in developing standards for English as a second language through Teachers of English as a Second or Other Language. And she has assisted many school districts in developing more authentic assessments of student performance. In all her work, she has promoted the forging of links between research and the classroom to support meaningful school change.

Edmundo Norte teaches for the Leading for Diversity Master of Science Degree program (a collaboration between California State University, Hayward, and Art, Research, and Curriculum Associates in Oakland, California); is an Education Specialist providing technical assistance in curriculum development to charter schools in Oakland; and is an educational consultant on issues of power and perceptions, educational leadership, Latino/a culture, and transformative education. He began his career as a bilingual, elementary level teacher yet has a wide range of experience working at every level of public education, spanning 20 years. He holds a master's degree from Harvard University and has nearly completed his doctoral work there in the department of Human Development and Psychology with a focus on risk and prevention. He acknowledges that by far his greatest learning experience and challenge to date has

xii HOW SCHOOL
LEADERS
PROMOTE
POSITIVE
INTERETHNIC
RELATIONS

been that of applying his knowledge and experience to the developmentally responsible parenting of his two children—an ongoing labor of love.

Susan E. Sather, PhD, is currently Regional Coordinator for Ventures Education Systems Corp., a whole-school reform model. She is from Montana and, prior to completing her doctorate, spent 18 years as a public school teacher and administrator in New Jersey, Colorado, and California. Those years of practice provide the lens through which she views educational research. She worked for ARC Associates in school reform as well as in the Leading for Diversity research and for West Ed in the Teaching for Diversity case methods project.

Ernest W. Walker is the Diversity Programs Coordinator with Alameda County Social Services Agency. He has a wide range of experiences in diversity and conflict management among African American churches. He has served as a facilitator of the film *The Color of Fear*. He has also worked with churches in conflict, and in strategic planning and team building for nonprofits and government agencies. He is a former consultant with the Alban Institute and is currently a contract mediator with the U.S. Postal Service's REDRESS worksite mediation program. He is past chair of Conciliation Forums of Oakland, a community mediation organization. He also worked as a researcher for ARC Associates, documenting best practices of public schools that manage diversity. He has a bachelor of arts degree from Rutgers University in New Jersey and a master of divinity degree from Princeton Theological Seminary, also in New Jersey. He is author of scholarly articles and is also a part-time instructor on African American religions at Contra Costa College in San Pablo, California.

Introduction

Are you a school principal or district administrator who is concerned about developing more positive relations among different ethnic groups in your school community? Are you a teacher who has taken on a leadership role in your school? Are you a counselor who is in charge of a new conflict resolution program or human relations program? This book is written for K-12 school leaders of all kinds who care about developing school communities that encourage students and adults to get to know one another across lines of difference. It is for people who want to learn not only how to improve the ways they address ethnic or racial conflicts but also how to create a strong foundation of inclusion, a healthy respect for differences, and strategies for addressing the underlying sources of interethnic conflict. When applied, the lessons from this book will help school leaders reduce the likelihood of ethnic or racial violence and, on the more positive side, it will help them create safe, secure, and respectful multiethnic school communities.

But who, one might ask, is a school leader? In this book, we have decided to be very inclusive in the use of this term because the nature of school leadership is shifting rapidly. The term *school leader* used to conjure up a stereotype of a principal, probably a European American man who was able to rally the team with a firm and commanding voice. The best principals, according to the stereotype, were those with charisma—a quality as difficult to measure as love, and harder still to replicate. They were not so much military leaders who ruled with an iron hand and used fear as their primary tool of control, but patriarchal figures who cared about the people in the school community and knew how to reward those who followed their dicta. Nonetheless, they remained the final authority.

Recent scholars and practitioners of leadership, however, question this worn-out image of the school leader. Lambert (1998) urges us to be more concerned with leadership than with leaders:

> When we equate the powerful concept of leadership with the behaviors of one person, we are limiting the achievement of broad-based participation by a community or a society. School leadership needs to be a broad concept that is separated from person, role, and a discrete set of individual behaviors. It needs to be embedded in the school community as a whole. (p. 5)

Furthermore, there is a definite advantage to thinking about leadership in this broad-based way when it comes to making schools more inclusive of diversity.

2 HOW SCHOOL
LEADERS
PROMOTE
POSITIVE
INTERETHNIC
RELATIONS

By making room in leadership for more people with different talents and interests, greater possibilities open up for people of color, and others whose voices have been relatively silent in school leadership, to step into the foreground. Teachers, counselors, parents, community members, and students all have the potential to play formal or informal leadership roles in schools, and they may be especially skilled at leading initiatives that have to do with interethnic relations. Throughout the book, we include examples of people in these less traditional leadership roles as a reminder that the sources of leadership must broaden. We also hope the book will be equally helpful to those who are still in the process of becoming leaders, who may be in administrator and other types of leadership preparation programs.

WHY LEADERS NEED TO FOCUS ON INTERETHNIC RELATIONS

In today's U.S. educational policy context, with its tremendous push toward greater accountability for student achievement, it may seem almost old fashioned to talk about improving intergroup relations. The focus has shifted away from diversity, self-esteem, and other topics that many consider "touchy-feely" or not germane to the bottom line concern with raising test scores. However, the focus on academic achievement and test scores has powerful implications for other areas of school functioning. If educators' efforts are primarily directed toward improving test scores, then less effort is available to focus on social issues in a school. Yet we cannot escape the fact that schools are socializing institutions as well as educating institutions. In fact, they socialize students whether we intentionally plan for that socialization or not. In the absence of any structured plan, schooling tends to reflect the social patterns of the larger society, including its structural inequalities based on class, race, gender, and so on. Not only does it reflect these unequal relations; it also tends to reproduce them over and over again. (Bowles & Gintis, 1976). Of course, social reproduction theories like these have been criticized for being too deterministic. "In such a view there is no room for human agency. Such a social theory, when applied to education, implies that neither the domestic minority students nor their teachers can do anything positive together educationally" (Erickson, 1987, p. 343).

If leaders see their task as managing the status quo of the school and following, to the best of their ability, the latest policy dictates to raise achievement, social reproduction theorists like Bowles and Gintis (1976) will probably be more right than wrong. Such schools will tend to remain vehicles for the reproduction of the class structure, race relations, and conflicts of the larger society. If, however, leaders and other educators take seriously their "human agency" as Erickson (1987) suggests, then there is a great deal that can be done in local settings such as schools and districts to alter the status quo of intergroup relations and patterns of dominance and subordination. We have seen evidence that local leaders, be they principals, teachers, students, parents, community activists, or other educators, can, in fact, make a profound difference in the way schools socialize students and adults.

There are at least three reasons for leaders to use their human agency to improve interethnic relations, as well as group relations more generally:

1. One reason is that students are unlikely to focus on academic learning if they feel unsafe or threatened at school. Maslow (1968) theorized in the 1950s that a sense of safety and security is a prerequisite for higher levels of human development. If we want to raise academic achievement across all groups and not leave low-income students of color and poor white students even further behind than they already are, we need to create a strong foundation for their learning. This foundation includes freedom from physical violence and freedom from slurs and harassment based on ethnicity, language, religion, and other aspects of identity.

2. Another reason is that in today's increasingly multicultural school and work environments, students and adults need more than ever to learn how to get along, and work productively, with those who are different from themselves. And particularly at times when there are crises such as the September 11, 2001, attacks on the World Trade Center and the Pentagon, we are reminded that relations across lines of difference are *always* in need of preventive attention so that they do not explode into hate crimes and violence.

3. A third reason, and for us the most powerful, is that we believe schools should become "laboratories for a more just society than the one we live in now . . . . Classrooms [and schools] can be places of hope, where students and teachers gain glimpses of the kind of society we could live in and where students could learn the academic and critical skills needed to make it a reality" (Bigelow & Miner, 1994, p. 4).

This book urges educational leaders to reinvigorate a focus on developing positive human relations as a serious part of the school's mission, along with promoting academic achievement.

HOW THE LEADING FOR DIVERSITY PROJECT GOT STARTED

The impetus that led to this book first emerged from a group of principals in the San Francisco Bay Area who, in 1995, met with several staff members from ARC Associates, a nonprofit organization in Oakland, California, to discuss issues they face as leaders in ethnically diverse schools and possible professional development that could help them resolve these issues. Of course, they raised many complex problems, none of which had easy solutions. Here is a sampling of the questions that were related to ethnic diversity:

- How do we address the persistent underachievement of African American and Latino students, especially males, in Bay Area schools?

- How do we increase the number of faculty members and administrators of color so that students will have more role models who look like them and understand their cultural backgrounds?

4 HOW SCHOOL
LEADERS
PROMOTE
POSITIVE
INTERETHNIC
RELATIONS

• How can we increase parent involvement among non-English-speaking parents?

• How can we deal with teachers who still hold racist, ethnocentric views of students of color?

• Many of these school leaders expressed a particular urgency when it came to interethnic or interracial conflict. How, they wanted to know, do effective school leaders address racial or ethnic conflicts? How do they develop positive relations among the different sectors of the school community? Are there any models we can look at?

Several of the leaders in this group explained that they had faced serious gang violence in their schools and were still seeking ways to respond more effectively. Others were concerned about tensions that seemed to be just under the surface. One high school principal described her concern about how quickly students and parents seemed to accuse teachers of racism whenever teachers referred students to the office for behavior issues. She felt the white teachers were becoming more and more lax and letting problem behavior slide rather than confront such accusations. A middle school principal described his frustration with the way students as well as faculty members tended to self-segregate at lunch and during breaks. On the one hand, he felt it was healthy for students to develop a positive sense of ethnic identity, but, on the other hand, he didn't like it that other students were sometimes actively excluded.

As these examples illustrate, the interethnic conflicts these principals were concerned about encompassed a range that included violent encounters as well as what might be more aptly described as simmering undertones of hostility or exclusion on the basis of race or ethnicity. They were well aware that the violent encounters represented a bubbling up of tensions that are always present in any sector of our society, given its history of racist policies and practices and our continuing struggles over present-day issues such as affirmative action, immigration policy, welfare, bilingual education, and democratic principles in the wake of terrorism.

One would think that issues of such great concern would be highly visible in the preparation of school leaders. Surprisingly, though, we learned that while diversity is given a certain degree of lip service in administrative credentialing programs, these leaders had not been prepared with tools to analyze racial or ethnic conflict, or with specific strategies for building positive interethnic communities. They were trying to acquire these competencies on the job, but they didn't know of any available models they could turn to for guidance. When we attempted to help them locate good models, we realized that this was an area in great need of research so that positive practices could be brought to light and shared.

As a result of these initial meetings and inquiries, the Leading for Diversity Research Project was developed. We focused on two central research questions:

1. How can leaders effectively address racial or ethnic conflicts?

2. How can leaders create a foundation for safety and respect so that relationships among diverse groups and individuals can flourish?

In order to answer these questions, we conducted case studies of 21 schools across the United States where the student population was diverse, where there was some history of racial and ethnic tensions in the school or surrounding community, and where the leadership had taken proactive steps to improve relations among the different groups. This research (Henze, Katz, Norte, Sather, & Walker, 1999) spanned 3 years, from 1996 to 1999, and was funded by two U.S. Department of Education grants.[1] Appendix A provides a description of the methodology.

WHAT THE LEADING FOR DIVERSITY STUDY CAN (AND CAN'T) TEACH US

What we have learned from this study is, in one sense, very simple: School leaders can, without a doubt, make a positive difference in interethnic relations. This message is a vital one to carry forward because schools, and the adults who operate them, are often blamed for everything that is wrong with the educational system. In particular, they are blamed for perpetuating inequalities that make racial tensions worse rather than better. While some of this blame is justified in some cases, it is important to keep in mind that individuals in leadership roles can do a great deal to create a local environment for positive change—even in the midst of larger, systemic inequities. How they create this positive environment is the subject of this book. The 21 schools in the study offer a number of insights that can help those in school leadership roles put into practice the ideals of safety, respect, and social justice in diverse schools.

The schools in the study spanned all levels—elementary, middle, and high school. We found that different levels of schooling called for certain differences in approach. For example, high schools tended to have more ethnic-studies classes than middle schools, and we found no such classes in elementary schools. There was much more emphasis on parent involvement in the elementary schools and middle schools than there was at the high schools. Differences such as these take into account both the developmental level of students and the different sizes and structures of elementary versus middle or high schools. Throughout the book, we share examples from all three levels of schooling in the hope that educators at all levels will find useful and relevant information.

Many people have asked us, on hearing about the study, whether we also studied practices that address homophobia, discrimination against differently abled people, classism, and so on. We agree that there is a need for more attention in schools to all these areas of intolerance and oppression. However, the vast range of *isms* in our society would have called for too large and unwieldy a study. Given our limited resources and time, we decided to remain focused on issues of race and ethnicity. On the other hand, we believe there are many commonalities linking all forms of intolerance and oppression, whether people are the subject of harassment because of race and ethnicity, gender, sexual orientation, physical disabilities, or any other kinds of difference. It is likely that many of the same approaches discussed in the following pages could be adapted to addressing other forms of intolerance.

Another question that sometimes arises is whether the study's findings can be applied outside the United States. Since we did not base the study in any other

6 HOW SCHOOL
LEADERS
PROMOTE
POSITIVE
INTERETHNIC
RELATIONS

countries, we are not able to generalize to non-U.S. contexts. This is not to say that school leaders in other countries will find nothing of value here. Certainly, those who work in ethnically diverse schools will find material here that they can adapt or use. However, the educational policy context may be very different in other countries—for example, many other countries have a national curriculum that all schools have to follow, whereas in the United States, there is still considerable choice at the state and local level. Even for U.S. readers, it is important to remember that most innovations cannot be lifted as-is from one context and placed into another. There is always a need for including local stakeholders in the process of decision making and adapting the innovation to fit the local context.

WHO WE ARE

In the traditions of contemporary anthropology and ethnographic research, which necessarily involve a great deal of interaction with the people and settings one is studying, it is important for researchers to grapple with their subjectivities. In other words, the idea that researchers are objective, uninvolved beings who somehow translate complex social realities into research findings without any bias or underlying values is untenable today. Rather than pretending complete objectivity, researchers in this tradition are urged to give readers some insight into their position or particular angle of vision, for this can "enable and inhibit particular kinds of insights" (Rosaldo, 1989, p. 19).

Without going into great detail about our personal lives, we want to give you, the readers, a flavor of who we are as individuals and as a team. Our biographical sketches in About the Authors introduce us. We are the same people who conducted the Leading for Diversity Research Project. We were all employed at the time by ARC Associates, a nonprofit organization in Oakland, California, which is dedicated to promoting educational excellence and equity for students of diverse backgrounds. We all had various experiences we brought to bear on working in the field of multicultural education, social justice, and leadership. We viewed our team as an important mirror for our work on the study. Because we are an ethnically diverse group ourselves, and because issues of race, ethnicity, and leadership formed the center of our study, we found many opportunities to examine our own beliefs and practices, both individually and as a team. When we had conflicts within the team, we often turned the observer's lens that we used in schools on ourselves. When we shared stories with each other about the schools we were spending so much time in, somebody always had a different perspective. Often, that perspective was filtered through the lenses of our racial and ethnic background (African American, Latino, or European American), our gender, or our economic background. But equally often, it was not a matter of any of the above but, rather, a matter of family history or personal style.

The point is that we saw ourselves as continuing learners, particularly about the power and depth of race, ethnicity, class, and other differences, and we had to be willing to confront some of our own biases in doing this work. We established an agreement at the beginning of the project to discuss differences openly. This internal work allowed us to see how difficult this must be for schools, which are much larger and more diverse than our small team of five. It also served as a reminder that school leaders, in order to be proactive in

---

Box I.1

Nationality:

Race:

Ethnicity:

Culture:

---

the area of diversity, need to practice internally what they are preaching externally. The idea that school leaders need to teach students about diversity and intergroup relations assumes a one-directional flow of information, from those with more formal authority and power to those with less. But proactive leaders recognize that the flow goes both ways; they, too, must participate in the learning process.

DEFINING KEY TERMS

Before we embark on an exploration of what school leaders can do to improve relations among racial or ethnic groups on campus, it is worth taking time to consider what is meant by *nationality, race, racism, ethnicity,* and *culture*—especially since these terms tend to be used loosely in many everyday conversations. Students in high schools frequently ask each other, "What's your race?" and the answers can vary enormously from "I'm half black and half Japanese" to "I'm from Lebanon." Any response that refers to skin color, ancestry, language background, or nationality may be deemed an acceptable answer. There are, however, distinctions that are important to understand if we want to move beyond fuzzy thinking in dealing with our differences. We open this section with an activity that is designed to reveal any problems associated with the terminology.

ACTIVITY 1: DEFINING TERMS

This activity can be done in any preservice or inservice setting. The purpose is to come to grips with the overlapping use of the terms *nationality, race, ethnicity,* and *culture* and to begin to sort out some distinctions. The facilitator should give every participant a 3-inch-by-5-inch (or 5-inch-by-7-inch) index card. On the left side, ask them to list the words *nationality, race, ethnicity,* and *culture* (or use the form in Box I.1). Then follow the steps outlined below.

1. **Individually:** Take a few minutes to think about, and write on the card, your own nationality, race, ethnicity, and culture. For the race category, try to use the racial categories in the U.S. census—American Indian or Alaska Native, Asian, black or African American, Native Hawaiian or other Pacific Islander, and white (U.S. Census Bureau, 2001).

8 HOW SCHOOL
LEADERS
PROMOTE
POSITIVE
INTERETHNIC
RELATIONS

2. **Whole group:** Did you have any difficulty deciding what to write for any of these categories? What problems did you encounter?

3. **Jigsaw:** Divide into five groups. Each group will be responsible for reading and summarizing one of the sections that follows (on nationality and the problems with the terms race, racism, ethnicity, and culture). Make a note of any comments or questions you have about this section.

4. **Jigsaw, continued:** Now form groups of five, each with one representative from the previous groups. Representatives should teach the rest of the group what they learned and discussed in the previous group. Again, make a note of any questions or comments that come up in the group.

5. **Still in the same groups:** Read Why School Leaders Need to Understand Terms Associated With Race and Ethnicity. As a group, discuss what you could do as leaders in your schools to help others understand these concepts better?

Nationality

Most adults will not have any difficulty understanding the term nationality. It means the country or countries of which you are a citizen. In some cases, people have dual citizenship. In order to know this, one has to know the citizenship laws of the countries in question. In the United States, one can be a citizen by being born in the United States or born of American citizens in a foreign country. Immigrants to the United States can also become naturalized citizens by applying for and taking a citizenship test. Many students in high school and earlier are not sure of their nationality and whether they have dual nationality or not.

Race

The term race is problematic. It has been used to describe physical differences of populations which are then erroneously associated with mental capacities and the ability to achieve a high level of civilization. In the 1800s, it was common to hear phrases such as lower races, inferior races, superannuated races, backward races, mongrel races, primitive peoples, savages, and so forth. Traditional racial classifications in the United States include white or European, American Indian, black, and Asian. Yet, biologically, science has shown that there are more genetic differences within so-called races than there are between them. "Such facts render the concept of race and the continuance of race classification erroneous and obsolescent" (Montagu, 1997, p. 46).

Although Montagu's work was originally published in 1942, the message that race is not a valid biological category is little known among the public. Many people in the United States and other countries continue to believe and behave as if there were separate, distinct races. For this reason, we can say that race is a concept that is socially constructed, even though it is not biologically valid.[2] One might well ask, if there is no scientific validity to the concept of race, why do we continue to use it in gathering data for the census, for school districts, health services, and other public entities? According to Park (2000), "If we don't have the data, we can't track inequities and patterns across social categories. We can't move policy without data and analysis." It is precisely because racial discrimination has been real, even though race is not, that we have to continue to monitor inequities by examining data across racial and ethnic categories.

Racism

A definition of racism that has been applied often in workshops on racism is the following: Racism is prejudice based on perceived racial categories plus the institutionalized power used to keep people of that group down. A short-hand formulation is racism = racial prejudice + institutional power (Lindsey, Robins, & Terrell, 1999, p. 98).

Interestingly enough, this definition itself can engender conflict because it has been used to argue that people of color cannot be racist. This makes some people who identify as white defensive, and they may cite examples in which they feel individuals of color have practiced racism against them.

This is a good point, and it leads to another useful distinction—that between *institutional racism* and *individual racial prejudice* (Nieto, 1996). Certainly, any individual can perpetrate acts of racial prejudice on any other individual. Thus African Americans as individuals can be racially prejudiced against white people, Asians can be racially prejudiced against Latinos, and so on. But African Americans as a group do not currently have the political or economic power in the United States to keep whites down, so in that sense, no matter how much racial prejudice individual African Americans might have for whites, they cannot be said to be practicing institutional racism.

Because racism has, typically, been framed in terms of black and white relations, it is important to point out that racism affects different groups in different ways. Asian Americans, for example, are subject to a different kind of racism than African Americans because of the perception that they do too well, as suggested by their overrepresentation in elite colleges and universities (Omi, 2000). As a result, Asian Americans may experience racism in the form of invisibility, marginality, and neglect.

Ethnicity

Ethnicity is a less loaded term than race. It refers to a social group that shares a sense of group membership, culture, language, political and economic

10 HOW SCHOOL
LEADERS
PROMOTE
POSITIVE
INTERETHNIC
RELATIONS

interests, history, and an ancestral geographical base (Wijeyesinghe, Griffin, & Love, 1997). Yup'ik Eskimos, Swedes, Haitians, Nubians, Basques, and the Irish are all examples of ethnic groups. Notice that some ethnic groups coincide with nationalities, as do Haitians in Haiti, whereas others exist as one of several ethnic groups in a nation-state (e.g., Basques in Spain), or across several nation-states (e.g., Nubians live on both sides of the Egypt–Sudan border).

The concept of ethnicity is a useful antidote to the biologically flawed concept of race. It helps people become more specific and historically grounded in their naming of identities. Instead of white people identifying themselves as a race, they can identify as Scots-Irish, German, Slavic, and so forth. Asians can identify as Malaysian, Japanese, Vietnamese, Laotian, and so on. A problem arises, however, when people are unable to trace their ethnic roots. In the United States, slavery and the forced break up of families and loss of native languages obliterated the historical record of which slaves came from which tribes or regions of Africa. In other countries—Cuba, for example, although there was also European colonization and slavery—families were allowed to stay intact, and, as a result, Cubans of African ancestry are much more connected to their ethnic origins as Yoruba, Congolese, and other ethnic groups.

Ethnicity is also a form of identity that people choose and construct to varying degrees to suit different purposes. For example, Hensel (1996) describes how Yup'ik Eskimos in Alaska may, in certain settings, pass as real or fictive whites.

> Successful passing carries its own risks as well as rewards. The reward is the ability to appropriate unevenly distributed cultural capital, such as knowledge, status, wealth, opportunity. . . . The costs are possible rejection by one's own group, as well as (possibly) increased stress inherent in such a bicultural balancing act. . . . People are likely to show themselves differently in different situations, for different purposes. (Hensel, 1996, pp. 84-85)

Given the many ethnic groups in urban and suburban schools these days and the increasing numbers of students who are multiethnic and multiracial, one can imagine that the possibilities for claiming different ethnicities vary enormously from moment to moment and from setting to setting. One of the implications of this variability for school leaders is that they cannot assume that people will stay fixed in a single ethnic or racial identity. Schools that force people to choose an ethnic identity and remain there merely reinforce old divisions. Schools where it is an accepted and valued practice to explore ethnicity and acknowledge how identities can shift depending on context are more likely to help students and adults bridge racial and ethnic divides.

Culture

Culture is a much-contested concept among anthropologists. Some have even suggested doing away with it entirely (e.g., Wolcott, 1991). In the past, anthropologists and others assumed that culture was a kind of package deal. Cultures were believed to have neat boundaries, and, inside those boundaries, were all sorts of traditions and structures, such as marriage practices, gender roles, religion, death rituals, childrearing practices, language, power and authority structures, food, and so on. "In the 1940's, when I began my fieldwork, everybody knew what culture was—culture was what everybody had in a predictable, bounded sense; everyone [was] recognizable by their laundry list of cultural traits" (Spindler, 1996). The one area anthropologists agree on is that culture is learned; that is, it is not an inherited trait. Most other notions of culture are now hotly contested.

Contemporary concepts of culture are beginning to take into account the following understandings:

1. There is tremendous variation in the cultural repertoire within a given cultural group, depending on age, gender, occupation, economic niche, and many other factors.

2. Cultural borderlands, with much sharing and borrowing, are more the rule than the exception these days, especially among industrialized nations and in our increasingly interconnected cyberspaces.

3. We all actively construct and change culture, as well as acquire parts of it through socialization—the only culture that remains static is a culture that has died.

4. Much of culture is implicit—foods-and-festivals depictions give a false picture of culture as a visible, ritualized set of practices and ignore the less-visible aspects of culture, such as the way we respond to a compliment or how we know when it is appropriate to hug somebody.[3]

Why School Leaders Need to Understand Terms Associated With Race and Ethnicity

The distinctions among terms such as race, ethnicity, nationality, and culture are important for school leaders to understand for at least two reasons. First, if race and racism are socially constructed (not biologically determined), then people have the power to socially deconstruct them. In other words, we do not have to accept racial divisions and racism as givens. We can work to change other people's misperceptions and misinformation. School leaders in positions of authority, such as principals, district administrators, and county superintendents, stand in powerful positions from which to influence others. Their policies and practices are highly visible and can shape the way others perceive human diversity.

Second, understanding the distinctions among the social terms race, ethnicity, nationality, and culture could potentially become part of the curriculum in all schools, providing an epistemological base from which students could learn about group relations. Studying about the biological fallacy of race could become part of the science curriculum in every state, while untangling concepts of ethnicity, nationality, and culture could be an explicit part of social studies curriculum. Professional development for teachers would need to ensure that they are well prepared to teach these concepts. Providing a more scientific, biological, and anthropological basis for the study of diversity among students would help to drive the "touchy-feely" reputation of diversity studies into a more academic vein, giving it greater prestige and respectability and

12 HOW SCHOOL
LEADERS
PROMOTE
POSITIVE
INTERETHNIC
RELATIONS

heightening the chances that district policymakers will see it as a valuable addition to the curriculum.[4] Curriculum leaders at all levels can use their positions to advocate for such changes.

ACTIVITY 2: MORE TERMS FOR GROUPS

This activity can be used as a follow up to Activity 1. The purpose is to extend the discussion of socially constructed terms to include other terms used to create distinctions among groups. For example, we know that class or economic differences can create divisions among people even if they share common ethnic origins.

1. **Small groups:** Think about students at your own schools and consider these questions:

   A. What group terms do you hear students using to categorize each other?

   B. How are these terms used to include or exclude people?

   C. How do students define these terms? Are their definitions or meanings different from the ones adults give to the same terms?

   D. What consequences are there to belonging or not belonging to specific groups?

2. **Whole group:** Share your responses to the above questions.

3. **Whole group:** What impact do these groups have on the climate at your school?

SUGGESTIONS FOR USING THIS BOOK

You might wish to use this book in several ways. If you are an individual reading it for your own learning, you can read it in the usual linear way from beginning to end, or you can skip around. If you read it from beginning to end, you will be moving deductively, from broad generalizations to specific instances of those generalizations. If you are a person who likes to process information inductively, from concrete experiences to broader generalizations, you might want to begin with a couple of the cases in Part II, which are based on actual dilemmas and problems that school leaders struggled with. The cases also have some learning activities embedded in them to help you make sense of the problem. These activities will refer you to some of the theories and tools in Part I.

This book can be used in a number of group formats. If you are a professor of educational administration or teacher education, you might include it as part of a course that deals with issues of equity and diversity. If you are a staff developer working for a district, you might consider using sections of the book (especially the cases in Part II) in professional development sessions for leaders. Or you might be a member of a school-based study group of practitioners looking for ideas and strategies to create a more positive interethnic school community. Most of the activities in the book assume that readers are already working in schools or district offices, or at least are familiar with a particular school. The activities include some space for writing down responses to questions, though admittedly these spaces are too limited to allow for much extended reflection. Readers are urged to go beyond the spaces provided.

At the end of the book, there are two resources that you might find useful. Appendix B is a list of Resources for Schools. This is a list of videos, curricula, and professional development materials that were used by schools in the Leading for Diversity research project. We have provided short descriptions and contact information whenever possible. Another resource is the checklist in Appendix C, which aligns content from this book with the educational administration standards developed by the Interstate School Leaders Licensure Consortium. Those who are using the book as part of an administrative credentialing program will find this helpful in mapping out how the content of the book addresses the six standards.

NOTES

1. This study was funded through two grants, one through the Field Initiated Studies program (PR# R308F60028), and another through the Center for Research on Education, Diversity, and Excellence (CREDE), PR# R306A60001. Both grants were administered by the Office of Educational Research and Improvement (OERI), U.S. Department of Education (USDOE). The content, findings, and opinions expressed here are those of the authors and do not necessarily represent the positions or policies of CREDE, OERI, or USDOE.

2. For more information about anthropological research on race, see the American Anthropological Association (1998).

3. Further explanations of these concepts can be found in Rosaldo (1989), González (1995a), and Henze and Hauser (1999).

4. For a case study showing how diversity studies were made a requirement in one district, see Henze (2001).

Part I

A Framework for Developing Positive Interethnic Relations

In theory, there is no difference between theory and practice, but in practice, there is.

—Anonymous

Developing positive relations among diverse groups of students and adults can seem like an overwhelming task. Since it involves virtually every student and every adult member of the school community (parents too), and since interethnic relations are potentially an issue in every setting—from classroom instruction and special assemblies to sports events, parent meetings, and faculty meetings—it can seem impossible to focus the task on anything manageable. Where does one even start such a process? That is why we wrote this book. In our own lives, we have noticed that the things that seem overwhelming tend not to get done because they are so daunting, they discourage us from even taking a first step. We don't know where to begin, so we don't begin at all.

Breaking these overwhelmingly large tasks into manageable chunks is one way to make them less daunting and more doable. Thus Part I is organized into stages that (more or less) represent the process we believe is necessary to improve interethnic relations. Within these stages, we will present various tools that can

16 HOW SCHOOL
LEADERS
PROMOTE
POSITIVE
INTERETHNIC
RELATIONS

be used at a school site or in a professional development course to help you think about and assess what is going on in your particular context. Because we believe that no journey of school change should be undertaken without self-reflection, we begin with a chapter that is intended to help present and future school leaders look at their own experiences, assumptions, and biases. Although the chapters that follow are presented as part of a process, they are not as linear as it might seem. The organization of a book requires one to choose an organizational scheme, and since change is essentially a process, it made sense to present it as such. But we also know that school change is a very complex process, not a simple matter of a first step leading directly to a second step and so on. In school change, the stages that comprise the process often overlap, and one often has to revisit an earlier stage, which then suggests a somewhat different direction. Rather than a straight line, the process is more like a spiral.

As we present different aspects of the change process, we will also present several theories that shed light on ethnic relations and leadership. Theory is traditionally separated from practice and is often considered irrelevant from a practitioner's standpoint. We think that this separation needs to change for several reasons. First, it assumes that theories have no practical applications, that they exist on some ethereal, scholarly plane that has nothing to do with the real world. But a good social theory explains a number of phenomena that can be observed in everyday life. It may not be the only explanation, and a better theory may be proposed later, but it helps us link diverse social phenomena into some kind of overarching explanation. The problem, from a practitioner's viewpoint, is that theory is often expressed in such a way that it cannot be easily translated into action. Secondly, the separation of theory from practice assumes that ordinary people (practitioners) aren't theory builders. In fact, however, all of us theorize from time to time, whenever we try to explain patterns, such as similarities, differences, interdependencies, and so forth, that we have observed among students, among schools, or among instructional strategies.

In Part I, our intent is to bring a number of different tools and theories to the attention of practitioners in a way that enables them to use these resources to solve problems and improve schools. Activities that can be used in professional development settings are included where they seem appropriate in the text.

1

Leading From Within

It would hardly be fish who discovered the existence of water.

—Clyde Kluckhohn (1949, p. 11)

One of the characteristics of proactive leaders in the schools we visited during the study was their courage. They were able to look within themselves and honestly confront their own biases and shortcomings, and they did the work they needed to do in the world. They seemed to share an assumption that internal work is necessary in order for external work in the school community to be authentic and effective. This courage to start with yourself and examine deeply held beliefs is also one of the essential qualities of leaders who foster resiliency in their schools (Krovetz, 1999). Robert Cohen,[1] one of the principals in the Leading for Diversity study, shared what was involved in his own process of self-reflection:

> When I went through my counseling program for my master's, we spent a lot of time in self-analysis, and it was eye-opening for me. We bought into the notion that in order to heal others we had to know ourselves and open ourselves. We needed to look at our values and beliefs, and at the difference between what we know and what we say and do. . . . I don't think you can just teach diversity; I think you have to live diversity.

RECOGNIZING ONE'S LOCATION

Key Question for Leaders

- How have my experiences and social and ethnic background influenced my perceptions, attitudes, beliefs, and behaviors?

Before we can begin to unravel how our perceptions, attitudes, and beliefs affect our work in schools, we have to first become aware of how our social context has shaped our worldview. One of the many advantages of traveling in other countries, or even in different communities within our own country, is that it can make us reflect on our own culture and social environment in a new way. When we return to our familiar surroundings, they don't seem so familiar anymore. Spindler & Spindler (1982) called this "making the familiar strange" (p. 23). The contrast between other ways of living and our own way raises awareness that our way is not the only normal way, and that our beliefs and assumptions are not universally shared.

The jolting experience of culture shock can lead eventually in two directions. For some, it results in an increased appreciation of how their social environment—the water in the quote by Kluckhohn—shapes their most basic attitudes, beliefs, and behaviors. They realize, for example, that not everyone values time in the same way that U.S. corporate culture does, or that middle class white ways of socializing children place a premium on the individual (as opposed to the family collective) and encourage competition between individuals. For others, spending time in other communities or cultures seems to have the opposite effect—increasing their sense that their way is definitely "the best" and that "those people" are disorganized, lawless, dirty, and don't care about education. Unfortunately, this book is not a ticket to another community or country, but we hope that you will find opportunities to travel somewhat outside your usual milieu so that you can experience more directly the ideas we are discussing here.

THE CIRCLE OF LIFE EXPERIENCES AND PERCEPTIONS

We all have a particular location or vantage point from which we look at and experience the world. Our location includes our culture and language, our socioeconomic position relative to the dominant culture, our informal and formal education, and the physical characteristics (gender, race and ethnicity, age, physical capabilities, sexual orientation, etc.) through which all of our personal experiences have been filtered. Figure 1.1 illustrates our different locations in relation to events in the world.

In looking at the circle of perceptions, you might wonder why the arrows are of differing lengths. Shouldn't all perceptions be considered equal? In theory, yes, but the reality is that in the social worlds we inhabit, some locations are privileged. A 30-something white male carrying a briefcase and wearing a

Figure 1.1 The Circle of Life Experiences and Perceptions

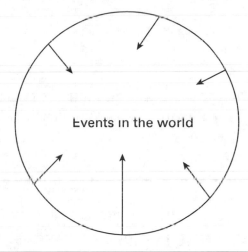

Events in the world

SOURCE: Developed by Norte (2001a).

suit, who is giving an account of a traffic accident, is more likely to be believed by the police than is an 18-year-old black male wearing baggy pants and a T-shirt. How we come to stand at a particular place on the circle, and how society differentially treats those in different locations, creates very divergent experiences among those who occupy different locations. Not only are our perceptions of events and their meanings different but also our society values some perceptions more than others, thus creating a second layer of difference. Our perceptions of the world are shaped in part by how the world has treated or responded to us. Knowing that one's perception is less likely to be valued can have numerous negative repercussions on individuals, from making them stronger in their pursuit of equal opportunity to making them reluctant to participate in the mainstream society or dominant culture or actively antagonistic toward it.

ACTIVITY 3: EXPERIENCING A DIFFERENT NEIGHBORHOOD OR COMMUNITY

Spend some time in a neighborhood that has a different ethnic and class makeup from your own. If you are working in a school with diverse students, choose a neighborhood that is home to some of the students. Do something you would ordinarily do in your own neighborhood, such as eat lunch in a restaurant, get a haircut, or go shopping for groceries. Pay attention to what people are doing and how they are doing it, including what languages or dialects they are using. Try to just observe, without judging. Also pay attention to how you are feeling. When you get home, try to answer these questions:

1. Was there anything that made you uncomfortable? What was it?

2. What does this discomfort tell you about your own socialization and worldview?

3. Were there things you saw or heard that you didn't understand? If so, what questions do you have? How could you try to find answers to these questions?

MULTIPLE PERSPECTIVES AND THE MYTH OF OBJECTIVITY

Key Question for Leaders

- How are my perceptions similar to or different from those of others at my school, for instance, people who play a different role in the school than I do and people whose ethnic and social backgrounds are different from mine?

You may have heard the parable about several blind Sufis who were all asked to describe what an elephant is. An elephant was brought before them, and each Sufi reached out and touched the elephant in order to describe it. One said, "An elephant is like a tree trunk." Another said "An elephant is like a big wall with a rough surface." A third said, "An elephant is like a snake." The fourth said, "An elephant is like a fan." And so on. Each Sufi was, of course, touching only one part of the elephant—the leg seemed like a tree trunk; the side of the torso like a wall; the trunk like a snake; and the ear like a fan. Each Sufi thought he was being objective but was actually bringing past experiences into his task of perception. Each Sufi, likewise, was unable to grasp the complexity of the whole elephant.

It is a recipe for conflict to act in the world based on the assumption that we have an objective view of it. In contrast, to assume that we each have a valid view of the world and have something to learn from each other's perspectives is the basis for mutual respect and appreciation.

Some will have an immediate reaction to this set of statements and will want to pose challenges such as, "Oh, so you believe anything goes, eh? How about female genital mutilation, are we supposed to accept that as a valid worldview? This sounds like cultural relativism gone amok!"

Actually, our point is more subtle. We are not suggesting that one needs to agree with any or all perspectives, but rather that it is useful and enlightening to try to understand why people have those perspectives. In other words, why and how did other people come to see the world in their particular way?

When we improve our ability to understand multiple perspectives, it gives us a more complete picture. As educators, it is especially important for us to recognize that we, too, are subjective and that this is a part of being human. We don't need to feel guilty about being subjective and, in fact, coming to terms with our subjectivity frees us to move around the circle of perception—to understand and respect other perspectives, to embrace more of the picture rather than only one small corner. We are supposed to be educating young people to be tolerant and respectful of others, so we need to cultivate those skills in ourselves first. Robert Cohen, Principal of Sojourner Truth High School, said, "It's so helpful for me to just try to shift, to just try to see the other perspective. That ability to empathize, to step outside of yourself and say, 'Well, of course, so and so is angry and resistant. I would be, too, if I were in his (or her) position.'"

Physically traveling outside our comfort zone, as suggested in the previous section, can be one way to learn about other perspectives. Another way, which can easily be accomplished in your school or wherever you are, is to consistently ask open-ended questions (as opposed to yes or no questions), with the aim of understanding how a person came to see the world in their particular way. Of course, doing this in an inquisition-like way or putting people on the spot isn't going to help. The best learning of this kind takes place within respectful, trusting relationships that are the basis for honest dialogue, especially across differences. Educational leaders can, as part of their roles, establish structural opportunities for sustained, purposeful, and positive interaction with those who are different from themselves. We will give examples of such structures in Chapters 6 and 7.

THE LEGACY OF RACISM

Key Question for Leaders

- What has been the impact of racism in my life?

Unfortunately, even though the practice of slavery and discrimination based on race are no longer legal in the United States, racism still affects all of us in this country, whether we are African American, European American, Dominican American, or a recent immigrant from India or Taiwan. The influence of racism is still clearly visible to most people of color, who can usually name recent incidents in which they felt they were targeted in some way because of their race or ethnicity. Young blacks and Latinos frequently recount experiences when they walked into a store and were followed by security guards, while young white people rarely have the same experience. When the economy is in a downturn, people of Asian, African, and Latino backgrounds are often accused of draining the welfare coffers and burdening the educational system, even though there is agreement among economists that immigrants actually contribute far more in taxes to the American economy than they use in government services (Simon, 1999).

However, people of color are not the only ones to experience the damaging effects of racism. European Americans are also hurt but in a different way. McIntosh (1989) eloquently explains this:

As a white person, I realized I had been taught about racism as something which puts others at a disadvantage, but had been taught not to see its corollary aspect, white privilege, which puts me at an advantage. . . . I have come to see white privilege as a package of unearned assets which I can count on cashing in each day, but about which I was meant to remain oblivious. (p. 10)

Some of these unearned assets are represented in such statements as

- I can be sure that my children will be given curricular materials that testify to the existence of their race.
- Whether I use checks, credit cards, or cash, I can count on my skin color not to work against the appearance of financial reliability.
- I can swear, or dress in secondhand clothes, or not answer letters, without having people attribute these choices to the bad morals, the poverty, or the illiteracy of my race.
- I can do well in challenging situations without being called a credit to my race.
- If a traffic cop pulls me over or if the IRS audits my tax return, I can be sure I haven't been singled out because of my race.
- I can choose blemish cover or bandages in "flesh" color and have them more or less match my skin. (pp. 10-11)

McIntosh points out that in recognizing these assets, she was also forced to give up the "myth of meritocracy. . . . If these things are true, this is not such a free country; one's life is not what one makes it; many doors open for certain people through no virtues of their own" (p. 11). She suggests that these unearned advantages for a small number of people "prop up those in power, and serve to keep power in the hands of the same groups who have most of it already" (p. 12).

When we realize that racism and its effects are part of the water we swim in—no matter what ethnicity we claim and what the color of our skin is—we are in a position to begin the next stage of our internal journey, unlearning racism.

UNLEARNING RACISM

Key Question for Leaders

- How can I develop the knowledge, consciousness, and vision that are essential to leading efforts to create more inclusive, just, and healthy communities in diverse schools?

A relatively new lens for understanding the roots of interethnic and racial conflict that offers a very pragmatic, yet ultimately hopeful approach, is that of unlearning racism. There is a generation of youth growing up today in the United States who, for the first time in history, are learning about the process of unlearning racism as part of their coming of age in diverse communities. The idea of unlearning racism is a very powerful one because its basic assumptions are that

1. The practice of and participation in racism are learned

2. Racism exists, to some degree, in all people who have grown up in societies that have racist elements

3. Racism is something that we all have the capacity to unlearn

These are powerful assumptions that differ greatly from many ideologies and social theories that have held dominance in the past, as we noted in the introduction where we discussed the social construction of race.

While the concept of unlearning racism may not, as yet, have reached critical mass as a generally accepted assumption in society, its acceptance seems to be growing, particularly among today's youth. One example is the People's Institute for Survival and Beyond (see Organizations in Resource B). It supports trainers who travel throughout the country conducting workshops in unlearning racism and white privilege, at colleges, schools, churches, and community-based organizations. Great possibilities for understanding and change open up when the problem of racism is framed as a matter of learning, unlearning, and relearning, rather than as a chronic, immutable fact of life.

Our premise here is that if we, as school leaders, are to be effective in making transformative changes in our school communities, we must also be willing and able to engage in a process of transformative change within ourselves. As Lindsey, Robins, and Terrell (1999) point out, this process may not be easy or comfortable, yet it is ultimately necessary to go through the process of unlearning racism and arrive at what they term "cultural proficiency." Although they do not use the term *unlearning racism*, their analysis of the processes involved in achieving cultural proficiency is complementary and has many parallels.

We can begin the process of unlearning racism and contributing to a more socially just world by accepting, without judgment, that we all have biases and blind spots and that this is part of being human. And while we are not responsible for what shaped us as we were growing up, we are responsible for consciously taking steps to unlearn the damaging beliefs and attitudes that societal racism causes us to breathe in. We are also responsible for finding new ways to act based on this unlearning.

The proactive leaders who were part of our study exemplified the kind of self-reflection we have been discussing here. Leaders have to know experientially what helps and what hinders in this process of change. They have to speak from personal experience when they work with staff members on issues of diversity. People recognize when someone is working *with* them rather than telling them to do the work without ever having done it themselves. Proactive leaders are able to acknowledge and speak about their process of error and change and, in doing so, they provide a model for others. In short, they walk the talk based on their own experiences of struggle and transformation.

Rick Sebastian, principal of Ohlone High School, exemplified this awareness when he opened up a staff development day focusing on diversity issues with the following statement:

Our school is on the front edge of what California is going to become. All of us need to reflect. My own experience in working with the multicultural collaboration group has helped me to explore my own core values. . . . It's healthy to do this kind of thing.

NOTE

1. In order to protect the confidentiality of information shared, all individuals and schools in the Leading for Diversity study have been given pseudonyms.

2

Assessing the School Context

It is not the richest societies that have the best health, but those that have the smallest income differences between the rich and the poor.

—R. Wilkinson (cited in Fullan, 1999, p. 8)

Before school leaders can develop a plan for the improvement of race or ethnic relations, they need to consider their particular school's context and the way it affects human relations in general and, specifically, race or ethnic relations. There are many areas of context that are beyond the immediate control of school leadership. These include, for example, the demographics of the school, the economic disparities of the surrounding community, the physical structure and condition of the school, the district's policies and practices, and the legacy left at the school by previous leaders. All these contextual features can have an impact, positive or negative, on interethnic relations and group relations more generally. In order to get a handle on what you can do to make change as a leader, you have to have a good sense of what is already given as well as how solid these givens are. Some givens are amenable to change over the long term—for example, if you found that a certain district policy was having a negative impact on interethnic relations at your school, you could organize a movement to change the policy. It might take some time, but it is possible. The demographics of the community, however, are not amenable to change, at least not by you and the other leaders of the school. This chapter takes you through a process of identifying these contextual features and considering their impact on race and ethnic relations.

SUPPORTS AND CONSTRAINTS

Key Questions for Leaders

- What kind of school is ours, and how does context affect the development of positive interethnic relations?
- What hinders the development of positive interethnic relations here?
- What supports are already in place that I can build on?

Each school leader steps into a different context and history which may have laid important groundwork for positive interethnic relations, created barriers that impede relationship building, or, more likely, some combination of these possibilities. Some schools and their leaders, because of preexisting contexts, face more barriers and rely on fewer contextual supports in their quest to promote positive interethnic relations, while others already have numerous supports in place. Two contrasting high school cases illustrate this difference— Rancho Verde and Ohlone.

Rancho Verde High School

Rancho Verde High School is a good example of a school that faced numerous contextual constraints as the leadership tried to implement changes that would improve interethnic relations. The term *contextual constraints*, as we are using it here, means elements over which the school leadership has no immediate control. Rancho Verde is a comprehensive high school with about 1,700 students from a wide range of ethnic backgrounds, located in a suburban area close to San Francisco. The physical structure, which was built in the 1950s and consisted of many long, one-story buildings designed in rows around a central court, was badly in need of repair. Leaking roofs, peeling paint, and other problems with the physical plant had a demoralizing effect on staff and students alike. The recent district bankruptcy had put the district in a deep hole financially, so repairs and upgrades were unlikely in the coming years. The bankruptcy had also put a cap on salary increases, so salaries were lower than in any other district in the area. When teachers had a chance to move out to other districts, they tended to do so. Attracting and retaining the best teachers was, therefore, very difficult. The large number of students and overcrowded conditions made it a challenge to personalize relationships between staff and students. There were just too many people for the space, and during passing times between classes, students would have to squeeze past each other in narrow hallways, creating a context for conflicts over who pushed whom, and so on. The staff members had some deep divisions, mainly along lines of veteran versus newer staff, and these divisions stood in the way of the principal's efforts to develop site-based leadership. The faculty voted it down twice because the majority were unwilling to commit to the time and collaboration necessary to make site-based leadership work. They were already feeling so beleaguered by low salaries, poor physical plant, and so on, that they just weren't willing to give any more, and they didn't trust the process. They were afraid it would be "pseudo-participation." Lastly, an open-enrollment policy meant that students came to

Rancho Verde from communities other than the immediate neighborhood and, therefore, tended to have less ownership over the school.

Of course, there were some contextual supports at Rancho Verde—it wasn't all totally bleak. One support was the fact that the communities where students lived were relatively homogeneous in terms of socioeconomic status, being mostly middle and working class. Large disparities in income, as we saw in several other schools in the study, tend to aggravate divisions among students as there are clear and visible differences (in clothing, transportation, access to computers at home, etc.) between those who have more and those who have less. This was not such an issue at Rancho Verde. Another support was the fact that, despite some gang activity in and around the school, the crime rate in the community was considered low and the climate was not conducive to crime and violence.

Ohlone High School

To understand how striking the differences in context can be, we now turn to another comprehensive high school, Ohlone, with 4,100 students who, like those at Rancho Verde, represented a wide range of ethnic backgrounds and were from middle-and working-class families. Ohlone was also situated in a suburban area near San Francisco. However, the contextual constraints were few by comparison. The enormous size of the school population was probably the greatest barrier, and as the school population grew, space was also becoming a problem. The other major constraint was the way math classes tracked students by ability and, to a large extent, by race or ethnicity. Most of the Asian and white students tended to cluster in the honors math classes, while the black and Latino students tended to cluster in the regular math classes. Even though other departments claimed they had done away with tracking policies, the master schedule was such that students in the regular math classes only had certain time slots for English, so they ended up in the same English classes as a cluster. Likewise, those in the honors math took English at a different time. So, despite the English department's efforts to detrack, their classes became examples of de facto, or unintended, tracking.

On the support side of the ledger, Ohlone benefited from additional funding from several recent school bonds, coupled with good financial management. The physical plant was large and spread out but well maintained. The district had a very well-respected superintendent who had been there 22 years. It was largely because of his vision that the district had decided to keep all its high school population at one site rather than splitting off into two high schools. Had they chosen to create another high school, this would have divided the school populations along ethnic lines, with Ohlone keeping the white and Asian students, and the other high school enrolling mainly Latino, black, and lower-income Asian students.

A key support at Ohlone was a districtwide structure known as "collaboration time." This was a weekly, 2-hour time set aside for faculty to collaborate every Wednesday throughout the district. Students came to school later on Wednesday mornings, and banking minutes on the other days made up the instructional time. Each school could decide how they wanted to focus and organize this time. At Ohlone, teachers had to apply to become a collaboration group with specific goals and activities that they would accomplish. Because the school leadership encouraged interdepartmental groupings, many of these groups included teachers from various departments who had never really worked together before. The collaboration structure turned out to be a major breakthrough in terms of creating a structure for diverse faculty members to work together, helping break down departmental fiefdoms and teachers' isolation from one another. By creating conditions that were favorable to faculty collaboration, this structure fostered more personalized relationships among adults at the school and, in turn, led to faculty initiatives which had a direct impact on improving interethnic relations among students (we will explain these initiatives further in Chapter 6).

As these examples show, the two schools differed markedly in terms of the context that existed beyond the immediate control of the school leadership. A school leader who is stepping into a new school for the first time, or a faculty member thinking about taking on a leadership role within a familiar school, needs to consider how the particular context is and is not conducive to building positive interethnic relationships. Whatever interventions or changes leaders intend to make, they have to make sure those changes are appropriate given the context.

Tables 2.1, 2.2, and 2.3 provide templates to help you and your colleagues identify and reflect on the contextual constraints and supports at your school site. These constraints and supports are drawn from the 21 schools that participated in the Leading for Diversity study, so while they may be typical of many schools, they are not intended to be a complete listing of all possible constraints and supports. You are encouraged to go beyond what is listed and add your own particular items. Because districts are so vital in providing certain kinds of supports, we created a separate table to display some common district supports (Table 2.3). This is intended to help leaders pinpoint ways in which their districts are currently supporting positive interethnic relations, as well as ways in which the district administration could become more supportive.

ACTIVITY 4: SUPPORTS AND CONSTRAINTS

1.   To use these tables as part of a collaborative planning process within a school, fill out the tables on your own and ask several colleagues at your school to do the same. (Note: By building a group with diverse roles and ethnicities, you will enhance the chances that the ensuing discussion will be rich and challenging.)

2.   Compare and discuss your assessments. You will almost certainly have some similar, as well as different, views about how the context of your school supports or constrains positive interethnic relations. How and why are your views different? How are they the same?

Focusing the discussion on similarities and differences can help you clarify issues and also learn more about how and why your perspectives might differ. A teacher, for example, might have a very different view of human relations

Table 2.1 Contextual Constraints That Can Inhibit Positive Interethnic
Relations

Contextual Constraints	Please make a checkmark in this column if you see this as a constraint at your school.
It is difficult to recruit diverse staff.	_____
Students are segregated due to de facto tracking, grouping by language, or other reasons.	_____
Large size of school leads to less personalized environment.	_____
School is in a low-income community with high crime, gang presence.	_____
Some students come from communities outside the neighborhood.	_____
There is longstanding divisiveness among staff members.	_____
Community has negative perceptions of the school.	_____
School has a problematic relationship with the district.	_____
School's physical layout is not conducive to relationship building.	_____
School buildings are in poor physical condition.	_____
School has low per-pupil funding.	_____
School population is rapidly expanding.	_____
Previous leaders have left a legacy of mistrust and divisiveness in the school.	_____
The mobility rate of students and/or staff is high.	_____
New pressures from state (e.g., graduation standards, new testing program) divert attention away from human relations efforts.	_____
Students spend only 2 years at the school.	_____
There is strong parental pressure against change.	_____
Union constrains principal in making changes.	_____
Student population has wide economic disparity.	_____
Many staff members are new to teaching.	_____
Small size of school makes it difficult to offer a wide range of program options.	_____
Other constraints:	_____

Table 2.2   Contextual Supports That Can Encourage Positive
Interethnic Relations

Contextual Supports	*Please make a checkmark in this column if you see this as a support at your school.*
Additional funding is available for human relations efforts.	_____
Per-pupil funding level is high.	_____
School staff members are ethnically diverse and some are culturally similar to students.	_____
Physical layout is conducive to a sense of community.	_____
The facility is attractive and well maintained.	_____
District provides supports of various kinds (see Appendix B).	_____
School has preexisting collaborations with outside agencies or local universities.	_____
Small size of school leads to greater personalization.	_____
Supportive community takes pride in school and district.	_____
Community is relatively homogeneous in income level.	_____
Previous school leaders have put into place structures that support positive interethnic relations.	_____
School participates in reform effort with a focus on equity, diversity, community building.	_____
State requires a foreign language for graduation.	_____
The community has a low crime rate.	_____
Other supports:	_____

than a counselor or an administrator. As noted in Chapter 1, professional roles, as well as personal, cultural and social backgrounds, can all influence what we perceive in the school and how we perceive it.

3.   Do the same things that constrain positive interethnic relations at your school also hinder relationship building across other lines of difference (e.g., gender, sexual orientation, religion, age, etc.)? Why or why not?

Table 2.3   District Supports That Can Encourage Positive Interethnic
Relations

District Supports	Please place a checkmark in this column if you see this as a support at your school.
District leadership has strong agenda supporting diversity, equity, community building.	_____
Positive district leadership has been in place for a long time.	_____
District drawing areas ensure that school population reflects diversity of the district.	_____
District provides paid time for teachers to collaborate regularly for curriculum development and other school efforts.	_____
District has high standards, good reputation in state.	_____
District sets clear behavioral standards and supports schools in upholding them.	_____
Name of school reflects social justice focus.	_____
District provides transition time for incoming principals to get to know the school while previous principal is still there.	_____
Other district supports:	_____

4. Do the supports at your school also provide a strong foundation for improving relationships across other lines of difference? Why or why not?

The goal of conducting this assessment of the school context is to help you develop a clearer picture of how rough or smooth the road ahead might be. Leaders who find that they face many contextual constraints and have few supports may encounter more difficulty initiating and carrying out changes in interethnic relations; they might have to start with more modest proposals for change, yet still keep long-term goals in view. Leaders who find many supports and few constraints, on the other hand, may be able to move more quickly toward reaching their goals, building on a foundation that is already strong. No matter what you discover about constraints and supports, it is important to keep in mind that there is a historicity to leadership. Your contributions, whatever they are, will be important but will not result in the complete realization of the vision or long-term goals. You may leave or be transferred to another school, but the next leader will be able to continue the journey and build on what you have put into place.

SEGREGATION AND INTEGRATION

Key Questions for Leaders

- What kinds of segregation exist in schools (and in my school in particular), and how does this affect interethnic relations?
- What conditions need to be present for positive relations to develop between ethnic groups?
- Which of these conditions are present at my school, and when?

Several times in the previous section, we pointed out that some schools have built-in segregated groupings of students which, intentionally or not, are organized along ethnic as well as class lines. Even though the school may be integrated, the classrooms are not. In the next sections, we look briefly at two kinds of segregation—tracking by so-called ability and grouping by language. While an in-depth discussion of these two topics is beyond the scope of this book, readers can refer for further exploration to the books and articles cited in this chapter.

Tracking

Tracking is defined by Haury and Milbourne (1999) as "the practice of separating children into different courses or course sequences ('tracks') based on their level of achievement or proficiency as measured by some set of tests or course grades" (p. 13). Many schools, particularly at the secondary level, are partially or entirely tracked. The problem with tracking is that low-performing students, rather than being targeted for high-quality programs that will help them make greater gains, often become trapped in inferior curricular pathways that limit their educational opportunities. Class and race become implicated because lower-track classes tend to be heavily populated by African American, Latino, and Native American students, while the higher-track classes are more white and Asian. Economic disparities overlap with racial and ethnic disparities so that it is often impossible to untangle what is a class issue and what is a racial issue. Relegating low-income students and students of color to a permanent lower level of education by placing them, year after year, in less academically demanding classes is clearly inequitable. Much has been written about this practice and the damaging effects it has on college and career opportunities for low-income students and students of color (see, for example, Lipman, 1998; Mehan, 1996; Oakes, 1985).

The continuing practice of tracking or ability grouping in U.S. schools, and the debate surrounding it, highlights one of the essential dilemmas within our educational system. Nieto (1996) explains that,

Schools are organizations fundamentally concerned with maintaining the status quo and not exposing contradictions that make people uncomfortable in a society that has democratic ideals but wherein democratic realities are not always apparent. Such contradictions include the many manifestations of inequality. Yet schools are also supposed to wipe out these inequalities. To admit that inequality exists and that it is even perpetuated by the very institutions charged with doing away with it are topics far too dangerous to discuss. (p. 317)

Yet such topics must be discussed if schools are to emerge as anything other than replicators of the status quo. It would be naïve to think that race relations could substantially improve in any society that allows its schools to deliver less-rigorous education to a majority of low-income and minority students. One of the challenges for proactive school leaders, then, is to raise their own awareness of tracking and other structures that perpetuate segregation and inequality within schools, and to raise critical questions about these practices with their colleagues.

Grouping by Language

Not all kinds of segregation are the same, however, and leaders need to be cautious in applying the principles of integration across the board. For example, take the issue of grouping students by language. Students may be grouped through various types of programs designed to meet special language needs, such as English as a second language (ESL) programs, transitional bilingual programs, newcomer programs, and so on. These programs are set up with the intent of providing equal access to education for students who are not yet proficient in English, and are consistent with federal case law. *Lau v. Nichols* (1974) made a very important distinction between equality of opportunity and equality of access. While it was true that the Chinese-speaking children in the case were exposed to the same books, materials, and classroom instruction as other children in San Francisco, the plaintiffs argued that since the children could not understand these materials or instruction, there was, in fact, no access and, therefore no equality of opportunity. Methods such as bilingual instruction, ESL instruction, and special newcomer orientation programs are means by which educators have sought to address this "inequality of access." These programs are designed to be temporary, until such time as the students are proficient enough to succeed in a regular classroom. However, one of the consequences of such programs is that students do, in some cases, spend significant parts of their day, for several years, in classes with others of the same ethnic background. One of the principals in our study commented on the dilemma this raised for her:

One of the limitations of a bilingual program is that some of the kids aren't as integrated as one might hope, because of the language needs. We've done some things to remedy it, but there's always a sense that it's not enough and sort of a tension between the needs to do a bilingual program in the primary language and the need to integrate children.

And, probably, the different people you talk to would line up on bilingual issues differently. And some might see it as a big problem and then it is a catch-22, because not having bilingual education is a racist stand, too. Some people who aren't in favor of it might not perceive it that way, but, in my view, bilingual education is an equity issue. So those things are juxtaposed.

It is important to point out that the principal quoted above was talking about a transitional bilingual program, which is one where students are taught in the native language until they are ready to transition to an all-English classroom. The usual period of time students spend in such a program is 2 to 3 years, and the primary goal is English proficiency. The native language is not maintained in school after the students transition out of the program. There are several other kinds of bilingual programs besides this model, some of which are designed to promote oral and written proficiency in both languages; two-way immersion or dual-language immersion programs have the advantage that they instruct native English speakers and native speakers of another language in the same classroom. Therefore segregation is not an issue as it is in a transitional program. Additional ideas on different types of language-based programs are addressed in Genesee (1999), Brisk (1998), and Lucas (1997).

Other Forms of Segregation

In addition to segregation by academic tracking and segregation by language needs, many students find that once they reach middle and high school, the sports and other activities they participate in are segregated more or less along ethnic lines. Some argue that these groupings are a matter of student preference, and, therefore, educators shouldn't intervene to change the composition of these extracurricular activities. However, to the extent that activities are ethnically segregated or less-accessible to certain groups, they represent yet another opportunity missed, both for furthering educational equity and for providing students with structured opportunities to meet and know others of different ethnic backgrounds. In the Leading for Diversity study, we were especially concerned when we saw student leadership groups that were primarily white and Asian, even though the schools were far more diverse than that. Why were so few Latino, African American, and Native American students getting involved in formal leadership activities?

EQUAL STATUS CONTACT THEORY

Allport's (1954) equal status contact theory provides a base that can help leaders in the early stages of planning how schools can improve interethnic relations. Allport's theory states that in order for positive relations to develop between two (or more) racial or ethnic groups, four necessary conditions must be met:

1. Equal status: the contact should occur in circumstances that place the two groups in an equal status.

2. Personal interaction: the contact should involve one-on-one interactions among individual members of the two groups.

3. Cooperative activities: members of the two groups should join together in an effort to achieve superordinate goals.

4. Social norms: the social norms, defined in part by relevant authorities, should favor intergroup contact. (Brehm & Kassim, 1996, p. 157)

When schools were first integrated after *Brown v. Board of Education of Topeka* (1954), many people assumed that all four of these conditions would be met by simply placing students of vastly different backgrounds in the same schools. The goals of integration would be achieved through the desegregation of schools. Unfortunately, this turned out to be quite naïve, and, in fact, many schools report that there is even greater fragmentation along racial lines than a few years ago.

One problem was that many teachers were not prepared to teach in ways that fostered personal interaction and cooperative activities among students, and they did not know how to create social norms that would favor intergroup contact. We have come a long way in developing teachers' capacities to do these things through classroom participation structures such as jigsawing and other forms of cooperative learning (Aronson, 2000; Holt, 1993; Shaw, 1992).

Nonetheless, using more cooperative learning approaches in classrooms was only a partial solution to the issue of how students in desegregated schools would relate to one another. It still didn't address the larger social issues that existed beyond the classroom. Fine, Weis, and Powell (1997) offer an incisive explanation for why "settings that are technically desegregated will corrode into sites of oppositional identities, racial tensions, and fractured group relations which simply mirror the larger society" (p. 249). They make the point that setting up students as "equal" in the classroom cannot possibly make up for the great economic and social divides they bring with them when they enter the classroom. They claim that there are three critical conditions left out of equal status contact theory which need to be addressed in order for multiracial youth relations to flourish. These are

1. Sense of community: Differences should be drawn upon to enrich the community and develop a shared sense of purpose.

2. Creative analysis of difference, power, and privilege: Adults should be prepared to confront and explore (rather than shut down) the clash of differences that occur when questions about race, power, and privilege emerge.

3. Investment in democratic practice with youth: Schools should create and allow structures and processes that encourage youth leadership, voice, and participation.

A very similar set of conditions is proposed by Tatum (2001); she calls these conditions the ABC's of intergroup relations: Affirming students' identities, building a sense of community, and cultivating youth leadership (p. 550). To affirm students' identities is to value pluralism, the multiplicity of differences that students, their parents, and staff members bring to schools. To build a sense of community is to value what we have in common—for example, the desire to nurture young people's intellectual and social growth. The twin goals of pluralism and unity *(e pluribus unum)* are sometimes difficult to embrace within a school setting. "Some see this as a zero sum game. That is, how do I honor my heritage on the one hand, and at the same time contribute to a larger multicultural society? If I do one, it detracts from the other" (Park, 2000). But proactive leaders find ways to move beyond this zero-sum game by expanding the conversation. In a study of multiracial coalition building in Los Angeles, coalitions were seen as a way of healing racism in the aftermath of the 1992 Los Angeles riots. Participants in the coalitions found that reaching across racial lines to accomplish common goals does not have to mean denying or obscuring the importance of race or ethnicity (Park, 2000).

The third goal in both Fine et al.'s (1997) and Tatum's (2001) frameworks is to encourage youth leadership. This is consistent with the goals of critical pedagogy expressed by the Brazilian educator Paolo Freire (1970). Young people need to become active subjects of their own history, not just passive recipients of the history written in textbooks. They need opportunities to exercise leadership within their schools and communities and to connect that leadership with real problems and decision making. In some schools, students identified problems in their immediate environment—for example, the poor condition of the building or the fact that security guards tended to favor certain groups—and led campaigns to address these problems.

Tatum's (2001) three conditions provide the additional advantage of being easy to remember with a simple ABC mnemonic device. However, we propose adding a fourth element—addressing root causes of conflict (making the mnemonic ABCA)—because without this, school leaders can easily ignore underlying sources of tension, such as racist attitudes on the part of staff members, tracking of certain groups in less-demanding classes, and segregation that prevents individuals from coming to know members of other groups. The four principles represented in Figure 2.1 consolidate much of the information we have discussed so far and provide a simple framework for organizing a multitude of more specific strategies and approaches.

Affirming identity means encouraging students and staff members to recognize and value their different identities as groups as well as individuals. This can include celebrating ethnic holidays and the contributions of people of different backgrounds and, also, learning about the history and struggles of one's own people through an ethnic-studies class or a student club.

Building community means finding and building upon what we all share—for example, high aspirations for our children, the need for safety and security, the need to feel as if we are unified while still respecting our differences. The visioning process itself is a good example of building community because, in seeking

Figure 2.1   Four Principles for Improving Interethnic Relations (ABCA)

SOURCE: Adapted from Tatum (2001).

a shared vision, we are trying to agree on some basic values. To do so, of course, we have to articulate some differences, or else we will have only a rubber stamp vision, when the goal of articulating these differences is to seek a consensus.

Cultivating student leadership means creating conditions that allow students to empower themselves. If we simply impose our agenda of positive interethnic relations on students, they will not come to see this as part of their own work. Changing the structures of school so that there are multiple ways for students to acquire leadership skills and multiple leadership roles for them to play encourages more diverse student leadership and teaches critical democratic values.

Addressing root causes of conflict is always necessary because, even if we practice all the previous three principles, there will still be conflicts from time to time. We still need to seek an understanding of the root causes, such as inequalities in the system of the school that confer privilege on some students more than others; segregating groupings, whether intentional or not; and racist attitudes and behaviors.

ACTIVITY 5: SEGREGATION AND INTEGRATION

This activity is designed for school leaders in order to involve staff members and students (middle school and older) in assessing how your school segregates and integrates students, and to what extent your school meets the seven conditions for positive interethnic contact proposed by Allport (1954), Fine et al. (1997), and Tatum (2001). A possible structure for this activity is a jigsaw, in which groups of four or five are formed with at least one administrator or counselor, at least one teacher, and at least one student. Participants complete the

Table 2.4   Structures That Result in Segregation

Structure	Who's involved?	When and for how long does it happen?
Example: Math classes are tracked (honors and regular).	White and Asian students tend to be in honors. Black and Latino students tend to be in regular sections.	Daily; students tend to stay in the same track year after year

Table 2.5   Structures That Result in Integration

Structure	Who's involved?	When and for how long does it happen?
Example: The multicultural choir	Filipino, African American, Latino, and European American students	Once a week after school

questionnaire for their role group (e.g., the administrator group). They then have to complete a shared matrix that combines the findings of each role group. Each group then discusses what they think the combined findings mean, and prepares a short summary to present to the whole group.

1.   What are some structures that result in students at your school being segregated by race or ethnicity? (See Table 2.4.)

2.   What are some structures that integrate students at your school (meaning that students from the full range of diversity at your school are present)? (See Table 2.5.)

3.   Consider the following conditions that researchers tell us are necessary to create and sustain positive interethnic relations in schools. To what extent do you think each of these conditions exists at your school? Where and how often do you see these conditions happening?

A. Equal status: The contact should occur in circumstances that place the two (or more) groups in an equal status.

I see this happening when

B. Personal interaction: The contact should involve one-on-one interactions among individual members of the two (or more) groups.

I see this happening when

C. Cooperative activities: Members of the two (or more) groups should join together in an effort to achieve superordinate goals.

I see this happening when

D. Social norms: The social norms, defined in part by relevant authorities, should favor intergroup contact.

I see this happening when

E. Sense of community: Differences should be drawn upon to enrich the community and develop a shared sense of purpose.

I see this happening when

F. Creative analysis of difference, power, and privilege: Adults should be prepared to confront and explore the clash of differences that occurs when questions about race, power, and privilege emerge.

I see this happening when

G. Investment in democratic practice with youth: Schools should create and allow structures and processes that encourage youth leadership, voice, and participation.

Table 2.6   Summary of Group Members' Findings

	Administrators' Perspectives	Teachers' Perspectives	Students' Perspectives
Structures that segregate students by race and ethnicity			
Structures that integrate diverse students			
Opportunities for equal-status contact among diverse students			
One-on-one, personal interactions among diverse students			
Cooperative activities involving diverse students			
Social norms favorable to intergroup contact			
Sense of community involving the whole school			
Creative analysis of difference, power, and privilege			
Structures and practices that encourage youth leadership, voice, and participation			

I see this happening when

4. Now, your group will need to summarize the findings from each member. Use the matrix in Table 2.6 to create your summary together, and then discuss what it tells you about your school's opportunities for positive intergroup relations. (If your groups are not composed of administrators, teachers, and students, you can change the headings to fit your role groups.)

MAKING SENSE OF DATA

Key Question for Leaders

- What can I learn by examining existing data for my school or district?

School leaders can learn a great deal by examining data for their school site, especially when the data have been disaggregated—that is, separated by categories such as ethnicity, gender, type of program, classroom, and so forth. Most school districts have only recently begun to provide this service to school

Figure 2.2 A Simple Cycle of Inquiry

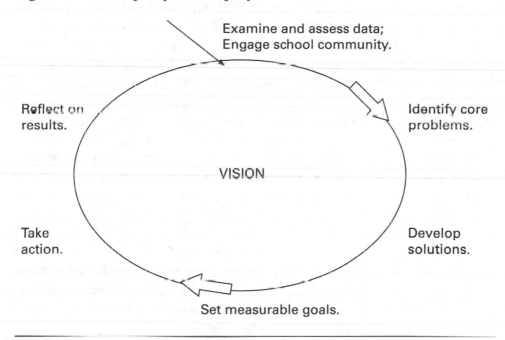

SOURCE: Adapted from Bay Area Coalition of Essential Schools (1999).

sites, and many people are still unsure how to use these data in productive ways. There are a number of potential pitfalls that need to be avoided, but wise use of these data can be a great help in understanding the context and setting priorities for educating students more equitably. In fact, examining and revisiting data in a cycle of inquiry is key to sustaining and building on any kind of proactive intervention in a school. In its simplest form, a data-based cycle of inquiry includes the following recursive processes: examining and assessing data; identifying core problems; developing solutions, setting measurable goals, taking action, assessing results and reflecting on action; identifying continuing or new problems, refining solutions, and so on. Figure 2.2 depicts this cycle.

In Chapter 6, we discuss how proactive leaders involved the whole staff in data inquiry as one of the approaches to developing positive interethnic relations. Here, we focus on using existing data to learn more about the preexisting context of your school.

What Data Can (and Can't) Tell Us

When data are disaggregated by ethnicity and other categories, one is able to look for patterns in the results, to see if students are proportionately represented in different programs, classes, and activities. One can also see whether certain racial or ethnic groups are performing less well on standardized tests than others. One can see whether low-income students (those participating in the free and reduced-fee lunch program) show significantly lower achievement on tests than students with higher family income levels. In some cities, data are disaggregated by zip code because the city's different income levels coincide rather closely with different geographic regions. In Berkeley, California, a city with wide income disparities, students living within certain zip codes consistently score in the lower quartile. They tend, not coincidentally, to be African American and Latino (Noguera, 1995). One can also look at discipline data such as suspensions and referrals to see whether certain ethnic groups are overrepresented. Disaggregated data spanning several years can enable one to see trends, such as steady, year-by-year increases in student achievement on standardized tests, a sudden drop in the number of suspensions from one year to the next, or a growing gap between the achievement of language minority students and native English speakers (Olsen & Jaramillo, 1999).

There are also a number of things these data cannot reveal. First, they cannot tell us the reasons for the patterns that appear. A drop in suspensions from one year to the next could mean a number of things—perhaps the new principal was lax and simply didn't suspend as many students. Or perhaps there was a concerted effort to crack down on behavior and, as a result, student behavior improved and fewer students were suspended. Or perhaps the number that were suspended the previous year of students was due to an overly strict principal, and the lower number the following year was more aligned with the disciplinary policy in other district schools. As this example shows, correctly interpreting the meaning of the disaggregated data patterns requires one to know much more about the school and the district.

Second, disaggregated data cannot tell us about individual students' performance nor about any subgroups that are contained within a larger group. For example, in many districts, all Asian students are lumped together in one category for purposes of reporting data. Yet the category might include groups as diverse as Cambodians, Vietnamese, Mien, Japanese, Filipino, Chinese, Indian, and Pakistani. Each of these groups has a very different history, native language, and educational background, not to mention the variation within each of these subgroups depending on economic status, reasons for immigration, how recently they immigrated, and so forth. In Oakland, for example, Asian students appear to do quite well according to the disaggregated data the school district provides. Yet some subgroups within the Asian category are not doing well academically at all, particularly Mien and Cambodian students. The high achievement reflects mainly students of Chinese origin (Asian and Pacific Islander Task Force, 2001). However, one would not know this unless the district agreed to provide subgroup data. Thus anyone looking at disaggregated data needs to bear in mind that the category may be hiding a number of subgroups whose results would look quite different if they were separated from the larger category.

Sharing Disaggregated Data
With Others in the School Community

Several of the schools in the Leading for Diversity study had leaders who understood the power of using data as a form of inquiry and as a tool in decision making. Not only did they examine the data themselves but they also shared data with faculty in an effort to build consensus about areas where the school needed to focus more attention. Chapter 6 provides an example of how this was done at Midvale High School, and the case about Fillmore Middle School (Chapter 12) also illustrates how data inquiry can become a focus for school change.

3

Understanding Racial and Ethnic Conflict

Conflict, if respected, is positively associated with creative breakthroughs under complex, turbulent conditions.

—Michael Fullan (1999, p. 22)

What have you been taught about conflict? Most of us have received a variety of different messages about conflict and what to do about it. For example, "If it ain't broke, don't fix it," is an adage that tells us to let the small stuff slide—but what constitutes small stuff? Some of us have been taught to "sweep conflicts under the rug" or refrain from "airing dirty laundry." On the other hand, therapists sometimes advocate for family members to have regular conflict resolution sessions, and conflict resolution programs in schools similarly make the assumption that it is healthy to air and resolve conflicts. These different views of how to handle conflict can occur even within groups who share a similar cultural background. When we add cultural differences to the mix, views about conflict can diverge even more.

In this chapter, we take a somewhat different view from either of the two extremes of hiding conflict or embracing it openly. Our research has indicated that conflicts involving race or ethnicity in schools can represent an opportunity for individual and organizational learning, as Fullan suggests in the quote above, but there are pitfalls that school leaders must be aware of. This chapter will prepare you to use some tools to analyze and better understand racial or ethnic conflicts at your school.

The conflicts that erupt in schools are similar to the symptoms a medical doctor is faced with every day. A proactive school leader, like a medical practitioner, understands that there are causes and mitigating circumstances that can bring symptoms to the surface. While some of these causes are well understood, others are still the subject of exploration. And, as in the medical world, there are alternative views of how the symptoms should be addressed. Western medicine is often seen as overly focused on symptoms and parts of the body; Chinese medicine, on the other hand, is said to focus more on underlying conditions and a holistic view of the human being, including physical, emotional, intellectual, and spiritual aspects. We do not wish to belabor the medical metaphor but simply to suggest that it can be helpful to think about issues of racial conflict with this comparison in mind. School leaders, rather than focusing only on the symptoms of conflict, can make more of a difference by turning their attention to the underlying causes of conflict.

THE ICEBERG MODEL OF RACIAL OR ETHNIC CONFLICT

Key Questions for Leaders

- What are the precursors of racial or ethnic violence?
- How can I do more than just react to overt conflicts?

In our study of proactive leadership in ethnic relations, a model has emerged that can help educators understand the progression of racial or ethnic conflict (see Figure 3.1). We use the metaphor of an iceberg to illustrate how some kinds of conflict are very obvious while others are less noticeable. Overt conflict, such as physical fighting or the use of racial slurs, sits at the top of this model. It is exposed and easy for others to detect. Underlying, latent, or potential conflicts or tensions are directly below the surface. The people affected by these conflicts and tensions may or may not be aware of them; for example, when people are excluded from participation in a group because of culture, ethnicity, language, and other factors, they may feel uncomfortable and hurt, but they may not recognize it as a form of racial tension. Such conflicts or tensions may remain hidden indefinitely or surface later as overt conflicts. The bottom of the iceberg represents the root causes of racial or ethnic conflict, which include such factors as

- Segregation, which allows for the development and maintenance of stereotypes about other groups with whom one has little actual contact
- Institutionalized racism and individual racial prejudice
- Socialization in which parents and other adults consciously or unconsciously transmit to children negative information about other groups
- Inequality, in which power, status, or access to desired goods and services are unequally distributed among groups. (Kreisberg, 1998, pp. 40-44)

Figure 3.1 The Iceberg Model of Racial or Ethnic Conflict

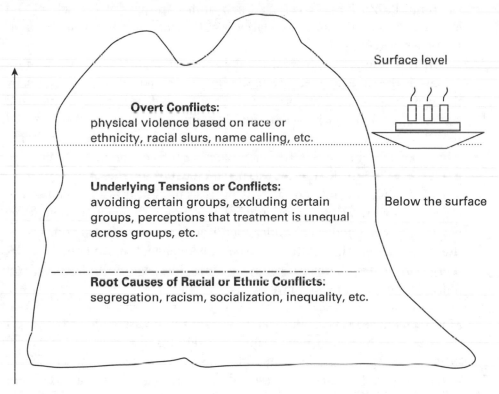

Surface level

Overt Conflicts:
physical violence based on race or
ethnicity, racial slurs, name calling, etc.

Underlying Tensions or Conflicts:
avoiding certain groups, excluding certain
groups, perceptions that treatment is unequal
across groups, etc.

Below the surface

Root Causes of Racial or Ethnic Conflicts:
segregation, racism, socialization, inequality, etc.

SOURCE: Based on 21 schools that were part of the Leading for Diversity Research Project.

Consider the following example:

Tyler, an African American security guard at a middle school, is having a discussion with Rosemary, one of the authors, about his role at the school and how he thinks the new school leadership has been very proactive in improving race relations among students. He is full of positive energy as he describes a number of new practices, especially in terms of how the three security guards now work with students on behavior issues. Each security staff member has a small office and can meet privately with students to discuss their behavior issues and develop a plan for improvement. Then Rosemary asks him, "How about in terms of race relations among adults at the school—how would you describe that?"

The smile leaves his face, and his voice becomes quieter. He describes an incident in which he was in the staff lunchroom getting ready to heat up his lunch, when a substitute teacher who was European American walked in and said, "You look like someone who knows where a mop and a bucket can be found."

Tyler says he just looked straight at him and said, "No, I don't." He walked away and went to a room where he could be alone to cool down. Later, he talked with the assistant principal (AP), who was Latino, and the AP was very helpful in a debriefing about the situation. Tyler isn't sure if any action was taken against the substitute after that. He never shared the story with anyone else and doesn't want to raise it as an issue with the rest of the staff. He is glad that it wasn't a permanent staff member who made the remark. But he also feels that substitutes are part of the school and should be held to the same standards as any faculty member when it comes to respect and dignity.

In this scene, no physical conflict has erupted. Yet the substitute's remark is the same as a racial slur. He had never met Tyler before (who, by the way, was very neatly dressed, with a tie and well-pressed shirt and slacks—i.e., the remark was not a reflection on clothing), and he implied that Tyler's looks made him think he must be a janitor. It is hard to imagine what about Tyler's looks, other than the fact of his being black, could have made the substitute think that this person must be a janitor.

What kind of conflict occurred in this scene? From Tyler's perspective, it seemed overt. We don't know what the substitute teacher thought or whether he even noticed or understood Tyler's reaction. For anyone else at the school, except the AP, this scene never happened. It was completely submerged in silence, therefore occupying the middle level of the "iceberg." Yet it deeply hurt and angered Tyler.

Most of us have been conditioned to work from the assumption that overt problems are the ones that need fixing. "If it ain't broke, don't fix it" is folk advice that serves well under many circumstances. However, when school leaders use this as their model for responding to racial issues, it places them in a reactive role, responding only to crises. As one teacher noted, "If you have a principal who's putting out fires all the time, that's not going to lead to a vision. You can prevent the fires by having a vision."

UNSILENCING RACIAL CONFLICTS

In the above case, only one school leader had any knowledge of the incident, and Tyler requested that he not share it with others. This is not uncommon, as racial conflicts are often painful for people to talk about. For this reason, it is often difficult for leaders to gain access to information about underlying conflicts. As in the scene with Tyler, people have many good reasons not to bring to the surface conflicts and tensions that have a racial or ethnic dimension. They may be afraid that doing so will lead to an increase in conflict or that they will then be targeted by the original perpetrators. They may simply not want to raise the issue because it is too painful to talk about or they know that other people will be uncomfortable. Many schools have a code of silence about race and ethnicity, a value system that says it's best to be color blind. In a color blind school, there is no safe place for someone like Tyler to discuss what happened, so it has to go underground. A student who participated in the study pointed this out when she said,

People would like to see our race problem disappear. And the way they think it's going to disappear is by *not* talking about it. But the real way you make it disappear is by talking about it, learning about it, and understanding it—and then you'll see a change—not just by ignoring it.

In general, the leaders in the study took a proactive stance, recognizing overt conflicts as symptoms and underlying tensions and root causes as the illness. They took many actions that communicated to staff and students that it was not only OK but also valuable to talk about and learn about race, ethnicity, and conflict. This is part of what Fine, Weis, & Powell (1998) call opportunities for "creative analysis of difference, power, and privilege" (p. 249) (see Chapter 2 on segregation and integration). For example, by modeling such open communication themselves, they enabled others to see that this was a valued practice at the school. Some leaders talked with their staff or with students from time to time about their own experiences with racism; they also attended and participated actively in events such as a trip to the Holocaust Museum and shared how the experience affected them afterward.

Leaders may also become targets of racial conflict. Tatum (1998) suggests that if leaders find themselves accused of racism, they should ask the person making the accusation, "Can you tell me what I did or said that made you think so?" In this way, the leader opens up a dialogue without immediately becoming defensive. Leaders can acknowledge the possibility that there might be some truth to the accusation without necessarily admitting guilt, and they can get onto more solid ground by finding out specific actions or words that were interpreted as racist. Often such honest conversations allow both parties to learn more about each other's perceptions. If there was indeed something the leader said or did that was biased or racist, it is important to listen and learn.

Often there are hot-button phrases and words that set off accusations of racism—for example, referring to a whole racial ethnic group as "you people" or attaching the racial or ethnic descriptor to any negative action (e.g., "That Latino kid who stole the VCR. . . "). Similarly, asking specific individuals of a particular racial or ethnic group to speak for their entire group is a prime example of stereotyping (e.g., "Vanessa, could you explain the black perspective on this issue?"). Often it is helpful to turn the situation around in one's mind, and consider whether it would be OK to ask, "Joseph, could you explain how white people feel about this issue?"

Accusations of racism are not, however, only based on words. Disciplinary actions against students and critiques of teachers can also lead to accusations of racism—sometimes for good reasons, sometimes not. If, for example, parents are questioning a leader because they think their child received more severe disciplinary consequences because the child is black, it is important first for the leader to be fully aware of all the details of the case. Second, the leader should hear the parents out and then review the details of the case with them. If the leader is convinced that there was no racial bias operating in this case, it can help to appeal to the parents' own standards of behavior. One principal in the study told us that in a situation like this, she said to the parent, "I know you don't want [your son] to be fighting in school and getting hurt or hurting other kids." She said this approach usually calms the parent down because it establishes a common ground; it shows the parent that the principal is on the parent's side, sharing certain basic values.

In addition to serving as models, proactive leaders in interethnic relations also create and support structured opportunities where students, staff, and parents can discuss issues related to race, ethnicity, and culture. The principal at a middle school, for example, worked with a district administrator to organize afternoon retreats three times a year, led by an outside facilitator, in which faculty, parents, and students shared stories about their own experiences with racial or cross-cultural prejudice. According to a district staff member who helped organize the retreats, "The rationale is that it's hard to be enemies with someone you know. Prejudice is the way you judge someone when you don't know their story."

Another way proactive leaders worked to create safe spaces for talking about race and ethnicity was through the people they hired. They made sure that students or adults who encountered racial conflicts would be able to find willing and open listeners. It is probably not an accident that Tyler chose to take his concern to the AP, who was a person of color and also a man (the principal was a European American woman). Tyler may have assumed that as a minority and a man, the AP had more in common with him and would be likely to understand and empathize. Leaders also have to be careful, though, not to assume that people's ethnic background accurately predicts whether they will be able to listen and talk in a helpful way about racism and discrimination. Some European Americans have learned how to do so very well, and some people of color are not willing to discuss such issues.

All of these strategies have in common the intent to take conflict out of hiding so that it can be understood and addressed. When a school provides multiple spaces and opportunities for people to air concerns and conflicts, leaders can more easily stay tuned to tensions that may be related to race or ethnicity, identifying trouble spots and developing activities and structures to build a stronger interethnic community. In this way, leaders shift from being reactive—reacting only to the most overt conflicts that have already done significant damage—to becoming proactive—anticipating needs and identifying problem areas early so that changes can be made that will improve relations in the school community.

CONFIDENTIALITY

Key Question for Leaders

- How can I maximize the learning potential of conflicts without breaching confidentiality?

Proactive leaders also understand conflict as a normal part of human social interaction, rather than as a destructive scourge to be eradicated altogether. Conflict need not result in violent or destructive outcomes; it can in fact become an opportunity for learning, both for individuals and for the organization as a whole. School leaders can play a key role in turning conflicts into opportunities for learning, but if they want to extend the learning beyond the individuals involved, they have to decide first whether to allow the conflict to be discussed more publicly.

There will always be situations when, for such reasons as confidentiality and safety, it is better not to discuss racial conflicts with others. Leaders need to become skilled at recognizing when sharing an incident with staff members or students might harm particular individuals. Sometimes they can work around this problem by fictionalizing—that is, changing certain aspects of the incident so that it won't be obvious who was involved. But some schools are such close communities or so small that no matter how hard a leader tries to conceal identities, people will figure it out anyway. The case study of Metropolitan High School in Chapter 14 highlights how such an issue was handled there.

IDENTIFYING TRIGGER ISSUES AND KEY PLAYERS

Key Questions for Leaders

- What issues trigger racial or ethnic conflict or tension at my school?
- Who are the players in racial and ethnic conflicts?
- How does a leader decide if a particular conflict has a racial or ethnic dimension?

Racial or ethnic conflicts, besides being fundamentally about intolerance or discrimination based on race or ethnicity, can be triggered by a number of different issues. In our study, we developed a typology that identifies these different issues. As Box 3.1 indicates, they fall into two general categories: (a) distribution of material or social resources, and (b) values, beliefs, and cultural expressions (Kreisberg, 1998).

Since this typology was derived from the 21 schools in the study, it is probably an incomplete list. There may well be other issues that trigger racial and ethnic conflicts in other schools. However, it is a good starting point for readers to expand on.

In order to use this typology to assess trigger issues at your school, leaders need to cast a wide net that includes the whole school community. Many people assume, whenever the topic of racial conflict comes up, that students are the only people having conflicts. However, we found that students were perpetrators in only about half of the conflicts reported to us in the 21 school sites we studied. The other half included conflicts between staff members, between staff members and students, between parents and staff members, and between parents and other parents.[1] Particularly in elementary schools, we found that students, by and large, were not the main perpetrators of racial conflicts; adults were the more salient conflicting parties at this level. As students grow older, however, they start to identify more with their particular ethnic group or race, and some students also begin to affiliate with gangs. As we explain in Chapter 4, this identification with others who are perceived to have similar experiences is part of a normal developmental process that adolescents go through in a diverse society.

When a school leader witnesses or hears of a particular conflict, it is not always easy to determine whether the conflict has a racial or ethnic dimension.

Box 3.1   Issues That Can Trigger Racial or Ethnic Conflicts

A. *Distribution of material or social resources*

- Distribution of **academic expectations**; low academic achievement of African American and Latino males, or of students of color generally; tracking.
- Distribution of **staff positions.**
- Distribution of **disciplinary referrals or consequences**; high referral rate for African American and Latino males.
- Control of **territory** on or off campus; gang related.
- Distribution of **power** (decision making, voice, etc.) based on ethnicity or race.
- Distribution of **assemblies** and other celebratory events.
- Inclusion of multicultural perspectives in **curriculum.**
- Distribution of **time and schedules.**
- Distribution of **financial resources.**
- Distribution of **respect**.
- Distribution of **sports opportunities.**

B. *Values, beliefs, and cultural expressions*

- **Talking about race and ethnicity** versus belief that we should all be color blind.
- Appropriate or best **instructional methods.**
- **Staying within group versus mixing with others,** (includes dating issues).
- Use of **racial slurs** within the group (e.g., *nigga* or *nigger*).
- Culturally appropriate ways to **discipline** students.
- Use of non-English **languages.**
- Expression of **religion** in schools.
- **Assuming preferences or dispositions** based on race or ethnicity.
- Cultural differences in **clothing.**

SOURCE: Based on 21 schools that were part of the Leading for Diversity Research Project.

Conflicts that involve racial name-calling make it evident, but some conflicts are far less clearly about race or ethnicity. For example, in one school, an AP talked about a parent whose child had apparently been given more stringent disciplinary consequences because he was Latino. If the disciplinary consequences were actually reviewed across cases and found to be the same, would this incident still be a case of racial or ethnic conflict or tension? Kreisberg (1998) points out that, "People act in accord with their definition of the situation" (p. 4) and if at least one party in the incident defines the situation as having something to do with race or ethnicity, then that person's actions will be based on that understanding. School leaders who address this situation must recognize it as having a racial and ethnic dimension; otherwise, they will miss the mark in terms of working out a resolution. It is the perspective of one or more individuals that makes it a racial issue.

Another example of how conflicts can sometimes be difficult to pinpoint as racial is the case of an argument between a Latino and a Chinese American student. The Chinese American student accidentally spilled some water on the other student's backpack. The Latino student insisted it was done on purpose. Initially, there was nothing racial about the conflict. But as soon as the two students' friends started overhearing the argument, they immediately took sides based on ethnicity. Then there were six or seven Latinos arguing with six or seven Asian students, and everyone made the assumption that the conflict was racial. A leader intervening at this point would have to consider race a factor in the conflict because that is how others interpreted it, and they behaved accordingly.

Sometimes, conflicts appear to be within traditionally identified racial groups (e.g., Latino, Asian). This is often the case with gang-related incidents involving two rival gangs of the same ethnicity—for example, Norteños (literally, *Northerners*—those of Mexican origin who have lived in the United States for a generation or more) and Sureños (literally, *Southerners*—recent immigrants to the United States from Mexico). While it appears on the surface that these conflicts do not have much to do with interethnic relations, this is only an outsider's view. The young people involved in these conflicts see themselves as having different cultural and historical backgrounds, with the Norteños being more closely affiliated with the United States and U.S. Chicano culture, including language, and the Sureños being more traditionally Mexican in language, clothing, and other culturally shaped behaviors. In this case, it is not ethnicity per se that is the defining difference but rather a combination of cultural and historical conditions that have led these two groups to perceive themselves as distinct. Similar differences arise between recent immigrants and longtime residents of other groups. Intergroup conflict then reinforces this sense of separate identity and serves to strengthen the boundaries between the two groups (Hensel, 1996). From a school leadership perspective, it is important to recognize the cultural and historical dimensions of these conflicts and not to dismiss them merely as a case of within-group conflict. In addition, school leaders should always try to seek insider perspectives on the conflicts in question, as these will often differ markedly from the perspectives of outsiders.

The questions asked about a conflict are also key. Sometimes, a slightly modified question will yield much richer results. For example, in one study of conflicts among high school girls, the interviewer began by asking the girls, "What was the conflict about?" This question yielded very little in terms of useful information. The girls typically responded with answers like, "nothing, little stuff." When the interviewer changed the question to, "What was the conflict for?" she was rewarded with much richer responses as the girls told her about the importance of protecting their friends, and preserving honor and status (Lustig, 1994).

In some cases, efforts to improve interethnic relations actually result, at least initially, in bringing conflicts that were hidden out in the open, giving the impression that the efforts created conflict rather than healed it (Walker, 2001). For example, providing a single staff development day on diversity and race relations in a school where many faculty members consider themselves to be color blind might bring to the surface differences among faculty members that were never discussed openly before. Because these issues are volatile and threatening to the status quo, professional development that focuses on race and diversity needs to be carefully planned over a series of sessions, with adequate opportunities for debriefing in a structured setting where people adhere to agreed-on guidelines for safety and confidentiality. Those in leadership roles need to be aware of this potential for surfacing conflict whenever they develop new initiatives that deal with diversity.

Activity 6: Issues That Trigger Racial and Ethnic Conflict

1. Individual reflection: Review the list of Issues That Can Trigger Racial or Ethnic Conflict (Box 3.1). Have any of these issues emerged at your school or a school you know of? Are there other trigger issues that have led to racial and ethnic conflict in your school? Who were and are the key players involved?

2. Group discussion: Share the results of your reflections with others in your group. Which trigger issues seem to be the most salient in your school? Does your group agree? If not, how are your perspectives different? Given the discussion about perspectives in Chapter 1, can you offer any reasons that your perspectives differ?

NOTE

1. This number is not based on an accurate count of all conflicts—we only knew of conflicts that people in the schools reported to us.

4

Identifying High-Priority Needs—Individual and Schoolwide

Making something more important than something else is very difficult. . . . Everybody's thing is the most important thing you should be doing.

—A principal in the Leading for Diversity study

DEVELOPMENT OF RACIAL IDENTITY

Key Questions for Leaders

- Why do younger students readily play together in diverse groups, whereas older students tend to self-segregate by race or ethnicity?
- What can school leaders do to share information about racial identity development with staff?

If you have spent time in diverse schools at different levels—elementary, middle, and high school—you have probably noticed that the older students become, the more they tend to cluster in groups of similar race or ethnicity. Students are aware of this tendency as well. A ninth-grade, African American boy commented wistfully about this pattern of increasing self-segregation:

In middle school, I hung out with a more diverse group, but [in high school], it's all in factions—we hang out with all the blacks. Me and my El Salvadoran friend from middle school, we made a pact that we would not let culture divide us. But I don't see from upper-class students any guidance or role models, except for a few. . . . The waters are real rough.

The tendency toward self-segregation is not limited to students, however. Many faculty lounges during lunchtime are similar showcases of how we cluster by racial or ethnic groups.

Is self-segregation really a problem? Should we as educators be doing something to change it? Scholars who have worked on racial identity development can help us shed light on these questions. Helms defines racial identity development as

A sense of group or collective identity based on one's *perception* that he or she shares a common racial heritage with a particular racial group. . . . Racial identity development theory concerns the psychological implications of racial group membership, that is, belief systems that evolve in reaction to perceived differential racial group membership. (Tatum, 1997, p. 3)

The term *perception* is important here. You may recall that in Chapter 1, we pointed out that no biological validity exists for the concept of race. Yet people's perceptions of belonging to a race are most certainly social facts that educators must recognize and deal with. A positive sense of one's self as a member of one's group is important for psychological health (Tatum, 1997), and racial identity development, when fostered appropriately, progresses towards this goal.

Stages in Black Identity Development

Like any other developmental progression, growth can be divided into several stages. Cross has developed a model of black racial identity development, and Helms has done the same for white identity development (Tatum, 1997). Although similar models have not, to our knowledge, been developed for other groups, some evidence suggests that the process for other nonwhite groups that have experienced oppression in the United States is similar to that described for African Americans. In Cross's model of black identity development, the stages are preencounter, encounter, immersion and emersion, internalization, and internalization-commitment. Box 4.1 describes these stages.

Stages in White Identity Development

White identity development differs from black identity development in some fundamental ways. While the task for African Americans and other people of color in a racist society is to resist negative social messages and develop an empowered sense of self, the task for people who are perceived as white is to develop a positive white identity based in reality, not on assumed superiority. In order to do that, each person needs to come to terms with what it means to be white in a diverse and racist society and, rather than ignoring their racialized position in this society or feeling guilty about it, to "feel good

---

Box 4.1   Stages in Black Identity Development

Preencounter. The black child absorbs many of the beliefs of the dominant white culture, including the idea that it is better to be white.

Encounter. An event or series of events force the person to acknowledge the personal impact of racism. As a result, the person begins to grapple with what it means to be a member of a group targeted by racism. During this stage, which often occurs in adolescence, racial grouping becomes a response to the environmental stressor of racism. Anger towards whites is often characteristic of this phase. Joining with those one considers one's peers (who share similar experiences of oppression) is a positive coping strategy. In addition, during this period, institutional structures such as tracking begin to shape and reinforce segregated socializing patterns.

Immersion-Emersion. Black adolescents or young adults seek opportunities to learn about their culture and history, with the support of same-race peers. The focus is on self-discovery, and white people become not so much objects of anger as simply irrelevant. Internalized negative stereotypes of black people begin to give way to a more positive sense of self and of black people.

Internalization. In this stage, the sense of security developed during immersion-emersion makes a person more willing to establish meaningful relationships across group boundaries.

Internalization-Commitment. In this stage, individuals find ways to translate their personal sense of racial identity into ongoing action to address the concerns of blacks as a group.

SOURCE: Adapted from Cross (Tatum, 1997, pp. 55-76).

---

about it in the context of a commitment to a just society" (Tatum, 1997, p. 94). Helms (Tatum, 1997) has identified six stages in white identity development, described in Box 4.2.

How can these models of racial identity development help school leaders in their work to improve race relations? For one thing, the models help to explain some of the socializing patterns we see among students as they move from elementary to secondary school. For example, a European American high school student who is in the pseudoindependent stage will not have much success trying to make friends with an African American student who is in the encounter stage. Educators often see minority students' tendency to self-segregate (particularly in the encounter and the immersion-emersion stages) as aberrant or problematic. African Americans and other students of color are often criticized for not socializing with a more diverse crowd. The models, developed by psychologists and counselors, suggest that these behaviors are part of a normal developmental

---

Box 4.2   Stages in White Identity Development

Contact. Individuals pay little attention to the significance of their racial identity. They assume that white is "normal" and that these days, racism is practiced only by individuals, not by institutions.

Disintegration. Personal encounters bring the social significance of race and racism into view. Often, individuals experience a close relationship with a person of color and see firsthand how racism can operate. The new awareness of how racism operates, either in personal prejudices or among one's family and friends, can lead to feelings of guilt, shame, and anger.

Reintegration. The uncomfortable feelings raised in the disintegration stage leave a person with a desire to retrench. Often, attempts to call people on racial jokes and slurs have resulted in pressure from white friends or family to lighten up and stop acting so socially conscious. The individual may respond by slipping back into collusion and silence or by resisting the recognition of whiteness by saying things like, "I don't want to be viewed as part of a group—I am an individual!"

Pseudoindependence. Individuals at this stage are sometimes characterized as "guilty white liberals." They have an intellectual understanding of racism as a system of advantage but don't know quite what to do about it. They often try to associate with people of color in a self-conscious way, as if this would relieve feelings of guilt.

Immersion-Emersion. Individuals search actively for new ways to think about whiteness that will take them beyond the role of victimizer. At this stage, they might join a group of antiracist white people or research the history of white protest against racism.

Autonomy. In this stage, the individual incorporates the newly defined view of whiteness as part of a personal identity, neither denying the uniqueness of each individual, nor minimizing the effects of racial group membership.

SOURCE: Adapted from Helms (Tatum, 1997, pp. 95-113).

---

progression that is related to one's position as a part of a dominant or subordinate group in the United States.

Self-segregation that is a normal part of racial identity development should not, however, be confused with allowing young people to exclude others or practice hatred toward others. It is one thing for a group of Latino students to choose to socialize together at lunchtime; it is something else when these students actively *prevent* non-Latino students from joining them. Self-segregation for the purpose of socializing with others who share your background also differs from groups that form in order to intimidate or bully other groups. For example, at one school, a group of Aryan Nation skinheads attempted to form an after-school club. The principal wouldn't allow it on the grounds that they were not forming simply to socialize but also to pursue an agenda of hatred toward people of color.[1]

One thing leaders can do, instead of ignoring or pathologizing students for their social grouping behavior, is to encourage staff to become familiar with the models of racial identity development. Simply helping other adults to see students' behaviors as part of a normal progression is likely to alleviate much of the negativity and blaming that takes place when we don't understand the reasons for people's behavior. For example, a study group of faculty members could read a relevant book (e.g., Tatum, 1997) and then do a workshop to involve the rest of the staff in an exploration of the content.

There is also no reason that high school students should not become involved in studying and exploring racial identity development themselves, possibly in a social studies or psychology course. Many high schools now have required ninth-grade courses that teach about a variety of social issues, and this topic would fit well within a course like this. The material should be worded so that it is accessible to adolescents and could be translated to other languages as needed.

As in all activities designed to involve people (adults as well as young people) in discussions about racial or ethnic relations, care needs to be taken to establish a sense of safety within the group. A group of students from Ohlone High School, with an adult facilitator, created the following ground rules for their discussion:

1. Take care of yourself.

2. Speak up and speak your mind.

3. Respect other people's opinions.

4. What gets said here stays here (no gossiping about this group).

The adult facilitator told the students he didn't think they could do #3. "It's incredibly hard to do it, even though we can say we do on the outside, but inside it's really hard to respect a different opinion." This challenged students to clarify what they meant by respect. In the end, they agreed on the following common denominators: "At least try to understand where the other person is coming from. You can at least listen to the judgment you have about it."

In Chapter 6, we will be exploring a number of different approaches school leaders have taken to improve race and ethnic relations in their schools. Many of these approaches, when combined in meaningful clusters, not only improve race relations but also encourage individual racial identity development to move toward more advanced stages. By taking action to improve race relations, we encourage individuals to develop positive racial identities, which in turn helps them survive and succeed in a society which still bears the marks of racism.

ACTIVITY 7: SOCIAL GROUPING PATTERNS

This activity is appropriate for participants who are already working in a school.

1. Individual reflection: Think about the cafeteria at lunchtime or the playground or courtyard during recess or breaks. How do students group themselves? What happens when a student outside the group attempts to join? How do adults at your school view the way students group themselves?

2. Group discussion: Share your reflections with others in the group. How are they different or similar? In light of what you've read and discussed together, do you think change should occur at your school?

3. Now work through the same process, but this time focus on adult groupings at your school.

MASLOW AND THE LEADING FOR DIVERSITY PROGRESSION OF NEEDS

Key Question for Leaders

- How can I identify the highest-priority needs at my school?

In the previous section, we looked closely at individual needs as individuals progress toward a positive racial identity. Schools, however, are made up of a multitude of individuals whose demands and needs can be quite different from one another. School leaders are faced with the seemingly impossible task of figuring out which needs and demands to assign a high priority to at a given time. For example, some students may argue that the lack of sports facilities is the most pressing need to be addressed, while some faculty members may argue that they need structured time to meet in grade level groups. Some of the parents may argue that the school's need for better security should take precedence over all other agendas. Faced with such diverse and often competing priorities, yet knowing that leadership cannot possibly take on everything at once, how can school leaders make sense of what to focus on first?

Since school leaders often do not know what kind of school context they will step into next—and since that they will most likely have to work in several schools in the course of their careers—they need to have a way of assessing what the high-priority tasks are in a given school and community context. However, in order to decide on the highest-priority tasks, one has to have a way of prioritizing the many needs of the school and community. In order to do this, it is helpful to have a framework in mind to guide and give direction to the work of school leaders.

Some schools face serious problems of safety and security in which students—or staff members—feel physically or verbally threatened. A first step for leadership in these schools is to contain overt conflicts so that students and staff can, at the very least, come to school and feel safe. These schools must not, however, stop with containment but must plan ahead to build a more positive environment. Other schools have either never had a high degree of overt conflict, or such problems were addressed a long time ago. These schools, because they are already safe and secure, can focus more on other efforts, such as creating a sense of community, celebrating and learning about different ethnic groups and cultures, and making sure every student is encouraged to reach his or her potential. All schools should reach this point; however, the context and needs of a particular school may mean that it will take a longer time to get there.

Rather than reinvent the wheel, we found it useful to draw on the well-known developmental progression delineated by psychologist Abraham Maslow (1968) in what he called a Hierarchy of Needs. Maslow differentiated between two broad category of needs—basic needs and growth needs. Basic needs include the environmental preconditions necessary for need satisfaction (freedom, justice, orderliness), physiological needs (air, water, food, shelter, sleep, and sex), and the physical need for safety and security. Maslow submitted that once these basic needs have been satisfied, higher-order needs unfold, which include love and belonging, esteem from others and self-esteem, and the need for a host of other experiences (truth, goodness, beauty, individuality, meaningfulness, justice, order) that result in *self-actualization*—his term meaning the capacity to experience one's full potential. Although the notion of self-actualization may seem a bit amorphous, most of us would not contest the educational ideal of helping people realize their full potential. As such, if we apply this framework not only to the individual, as Maslow intended, but also to the collective of individuals and conditions that comprise a school community, we can begin to define a progression of school needs, through which schools must progress in the pursuit of realizing the full potential of all members of the school community.

Due to associations of the term *hierarchy* with notions of arbitrarily imposed standards and fixed categories, we prefer to consider this framework a *progression* that is dependent on context. This means that the stages in the progression are not rigid or mutually exclusive. One can work on an early stage in the progression while simultaneously beginning to address a later stage. The progression is represented in Figure 4.1.

Level 1

A school at Level 1 in this progression would place a high priority on meeting the physical needs of students—including the needs for food, shelter,

Figure 4.1 A Progression of School Needs

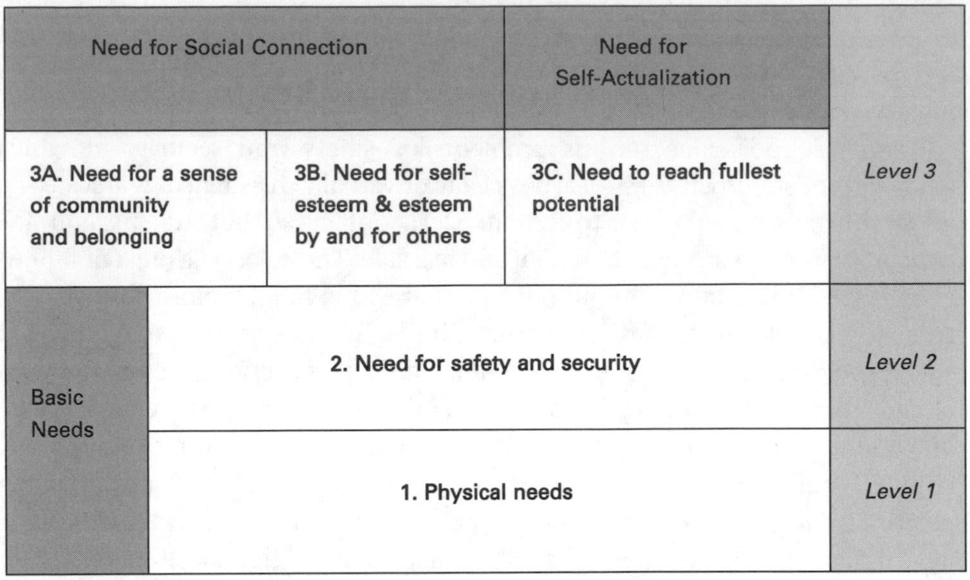

Need for Social Connection		Need for Self-Actualization	
3A. Need for a sense of community and belonging	3B. Need for self-esteem & esteem by and for others	3C. Need to reach fullest potential	Level 3
Basic Needs	2. Need for safety and security		Level 2
	1. Physical needs		Level 1

SOURCE: Adapted from Maslow (1968).

clothing, and transportation to and from school. While many schools do provide free lunch for students, transportation, and other physical services, this area is not the main emphasis of most schools.

Level 2

A school at Level 2 would place a high priority on ensuring that students are safe from violence and verbal threats and that they feel secure coming to school. Several schools in our study found it necessary to focus on this level because violence and security problems had so destabilized the school that nothing much could be accomplished until this level was under control. Some of the strategies schools were using to address this area included establishing stricter and more consistent behavioral standards; placing security personnel at key points, including exits and entrances; improving the training of security personnel; and closing the campus so that students could not leave at lunchtime. Proactive school leaders, however, try to couple such strategies with positive rewards and incentives so that efforts to establish safety and security are not seen as punitive. Thus, for example, a principal in a middle school who established much stricter and more consistent behavioral standards tied this to the creation of more positive activities for students to become involved with at lunchtime and after school.

Level 3

A school at Level 3 has typically established an environment where students' physical needs are met and where students and staff feel safe and secure from violence and verbal threats. While a proactive leader never entirely stops attending to these issues, they are no longer (or never were) the central focus of the school's efforts. At this level, a school can turn its focus to one or more of the three areas that Maslow called "higher-order needs." These include the need for a sense of community and belonging, the need for self-esteem and esteem from and for others, and the need to reach one's fullest potential.

Level 3A. One can think of community and belonging as the unity part of improving race relations, while self-esteem and esteem for and from others is the pluralism part. Schools that are focusing on community and belonging might, for example, work on building a diverse leadership team that includes different ethnic groups and different stakeholders such as teachers, students, parents, and instructional assistants. Providing structures such as houses, families, or teams where personalized relationships can develop would be another example of a focus on community and belonging. These approaches tend to highlight similarities among people and the sharing of similar goals, such as student achievement, safety, and respect.

Level 3B. A focus on self-esteem and esteem for and from others might be exemplified in a school where students have opportunities to study and appreciate their own and other's history and culture. Curriculum and special courses are one way to do this; celebratory events are another, though these have a tendency to be more superficial; professional development for staff in the area of diversity and race relations can also help toward the goals of self-esteem and esteem for others. These approaches tend to highlight differences and to point out that these differences are valuable resources.

Level 3C. A focus on all individuals reaching their highest potential is almost synonymous with the ideal of education—that it should help people expand and deepen their talents and skills, preparing them to reach their goals and to make a difference in some area, such as academics, arts, or social justice. At one elementary school in the study, this focus was exemplified by sixth graders who all worked on a yearlong project to solve community problems of their choice, and then presented the projects to an outside audience. This focus on reaching potential includes the traditional focus of schools on academic achievement; however, it is also larger, as it encompasses other forms of achievement as well as academics.

The following example from our study illustrates how one elementary school in the study, Cornell, moved through different stages in the progression of school needs. A more extended example can be found in the case study of Gladiola Middle School in Chapter 11.

In the 1970s and early 1980s, Cornell went through a lot of changes as the student population shifted from mostly white and African American students of working class families to more Latino and Southeast Asian immigrants, many of whom were on welfare or lacked a steady family income. Between 1970 and 1985, the school population also grew dramatically, from around 600 students to over 900. Several principals were at a loss as to how to deal with the changes, and by 1985, the school, as well as the surrounding community, was in considerable disarray. Within the school, students were disrespectful and sometimes violent toward each other and toward teachers. Disciplinary practices were unevenly applied and tended to be more punitive than educational. Outside the school, guns were increasingly common, as were reports of drug and gang activity.

In 1985, an upward trend began in the school when the new principal, Mr. Corey, made it his agenda to tighten up on discipline and create a safer, more orderly environment for learning. He began following through more consistently on the school's disciplinary policies, so kids didn't "get away with things" as they had before. He also focused on cleaning up the school's physical plant, installing light bulbs in dark hallways and making sure all drinking fountains and bathrooms worked.

When Ms. Gardner became principal in 1986, she was able to build on Corey's work rather than start from the beginning again. She made it her focus to develop the school's relationship with the community, as many community-based organizations (CBOs) had sprung up to assist immigrants and refugees from Mexico and Latin America as well as Southeast Asia. She began a Healthy Start project that linked these CBOs and the school in a partnership. She also laid the foundation for the school leadership team (which would be developed further by the next principal), and set up both conflict resolution programs and Tribes, two programs which teach prosocial skills to students. All of these initiatives served to build a stronger sense of community both in the school and between the school and the larger neighborhood.

Ms. Haas-Garcia became principal in 1993 and was able to set priorities for the school that built on both previous principals' work. By this time, the school was already considered relatively safe and secure, and a definite feeling of community existed among staff members and students. Haas-Garcia, together with the now-functioning leadership team composed of teachers, instructional aides, and parents, developed a school reform agenda and funding to make the school more of a community center. A Family Resource Center was created to address the health needs of the schools' families through onsite clinics, and she brought in many more after-school activities for students.

By the time we visited the school in 1997 and 1998, these initiatives were well underway. A new priority, however, had emerged: While students and families were happy with the sense of safety and community they felt at the school, students still had a long way to go academically. The need for a more focused effort in literacy and math had become evident, and staff members were working hard to develop more appropriate programming and teaching strategies to improve students' academic performance.

In this sketch of different leadership eras at Cornell Elementary, several things become evident. First, it is often the case that different leaders give various needs different priorities. This was most clear in the transition from Corey's law and order regime to Gardner's focus on developing a sense of community. Some schools, on the other hand, see the entire progression of needs unfold within the tenure of a single leader who remains in the school for a long time, assigning different priorities to different areas as the needs shift.

Another lesson we can glean from the Cornell sketch is the "necessary but not sufficient" principle. That is, the more basic needs may be a necessary step to satisfying the higher-order needs, but they are not in themselves sufficient to achieve the desired goal. Thus establishing a safe and secure school was a necessary step at Cornell, but it was not sufficient to make the school a place where all students can achieve to their fullest potential. Similarly, creating a strong sense of community and belonging was necessary but also not sufficient to achieving the higher goals of academic and other kinds of achievement. The school still had more work to do in this area, but the basic elements of safety and security and the strong sense of community were now in place as a foundation. Because school leaders have so many different constituencies to serve and so many potential areas for action, developing clarity about where to focus one's energies is a must. A few well-chosen focus areas, selected in collaboration with key stakeholders in the school community, can link the school leaders' work to the areas where the school has the greatest needs, making the leadership's efforts highly relevant.

ACTIVITY 8: PRIORITIZING NEEDS

This activity is designed to help those in school leadership roles go through a process to prioritize needs within the school community. The activity requires you to gather some information from students, staff, and parents in the form of focus groups or individual interviews.

1. Conduct focus groups or interviews.

The purpose of these information-gathering activities is to obtain input from a range of stakeholders in the school community. It is important to get input from sources who are diverse, not only in terms of the role they play at the school (parent, student, staff member) but also in terms of ethnicity, gender, English language proficiency, and other categories that might represent major forms of diversity in your school.

You can gather input through group interviews (focus groups of four to six people) or individual interviews. You can also gather it in meetings, such as staff meetings and student council meetings, through an open discussion, or through a questionnaire. Here, we assume you will either use focus groups or individual interviews. Focus groups have an advantage in that people get to hear what others think and may revise their own opinions based on what they hear. Sometimes, the discussions that go on in focus groups can be very helpful for clarifying and sharing information. On the other hand, if people have things to say that might be confidential, they will not speak openly in a focus group. In these cases, individual interviews with a nonjudgmental interviewer offer a way to elicit information that otherwise might not be shared. In any interview, it is important to state a few ground rules at the outset, such as clarifying that "what gets said here stays here" or that people's names will not be reported with the information they share.

Decide how many people you would like to interview and how you will select people and set up the interviews—the logistics.

2.   Develop some questions that can serve as a guide during the interviews. Of course, you can always depart from these questions as the need arises, but they form a structure that helps you stay on target as it is easy to get distracted once people start talking. It is also useful to think ahead of how you will probe for additional information. For example, if someone says, "I really think we need to pay more attention to security," you don't automatically know what they mean by security. You might probe further by asking, "Could you say a bit more about that?" or "Can you give me an example?"

Here are some sample questions that might be useful in an interview about school needs:

● What are the strengths of this school? (For young students, this might be reworded as "What do you like most about the school?")

● What are the areas that most need improvement? Why do you say this? (The second question will help you sort out whether the improvement is related to students having better learning opportunities or whether it is related to more comfort for a particular individual.)

● What do you think is the first thing that leadership should concentrate on in this school? Why?

Other questions to ask:

3.   Conduct the interviews, being careful to keep track of who says what, as you will need to tabulate this later. A tape recorder can be useful if you are willing to review the tape afterwards. You also need to ask people's permission before you tape record any conversation. If you don't tape record, then good note taking is adequate.

4.   Analyze the results. Use Table 4.1 as an analytical tool, grouping responses according to where you think they fit in the progression.

5.   Interpret the results. Which levels of need seem to be the highest priority according to the interviews you conducted? How closely does this match your own understanding of the school's greatest needs?

6.   Share the results. Let other stakeholders in the school community know the highest-priority needs that have emerged from your inquiry process.

Table 4.1   Summary of Priority of Needs

Directions: Summarize the results of your interviews in the appropriate spaces.

	Students	*Staff*	*Parents*
3C. Need to reach fullest potential—e.g., academic needs, career needs, creativity needs, social justice and equity needs			
3B. Need for self-esteem and esteem from others—e.g., focus on recognizing and valuing differences			
3A. Need for sense of community and belonging—e.g., need for unifying structures, recognition of common ground			
2. Need for safety and security—e.g., need to stop racial harassment, name-calling, violence, bullying, intimidation			
1. Physical needs—e.g., need for food, clothing, shelter, transportation to and from school			

SOURCE: Adapted from Maslow (1968)

Ask people to comment if they want to. Try to develop a broad consensus that these are the needs that must be attended to first. This information can then be the basis for collaborative decision making about what to do to address the needs.

NOTE

1. The legality of this principal's action is somewhat questionable, according to Taylor (2000), who explains the Equal Access Act of 1984: "Equal access may not be denied to groups whose ideas are unconventional or unpopular. The only groups that may be denied equal access are unlawful organizations or groups that materially and substantially interfere with the orderly conduct of educational activities. However, a school retains the authority to take proper disciplinary steps against a group that creates a material or substantial interference with school activities, as long as this discipline is not based upon purely speculative harm" (p. 70).

5

Envisioning Positive Interethnic Relations

It is necessary to dare to say that racism is a curable disease.

—Lilia Bartolomé and Donaldo Macedo (1997, p. 244)

We have covered a lot of ground in the previous chapters, all of which should have prepared you (as much as anyone can be prepared for action by reading a book) to develop a plan to promote positive interethnic relations in your school. Of course, this is not something you should attempt to do by yourself. No matter how good your intentions are and how sound the resulting plan might be in theory, it will not work if key stakeholders have no ownership in it.

TEAM BUILDING

Key Questions for Leaders

- Which members of the school community can I identify as potential collaborators for developing positive interethnic relations?
- What resources can I draw on to support the work of such a team?

Because this plan is about diversity and human relations, the process of creating it should reflect the diversity of your school as much as possible. This

67

means that the planning team should reflect a diversity of roles within the school as well as ethnic, economic, and other kinds of diversity. In terms of roles, ideally, the team should include school administrators, district administrators, teachers, support staff, parents, interested community members, and students (especially if you are at a middle or high school). Your school may already have a leadership team that fits the criteria noted above, in which case you are one step ahead. If you don't have a leadership team that fits these criteria, or if you have one but it doesn't function very well, you may need to spend some time forming an appropriate team. If you expect people to put in significant time beyond regular work hours, you should make an effort to locate some funds to pay them. This will send a message that the work is an important part of the team's professional duties. It will also, if you are an administrator and plan to be the leader or facilitator of the group, give you the right to expect more of the team (including yourself).

If people ask you what they are expected to do on this team, the true answer is, "It depends." It depends on what the team chooses to do and how much work they decide to take on. Most likely, it will be a team that spends some time developing a shared vision and values that are tied explicitly to human relations, diversity, and equity or social justice. It is also likely that you will need to do some team-building activities to enable the team to function effectively. If you are not already familiar with team-building processes, resources such as Shaw (1992) and McCall (1994) can provide guidance. Then, members will take responsibility for some part of the larger effort, and come back together periodically to share what they have accomplished and set goals for next steps. If you have already involved team members in doing some of the assessments and preparation covered in previous chapters, you are several steps ahead. If not, you will have to bring the team up to speed on what you have been doing to prepare.

DEVELOPING A SHARED VISION FOR INTERETHNIC RELATIONS

Key Question for Leaders

- How can we develop a shared vision for positive interethnic relations in my school?

Let's say you have already assembled a team that has the task of developing a plan for improving interethnic relations. The team has reviewed the material in the previous chapters and has seen the results of the various activities, so they have a good sense of how the school context affects interethnic relations, what kinds of racial or ethnic conflict exist at the school, and what the priority needs are at this time. You are now ready to begin developing a plan to improve interethnic relations. But don't expect this to be a smooth, linear journey. As you go through the processes that follow, you will necessarily revisit the earlier steps several times, as things that weren't clear the first time will need to be defined or fleshed out more carefully.

When a school leadership team begins to develop a vision of interethnic relations, a framework to guide the discussion is helpful. The field of multicultural education has produced several frameworks that identify different levels or degrees of inclusion of diverse and marginalized groups in schooling. These frameworks can serve as a point of departure. Team members might want to read books about multicultural education, such as Banks (1989) and Sleeter (1996), and then come together to discuss them in relation to their own visions for interethnic relations in their school.

Before we discuss these frameworks, we should clarify the distinction between *multicultural education* and the improvement of *interethnic relations*. We see multicultural education as a larger endeavor that seeks "full and equal participation of all groups in a society that is mutually shaped to meet their needs" (Bell, 1997, p. 3). In other words, multicultural education is a pathway toward social justice. Banks (1989) defined multicultural education as

> An educational reform movement and a process whose major goal is to change the structure of educational institutions so that male and female students, exceptional students, and students who are members of diverse racial, ethnic, and cultural groups will have an equal chance to achieve academically in school. (p. 1)

Sleeter (1996) defines multicultural education as "a form of resistance to dominant modes of schooling" (p. 2) and asserts that this resistance, in order to be effective, must go beyond educational reform; it should be thought of as a social movement because the change process must include not only educators within the education establishment but also community members and parents. In these definitions, positive interethnic relations are one subgoal, among others; pursuing the larger goal of creating a more just society should, in theory at least, lead toward more positive relations across lines of difference, as well as other benefits.

Banks (1997) focuses his model primarily on curriculum as the locus of change and posits four different "levels of integration of ethnic content." These are displayed in Figure 5.1.

Grant and Sleeter (1989) outline a somewhat different framework for multicultural education. They identified five levels, some of which go beyond curriculum to include the whole school:

1. Teaching the exceptional or culturally different, in which the goal is to help these students acquire the cognitive skills and knowledge of the traditional curriculum

2. The human relations approach, which focuses on attitudes and feelings students have about themselves and each other

3. Single-group studies, which provide in-depth portraits of specific groups and critical examinations of their oppression

4. The multicultural education approach, which advocates reform of the whole school in order to be consistent with its goals of social justice

Figure 5.1 Levels of Integration of Ethnic Content

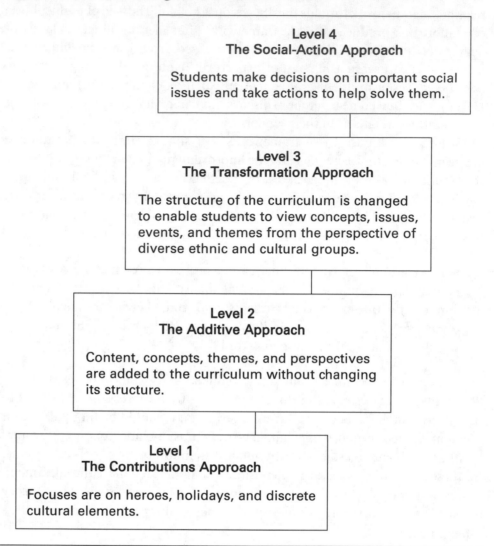

5. Education that is multicultural and social reconstructionist, which extends the multicultural education approach "by educating students to be analytical and critical thinkers who can take action toward greater equity in race, class, gender, and handicap." (p. 54)

As a member of the leadership team in your school, you will need to wrestle with the questions these frameworks imply. How far does your team want to go in the pursuit of positive interethnic relations? Are you willing to address underlying inequities in the system of education and challenge assumptions that the playing field is level? Do some individuals want to go further than others? Also, the language used to talk about the desired changes can be critical in terms of how the changes are accepted or rejected. Sleeter (1996) notes that:

The politics of bringing about change has necessitated frequently couching arguments for school reform in language that white educators would attend to. Many advocates have deliberately chosen terms like *human relations* because nobody opposes good human relations, while the term *multicultural* signifies a red flag to many people, and the term *race* literally scares many more away. (p. 8)

Leaders have to think strategically and politically, not only in terms of their own vision for the school. They have to consider the local politics and climate to determine how best to introduce and frame the desired changes. Sleeter (1996) quotes one of her colleagues, Yamane, who said, "Rather than looking for the sharpest needle, it is more strategically effective to look for one that sews" (p. 9). This doesn't mean you should throw out your vision if it isn't compatible with the values and attitudes of the powers that be in your district. But it does mean that you shouldn't get so invested in using certain terminology that you are unwilling to budge. If certain words are hot buttons, try other words—but stay true to your ideas.

As you begin to shape a school vision, it will also be useful to recall the four principles of the framework which we introduced in Chapter 2—affirm identity, build community, cultivate student leadership, and address root causes of conflict (ABCA). As a team, you should discuss each of these areas and come to some shared understandings of these four principles and also recognize any differences in your understandings of them.

ACTIVITY 9: VISIONING

A visioning activity is a good place to begin your work as a team. It will help you clarify different assumptions and values you hold about diversity, equity, and social justice, and should lead to some exciting and rich discussions—and possibly some conflict as people may surface feelings and attitudes that weren't safe to express before. As noted in Chapter 3, conflict can be a springboard for creative growth, so as a leader, you should try to be prepared but not afraid of conflict. Set some ground rules for the activity with the group. If possible, ask someone who has experience with conflict resolution to facilitate or to step in if needed. The following questions can be used as a stimulus for discussion.

1. What kinds of relationships do we want our school to foster between individuals and between diverse groups?

2. How do we want to develop and sustain these relationships?

3. How do we want to view and address conflict in our school?

4. What knowledge, dispositions, and skills related to ethnic diversity do we want to nurture among students and adults in our school?

5. Do we want to take a human relations approach which focuses on attitudes and feelings towards self and others, or do we want to go beyond that to address inequities in our system?

You might want to use a think-pair-share structure to facilitate this discussion. Ask each person to reflect and write about the questions for a few minutes. This helps people clarify their own thinking before engaging in dialogue. Then, ask people to find a partner (preferably someone they don't talk to all the time) and share each other's reflections. If your group is large (say 20 or more) you might want to then form small groups of four for further sharing and dialogue. If your group is small, then you can go directly to the last step, which is a whole-group sharing. Be sure to record the ideas people have for each question— either on chart paper or individual Post-its that people can stick underneath each question. Further discussion, after people share their ideas, can focus on clarifying the ideas offered and on similarities and differences among them. Final questions for whole-group discussion and closure of the session might be

• What are the unifying themes in our collective thinking about a school vision for interethnic relations?

• Where do our ideas fit in terms of the ABCA principles?

• Where do our ideas fit in terms of the frameworks developed by Banks or Grant and Sleeter?

• What are the areas we need to discuss further?

- Who else should be part of these conversations?

- How is our vision of interethnic relations going to be tied to the school's overall vision?

- How will we share the draft vision of interethnic relations with others at the school and in the community, and what kind of input do we want?

- What next steps do we need to take in developing our plan?

As with any action plan, the last question needs to be addressed specifically in terms of who, what, when, and how. People should take the lead on specific tasks and agree to a time frame for accomplishing them. You should also identify resources (time, money, materials, assistance) that you will need to get the tasks done.

If the team agrees that they are ready to begin sharing a draft of the vision with others at the school and in the community, then it needs to be written up in a form that others can respond to (this includes translating into other languages as needed). You might consider holding several forums or focus groups to get input. You also need to decide how you will handle the input you get. This can vary from, "Thank you for your input; now we'll do it our way anyway," to a more authentic form of participation in which you take the ideas offered seriously and, if they differ from or add to what the team has devised, you invite those people to the next meeting to discuss their ideas further.

In a critique of what often passes for participatory decision making, Anderson (1998) claims that many participatory decision-making processes only serve to recreate the earlier power structures under a different organizational structure. One reason for this, he says, is that, "The role of conflict in participatory approaches to institutional change may be undertheorized," and that there has been a bias toward "managing conflict, culture, diversity, and anything else that could potentially lead to authentic change but which might upset the balance of power in the institution" (p. 593). In other words, leaders often give lip service to participatory approaches, but in the end, they still make the final decisions.

Obviously, the more authentic forms of participation make the process of developing a vision take longer, but the results can be well worth the effort in terms of greater ownership among diverse stakeholders. Authentic participation results in more solid decisions and a greater likelihood that they will be acted on and implemented. Also, the discussions themselves are a rich learning opportunity—professional development for all involved.

DEVELOPING COHERENCE AMONG DISPARATE APPROACHES

Key Question for Leaders

- How do proactive leaders create coherence in their efforts to improve interethnic relations?

The approaches we will describe in the next chapter offer many avenues for leaders to consider as they work toward building positive interethnic relations. Yet no single approach is adequate by itself, and it is not advisable for leaders to pick a few approaches that sound good and implement them without thinking carefully about coherence. This can lead to a scattered or hodgepodge effect, with disparate approaches lacking any clear linkage to one another or to a larger vision. For example, when we first began to talk with people about the study, explaining that the purpose was to document what schools are doing to improve race and ethnic relations, people often responded by saying, "Oh, yeah, we have a conflict resolution program at our school, and it has really taken care of any racial problems we had before." But even the best conflict resolution program by itself is not enough, because it only addresses one aspect of the complex issue of race and ethnic relations. Conflict resolution programs can be a wonderful asset, but they tend to focus on overt conflicts, and, as we explained in Chapter 3, overt conflicts are only the tip of the iceberg.

The proactive leaders in the study created what one principal called a "mosaic" of approaches to intergroup relations. The approaches that a particular school used were linked together through unifying themes, such as personalization, community building, and nonviolence. Themes like these, when they are embodied in the everyday practices of a school, build strong coherence, one of the key assets of high-performance schools as well as businesses.

> Coherence doesn't happen by accident, and doesn't happen by pursuing everything under the sun. Effective organizations are not ones that innovate the most; they are not ones that send personnel on the most number of staff development conferences. No, they are organizations that selectively go about learning more. In all of their activities, even ones that foster diversity, they create mechanisms of integration. Moral purpose, communication, intense interaction, implementation plans, performance data all serve the purpose of coherence. In examining new policies or possibilities integrative organizations not only worry about the value of each opportunity, but they also ask how the new idea connects with what they are doing. Shared meaning and organizational connectedness are the long-term assets of high performance systems. (Fullan, 1999, p. 28)

Allaneq Middle School provides a good example of how two successive principals at a particular school developed and implemented a coherent plan to improve interethnic relations. Their goal was to build a violence-free, personalized community at Allaneq Middle School.

At Allaneq Middle School in Alaska, personalizing the school experience for students as well as adults was an important value held by the previous principal, Mary Chauncy and her successor, Terri Turner. Personalization was seen as one avenue leading to the improvement of both intergroup relations and academic learning. Since the school served a very diverse, low-income population of around 850 students in Grades 7 and 8 only, they had less time than the average school to make a tangible difference in students' lives. If the staff didn't create connections with students quickly, they would miss the opportunity. To create greater personalization, the leaders used several approaches. First, Chauncy designed a team structure that assigned students to grade level teams of 120 to 140 students each; a particular group of five teachers and a counselor and Title I resource specialist were responsible for each team of students. This enabled the staff members of a given team to know their students better and also develop better connections with parents. Block scheduling was instituted for core subjects so that interdisciplinary themes could be explored in depth by the teams, and there was time each day, while students were in their applied academics class (e.g., health), for the faculty on each team to meet for curriculum planning and monitoring of student progress. While at first the teams were somewhat ethnically homogeneous, the staff viewed this as problematic since students weren't developing familiarity with other cultures to the degree they could if they were more integrated. So when Turner came in as principal, she reorganized the teams to be more internally diverse. By doing so, she aligned the team structure more closely with the goal of developing positive interethnic relations.

Another strategy to increase personalization was a concerted effort to hire more staff members with cultural backgrounds similar to students.' This helped the school become more accessible to the growing number of Native Alaskan, African American, Latino, Pacific Islander, and Southeast Asian students. Bilingual staff were able to do home visits and outreach with populations that had not been well served initially. A third approach, which Principal Turner used when she first started, was to conduct a needs assessment by meeting individually with every teacher and with every student in focus groups to find out what they thought the school's greatest needs were for the coming year as well as what they liked about the school and wanted to continue. This gave her high visibility from the start and ensured that when she implemented new initiatives, she had the necessary support from staff and students. One of the issues almost everyone identified was violence, including interethnic and gang conflict. This led Turner to declare a campaign for nonviolence, which then became a second unifying theme alongside personalization.

The theme of nonviolence was realized through several approaches, including a peer conflict resolution program, more consistent and stricter behavioral standards coupled with rewards for positive, nonviolent behavior, and a business partnership with the local telephone company to provide phones in all classrooms to support safety. The peer conflict resolution program, Resolving Conflicts Creatively (see Resource B) taught students a process for resolving their own conflicts whenever possible. The training provided for students and faculty advisors included a component that addressed race and ethnicity as possible dimensions in student conflicts. The increased strictness and consistency of behavioral standards involved several strategies. First, the administrators, counselors, security staff, and teachers had to agree on the standards for behavior, and the administrators had to agree to back up teachers if they referred students to the office for behavioral problems. Second, the three security staff members were given private offices where they could meet with students individually and provide support for students who were having behavior problems. In effect, this created another tier of personnel who could serve in a counseling role. Like many schools that tighten up on behavior, the number of referrals and suspensions initially rose, then dropped below the previous year's figures. Students first have to get the message that the administration is serious about giving consequences for behavior problems and that the consequences will not be subject to favoritism based on race or anything else. Once the message is clear, the number of referrals tends to drop off dramatically. The other side of the behavior strategy, however, is that it must not be seen as punitive only. Students who follow the policies need to receive positive attention from adults. At Allaneq, the leaders did this by having monthly reward assemblies for nonviolent behavior (such as a rock concert at lunchtime) and more student activities during regular lunchtimes.

The twin themes of personalization and nonviolence at Allaneq illustrate the concept of coherence in practice. Each approach that was used at Allaneq—whether it was a conflict resolution program or a team structure or any other approach—existed to serve a larger purpose that was part of the school's vision. There were other unifying themes at Allaneq as well, but these two give a glimpse of how a particular set of approaches can be united within a shared value system and vision (see Figure 5.2).

As school leaders consider how they might create greater coherence in the area of intergroup relations, it is important to keep in mind that schools serve not only students but adults (staff and parents) as well. It is a common mistake to plan intergroup relations efforts for students only and to overlook the fact that adults, as much or perhaps more than students, also need to improve in intercultural communication skills and ways to combat racism. A coherent set of approaches to improving interethnic relations will address both students and adults in the school community.

LEVERAGING RESOURCES

Key Question for Leaders

- What resources—financial as well as in-kind services or goods—can I leverage in order to support our plan?

Figure 5.2 Organizing Themes—the Connection Between Vision
and Practice

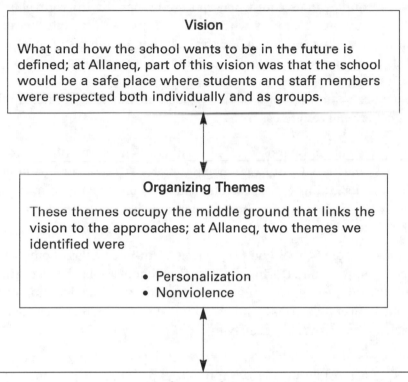

Vision

What and how the school wants to be in the future is
defined; at Allaneq, part of this vision was that the school
would be a safe place where students and staff members
were respected both individually and as groups.

Organizing Themes

These themes occupy the middle ground that links the
vision to the approaches; at Allaneq, two themes we
identified were

- Personalization
- Nonviolence

Approaches

Approaches are clusters of practice which together embody a particular
theme.

The theme of *personalization*
was embodied through

- Teams
- Diverse staffing to improve
  communication with
  students and parents
- Inquiry to assess needs

The theme of *nonviolence* was
embodied through

- A peer conflict resolution
  program
- Consistent and strict
  behavioural standards
- Rewards for nonviolent behavior
- Positive activities for students
  during lunchtime
- Partnership that provided
  phones in classrooms

By now, it has probably become obvious that in order to implement your
plan, you might require additional funding or in-kind services. While the next
chapter will deal more specifically with concrete approaches, it is not too early
to begin strategizing about how you might secure the additional resources you
might need. Can the district help? Do you already have Title I, Title VII, or other
federal and state funding that could be used to support your plan? Is there a
private foundation that might support some part of your plan? What about
business leaders in your community—should they be approached to ask about
in-kind or financial contributions?

Most organizations and businesses will not contribute to something that is not defined, so don't approach them yet. At this point, just start a list of potential resources to explore when you are prepared with your plan. Some cities have foundation centers where you can browse through literature on thousands of funding sources to find the ones that are interested in supporting the kinds of things you are planning. There is also a Web site you can use to explore funding possibilities: www.fdncenter.org.

Below are some examples of how leaders in the study reached out and received additional resources:

> The principal at Buena Vista Elementary School recruited two major business partners to support ongoing efforts at the school. One of these partners, for example, underwrote field trips for students to multicultural events or attractions. Another partner supplied paper goods for monthly lunches to celebrate students with 100 percent attendance.

> Allaneq Middle School had no phone system in the classrooms when we first began the study. During the study, the school established a partnership with the phone company and received a very welcome donation of a telephone in every classroom and an intercom system, which helped alleviate teachers' concerns about safety in their classrooms.

> At Dolores Huerta Middle School, in order to address gang presence, a partnership was established between the local police and the school. A multicity, gang taskforce was set up involving the schools, neighboring cities, and the police department. At the middle school, a new program called the Frontline Academy was established to give special attention and structure to at-risk students. The academy courses were taught by a police officer who, in addition to the more structured environment he provided for students, also attended to their social and emotional needs by providing counseling and support for them to achieve their goals.

When seeking potential funding or contributions, it is always important to have a short, written proposal you can give potential donors, outlining what you want the funding or in-kind contribution for, how much it will cost (or quantifying the services or goods you hope they will contribute), and what the benefits will be. Also, it is important to follow up by keeping supporters and funders informed of progress and sending thank-you letters. People and organizations who contribute to schools have a right to know how the money, services, or goods they contribute make a difference.

6

Selecting Approaches for a Coherent Plan

Effective organizations do trust the process, but not completely; they design their work in a way that is not left up to chance.

—Michael Fullan (1999, p. 24)

Your team has now wrestled with the development of a shared vision for interethnic relations and has, we hope, emerged from that process with a sense of what you would like your school to look like in the future in terms of relations among diverse groups. You have also considered the issue of coherence, or how the plan you develop will need to hang together somehow. Now it's time to consider specifically which approaches to improving interethnic relations make the most sense, given your context, priority needs, and vision. Your school may very well already be using some of these approaches. However, it is important to remember that there are degrees of implementation. Having held a half-day workshop for staff on racism in 1999 doesn't mean your school has the professional development approach sewn up.

Leaders in the 21 schools that participated in our study used a wide range of approaches to improve interethnic relations. These approaches, when combined in meaningful clusters, helped leaders address conflicts related to race or ethnicity and enabled them to develop a stable foundation for positive interethnic relations. Box 6.1 presents a summary of the approaches. In our view,

---

Box 6.1   Approaches for Improving Interethnic Relations

---

1. **Approaches that affect all members of the school community:**

    -   *Data Inquiry:* Use data inquiry, such as an examination of disaggregated student outcomes, as a starting point leading to various kinds of change.*
    -   *School or District Vision:* Use the school vision as a lever to keep goals, such as social justice, unity, and respect, in view.*
    -   *Organizational Changes:* Change physical or organizational structures in ways that encourage relationships across lines of difference.
    -   *Diverse Staffing:* Increase the ethnic, cultural, and linguistic diversity of the staff as a path toward greater inclusion.*
    -   *Professional Development:* Seek to educate staff members about interethnic relations.*

2. **Approaches designed to have a direct impact on students:**

    -   *Curriculum and Instruction:* Embed interethnic-relations topics in curriculum and use instructional methods that encourage interethnic cooperation.
    -   *Special Events:* Provide special times to celebrate the diverse cultures of the school, build awareness of differences and similarities, or focus on intergroup relations.
    -   *Programs:* Include conflict resolution, mentoring and tutoring, and after-school and extracurricular programs.
    -   *Behavioral Standards:* Focus on developing consistent standards of behavior across all diverse groups of students.*

3. **Approaches designed to reach extended audiences:**

    -   *Parent Involvement:* Develop meaningful connections between diverse families and schools.*
    -   *Expanding the School Community:* Link the school with local, national, international, and electronic communities.

---

*NOTE: The asterisks indicate approaches the authors consider essential; those without asterisks are more context dependent (e.g., necessary in some schools and optional in others).

---

certain approaches (the ones with asterisks) should be required in all schools, because we cannot imagine developing positive interethnic relations without them. Other approaches may be more context dependent.

It might be tempting to view this list as yet another cookbook style set of prescriptions, such as, "Pick any three of these approaches and implement them, and you will have a harmonious school where everyone gets along." However, as we pointed out in the previous discussion of coherence, the reality of school change is far more complex. Below are some questions to ask in your planning teams to help you focus on whether a particular approach would make sense in your school.

Key Questions for Leaders

- Are we already using this approach in our school? If so, how well is it working, and are there ways we would like to improve it?
- Does this approach fit with our vision for how we want interethnic relations to be at our school in the future?
- If we choose this as one of several approaches, how will it fit with the other approaches in our mosaic? What theme does it embody?

DATA INQUIRY

Schools using a data inquiry approach collect and analyze data and share the results as a basis for making improvements related to equity and ethnic relations on campus. This can take the form of examining existing data or gathering new data, such as information about student and faculty needs. In Figure 2.2, we provided a graphic image of the cycle of inquiry. To quickly recap, the key stages in the cycle are the following:

- Engage the school community in examining and assessing data.
- Identify core problems as well as areas of success.
- Develop solutions.
- Set measurable goals.
- Take action.
- Reflect on results and continue to refine your efforts, passing through the cycle with the new knowledge you have gained.

Midvale Township High School invested a great deal of time and energy in both collecting and analyzing data on student participation and performance. In 1995, the school leadership began compiling a series of reports on minority student achievement, which were shared with faculty members and the community. The reports were developed because "students with a poor high school education are frequently relegated to a second-class lifestyle in modern America" and because Midvale leaders and community members recognized that despite the school's prominence in a number of areas, they were still failing to reach a large pool of minority students, many of whom were African American. The first report described current programs designed to support minority student achievement; documented statistical evidence of minority student academic progress by examining honors and advanced-placement (AP) class enrollments, failing grade distribution, and standardized test results; presented student and faculty survey and focus group results; and provided conclusions and recommendations. Several of the recommendations focused on addressing problems in the academic tracking system, which was recognized as a key contributing factor not only in the segregation of students by ethnicity but also in the delivery of less-rigorous levels of curriculum and instruction to many minority students. Other recommendations focused on creating stronger connections with parents and on developing greater clarity and consistency in behavioral standards.

The second report focused on a study of 20 African American and 20 majority students who were achieving at high levels. The report found that the majority students took a significantly higher number of honors and AP courses than the African American students, and that this was not merely a reflection of individual student motivation or desire. Most of the majority students actually were better prepared going into high school because they had already completed Algebra 1 before entering. The successful African American students, in contrast, began their more rigorous courses later and, as a result, "seldom got to the capstone course in a discipline."

Subsequent reports included an action plan for the improvement of minority student achievement, following many of the initial recommendations from the first report. In addition, a follow-up study of graduates was completed. The point here is not that many reports were written but that the school engaged in serious data inquiry over many years in order to learn what factors contributed to low achievement among minority students, and what could be done to address this gap. The reports are merely one kind of tangible evidence of the process that leaders undertook at Midvale. The process involved many stakeholders, and while it was too early to see results in terms of student achievement, it was clear that everyone at the site had increased awareness of the issue and a commitment to work together to address inequities in the system. This in itself is a remarkable step.

We view data inquiry as one of fundamental tools for creating any type of lasting change in schools. Without this necessary base, decision making tends to be subject to the whims and latest fads of whoever is in control at the time. Basing decisions on data gives those decisions a much more solid rationale, and, by including many stakeholders—parents, teachers, students, and others— leaders create a more inclusive school. Leaders who pursue data inquiry with a focus on diversity, equity, or social justice can find excellent resources on how to do this in Olsen and Jaramillo (1999). In a chapter entitled "Opening the Door to Data and Inquiry," the authors provide specific guidelines for a process to engage school staff members actively in data inquiry as the basis for school improvement. Although the focus is on immigrant students, the processes they suggest can be used to gather and interpret data about students of any group.

SCHOOL OR DISTRICT VISION

In Chapter 5, we discussed how school leaders can develop a vision for how they want to see interethnic relations in their school's future. We see this visioning process as an essential part of any plan to improve interethnic relations.

Some schools take a further step and make this vision an explicit part of the school's or district's overall vision or mission statement. For example, the school might have a mission that identifies its academic expectations for student learning, but also identifies social learning, equity, and respect as part of the mission. Cornell Elementary School had a relevant motto: "Respect, Literacy, and Lifelong Learning." A mission statement that includes equity, social justice, and positive interethnic relations can be a powerful lever for change because it can be used to hold the school accountable for the goals it has set. However, leaders cannot rely only on a mission statement or motto to communicate the school's sense of purpose. The statement must also be embodied in policies and practices throughout the school; otherwise, the statement is just so much empty rhetoric.

Royal Middle School (not the real name) was named after a slain civil rights leader. Often the naming or renaming of a school provides a clear turning point that allows the entire school community to focus on whatever it was the person stood for. The school name can thus become wedded to the school vision, as was the case at Royal. The school culture became organized around the philosophy and ideals of this civil rights leader. Posters delineating his principles were placed throughout the school and in every classroom. These principles included equality, academic excellence, community action, respect for self and others, nonviolence, and leadership based on democratic principles. Teachers referred to the posters when teaching history and social studies, when establishing classroom rules and guidelines, and when working with individual students on behavior issues, motivating them to work harder. The school also established an annual awards ceremony in which students received honors corresponding with each of the principles.

Sojourner Truth High School's motto was "High expectations plus high standards yield high achievement." This very large (4,500 students) school in New York City served students from low-income backgrounds who were mostly Latino, African American, and Asian. While such a vision might be commonplace among suburban and upper-income schools, it was unusual to find it so embedded in an inner-city school, where a focus on high expectations and high standards has the potential to change stereotyped negative images of black and brown students as low achievers and as unmotivated. Among other things, the principal eliminated all fundamental, modified, or general classes, and created a house system to increase the personalized attention to students' needs, allotting extra money in the budget for tutoring to prepare all students to take the rigorous New York Regents exam. One of the counselors explained, "We're hearing these kids don't have a chance in hell to pass the Regents. [The principal] puts his money where his mouth is. He pays teachers a lot of money from the budget for tutoring sessions. We want kids to pass exams . . . but you know, many of them were victims of a mindset in their elementary and middle schools, and when they come here, you can't just automatically push a button and say, 'We believe in you and you can do it.' That's the guidance counselor in him . . . he makes sure we provide the services."

ORGANIZATIONAL CHANGES

Leaders who commit resources to restructuring time, space, and personnel for teaching and learning at their sites are using organizational approaches. The organizational changes we saw in the study schools were quite varied. They included the following possibilities:

- Houses, families, pods, and academies
- Teaming or coring between teachers
- Looping
- Paid time for teacher collaboration
- Detracking
- Changes in the way physical space in the school is used

We consider organizational changes a context-dependent approach because some schools may already have organizational structures that promote the personalized attention to students and teachers that are the underlying goals of these structures. In other words, it is not the organizational structures that are the goal here—rather, organizational structures are *vehicles* for achieving certain goals related to personalization and equity. However, leaders should also keep in mind that without the organizational structures that allow time and space for people to meet and collaborate, change efforts will be short lived. In this sense, organizational structures such as teacher collaboration time are a necessary (but not sufficient) element of the change process.

Many schools in the study had instituted structures such as houses, families, pods, and academies in order to cluster students in smaller groups and provide a more-personalized school experience. Another common structure was teaming or coring between two or more teachers who shared the same group of students. This, too, reduced students' sense of anonymity while increasing opportunities for the teachers to share and discuss individual students' issues and needs. In some cases, teaming was also used to reduce the segregation of two groups of students, as in an elementary school where a Spanish bilingual teacher (with all Latino students) teamed with a teacher who had a more diverse group of English language learners from various language backgrounds. Several elementary and middle schools increased personalization by using a looping structure in which students stayed together for 2 or 3 years with the same teacher or set of teachers. Creating paid time for teachers to collaborate on a regular basis was a key organizational change in several schools and was necessary in order for structures like teaming and interdisciplinary coring to work properly.

How do these organizational structures make a difference in interethnic relations? By creating a more personalized environment, with more opportunities for getting to know individual students and teachers, they build a foundation for more positive relations. When the groupings (e.g., houses, teams, families, loops) are composed of diverse students and faculty, then the personalized contact that ensues is necessarily going to involve getting to know people with different backgrounds and histories. If we recall Allport's (1954) theory of equal status contact (Chapter 2), personalized interaction was one of the conditions for improving interethnic relations. Personalized interaction, in many cases, helps people break down their stereotypes of the "other" and recognize the uniqueness of each individual. It can also, as Tatum (1997) suggested, spur growth in individuals' developing racial identity as they become more aware of the perspectives and experiences of people of different ethnic backgrounds. Some evidence also indicates that increased personalization enhances academic achievement (Wasley et al., 2000).

Detracking, as discussed in Chapter 2, is another reorganizing process that can radically change the nature of intergroup relations as well as increase students' access to rigorous classes. It involves undoing some or all of the ability grouping that pervades many middle and high schools. Detracking in some contexts can be a highly political issue that brings out underlying class and racial conflict in the community as well as the school. There may be backlash from affluent parents who are convinced their children will suffer if they are placed in classes alongside "less able" students. There may also be considerable resistance from some teachers who, accustomed to teaching in more homogeneous classrooms, find it difficult to modify instructional practices to be effective with a more diverse group with different levels of background knowledge. To become effective in a detracked environment, these teachers may need not only to have access to sustained, high-quality, professional development that hones their skills for multilevel classrooms but also to examine some of their underlying attitudes and assumptions about student abilities, equity, and the purposes of schooling in a democratic society. In conducting interviews for the Leading for Diversity study, we heard some of the most racist, classist comments and jokes when the subject of detracking came up. Leaders who pursue detracking, therefore, need to do so with a clear understanding of why they are doing so (what is the vision and how does detracking embody the vision?) and should be prepared to encounter and address resistance. As one principal said, "You have to make sure your value system is in place," especially when taking unpopular or controversial stands. For leaders who decide to take on the tracking system, there are a number of good resources (e.g., Oakes et al. and the video *Off Track*—see Appendix B).

A third way that schools use organizational structures to improve intergroup relations is by altering the use of physical space in ways that promote interaction and community building. Several schools in the study were built in a pod design with a central area surrounded by extensions that radiated outward. But the design, while it was built with the intention of fostering community, was not always used to best advantage.

At Gladiola Middle School, the new leadership team changed the way classrooms were assigned to pods. Classrooms had been grouped in pods by subject matter, but the new leadership team felt grade level would be a more effective organizing principle. Thus all the sixth-grade classrooms were assigned to one pod, seventh-grade classrooms to another, and so on. This allowed teachers who shared the same grade level to easily converse with one another while still keeping an eye on kids. It fostered more community building among teachers of different subject areas who shared the same students. It is a good example of how the design of the space can be an important, but not sufficient, feature leading to community building. Proactive leaders figure out ways to put physical spaces to their best use.

DIVERSE STAFFING

Many of the schools in the Leading for Diversity study made diverse staffing one of the cornerstones of their efforts to improve interethnic relations. We have labeled this as an essential approach, not an optional one, simply because to ignore it is tantamount to ignoring the increasing diversity of our students. On the other hand, we hope this section will caution educators against taking an overly simplistic approach to increasing staff diversity. It has become somewhat of a truism these days that the more diverse a school's staff is, the more culturally responsive that school is. How much truth is there in this assumption, and why is attracting and retaining a diverse staff important in efforts to improve interethnic relations?

Several rationales undergird the diverse-staffing approach. As a leader, you should be familiar with these rationales, as you will certainly be questioned about your reasoning from time to time. The reasons can be summarized as follows:

- Providing role models for diverse students and demonstrating a society where everyone (regardless of class, ethnic origins, and gender) has access to such positions as teacher, counselor, and administrator
- Improving communication with diverse students and parents and increasing their access to school
- Providing more opportunities for staff and students to learn about different cultures, religions, and lifestyles

The first rationale has to do with role models and making a vision of a democratic society more tangible. Children and young adults need to see people like themselves in a variety of roles and positions in society. If all the teachers and administrators are white, and all the paraprofessionals, janitors, and cafeteria workers are people of color, what message does this send to children? The idea that "people like me don't become teachers" can easily become ingrained in a child's consciousness. "Children," according to Dreikurs, "are good perceivers but poor interpreters" (cited in Nelson, 1996, p. 21). They can see that people who look like them have a lower station in life, but they don't know why and may interpret this information as a sign that they are not worthy or capable of assuming a wide range of roles in society.

Another rationale for diverse staffing is that it can improve communication with both students and families, especially when language barriers exist. Having bilingual staff on site is critical in providing access to the school and its services. But even if the language differences are not so great as to be mutually unintelligible, still there can be an ease and comfort for students and parents in finding someone at the school who is from a similar cultural background and can explain the school system and the curriculum in understandable terms to a confused child or parent. Communication with parents and community should not, however, be a one-way street in which the school is perceived to have all the resources and the parents need only to get access. Parents and other community members also have important funds of knowledge that they can be invited to share with the school. The Funds of Knowledge project, developed in Tucson Arizona, is a good model for developing family-school connections in this regard (González, 1995b).

A third and often-overlooked rationale is that when the school staff is diverse, staff members have more opportunities to learn from one another about different ethnic experiences in the United States. They also have the opportunity to model for students what interethnic collaboration looks like.

All this presupposes that leaders can easily find and retain faculty and support staff members of diverse backgrounds. Yet we know that this is not the case, and in some parts of the country, it is much harder to attract teachers of color than others. Thus percentages that look good in the Midwest or in mostly white suburban areas might be appallingly low to a school in a metropolitan area of the East Coast.

At United Nations High School in a Southern California suburb, the staff was almost entirely European American when the principal began. Seven years later, 26% of the certificated staff was nonwhite, and several of these teachers were also department heads. The principal said he recruited teachers himself and relied more often on universities than on the district personnel office because "they were not the best source." He spent considerable effort contacting teacher-training universities and going to career fairs to try and locate the best teachers. At Crispus Attucks High School in an East Coast city, 50% of the certificated staff members were people of color. The principal explained, "We went to New York, we went to California—we not only physically went but also we called, we wrote, we put it out on e-mail. We went to the Coalition [of Essential Schools] network. We made it very clear in our advertisements that it was a very demanding job, number one, and number two, we were extremely committed to finding, placing, and supporting teachers and administrators of color."

Several schools had teachers of color who had started out in the school as paraprofessionals. They had then received support from the district to get their teaching credentials. This kind of career ladder approach often works well in districts where a large pool of paraprofessionals reflect the diversity of the student population.

Recruitment of staff is one challenge for administrators, but retaining those staff members once they are hired can be an even greater challenge. Well-qualified staff can easily be pulled away to districts with higher salaries and better benefits when opportunities arise. Proactive leaders can make a difference in whether recently hired staff members, regardless of their ethnic background, stay on. By working with the district office, leaders can create mentoring programs that pair new teachers with more-experienced teachers; provide professional development opportunities; and offer peer coaching, modeling, and other forms of support to ensure that new teachers succeed in their work with children and feel the school provides a supportive environment for their professional growth.

A word of caution is in order before we close this section on diverse staffing. Faculty members who fit the stereotype of the U.S. teacher—a European American female—and who don't fully understand the value of a more diverse staff can easily feel threatened when administrators begin talking about hiring more diverse staff. They may feel they are being victimized or undervalued because of the color of their skin and gender, and that someone else who is Latino, Filipino, or American Indian is more highly valued simply because of their ethnic background.

This is a good time to point out again that there is no gene that comes with being black, Latino, Asian, or any other ethnic and racial group that makes one sensitive to kids' needs, a good teacher, a good colleague, and skilled in doing diversity work. However, knowledge of the students' culture and language does help a great deal, as one Latina paraprofessional pointed out:

When you can relate to the students, they act better and do better. . . .
Bilingual teachers who are not Latino, they can do a good job too. But
they have to really think and learn a lot about the culture. Where
Latino teachers, they know how to get to the kids.

Similarly, the stereotype of the white teacher who is clueless about minority students is just that—an overgeneralization. There are certainly a number
of European American teachers who are culturally sensitive, speak languages
other than English, work well with children of many different cultural backgrounds, and practice antiracist teaching in their classrooms.

As a leader who is committed to making the school more inclusive of diversity, you can reassure teachers that these are the qualities you are seeking when
you recruit new staff members. If the present staff members fit these criteria,
then they have nothing to worry about. You can remind teachers of the reasons
for seeking a more diverse staff, as noted earlier in this section. Furthermore, if
you have a shared decision-making structure at your school that invites teachers
to be involved in hiring decisions, then staffing issues become more open for
dialogue rather than conflict between administrators and teachers.

PROFESSIONAL DEVELOPMENT

Ongoing professional development is an essential approach for deepening and
enhancing the skills and knowledge of existing staff members (including leaders) in the area of diversity, interethnic relations, equity, and social justice. In
planning professional development opportunities, leaders need to consider both
content and process.

First, in terms of content, leaders need to consider the following questions:

- What is the knowledge, skill, or disposition that is in need of development?
- How does the content of various professional development offerings we
  are considering further the vision the school has created for interethnic
  relations?
- Is the content likely to be substantive enough to promote real growth
  among those who participate?
- Can we talk to people who have experienced this professional development
  and find out what they thought of it?

Secondly, in terms of process, leaders need to consider the benefits and
disadvantages of different formats. While a one-shot workshop by an expert in the
field can be very stimulating and can raise people's awareness, it rarely has much
staying power. Models that provide sustained professional development over
several sessions, and that incorporate coaching or follow-up of some kind, are usually preferable. Also, models in which outside trainers develop a cadre of experts on
site can help the school build its capacity to continue offering similar professional
development in the future, without relying so much on continuing outside help.

Many educators who participated in the Leading for Diversity study
had tales to tell about professional development training on diversity that did not
work out well. A common scenario was that a school hires an outside consultant

to do a workshop on racism or a similarly complex, emotional issue. The workshop raises awareness and also opens some wounds but goes no further. Participants are left with their emotions in flux and no resolution. Such a scenario is a setup for failure and does more harm than good as staff members may be reluctant to participate in future efforts on a similar topic. Leaders need to be prepared to follow up with additional sessions with qualified facilitators or staff developers.

Here are two examples of more extended professional development foci and processes we documented in the Leading for Diversity schools:

Teachers at Blue Ridge Elementary School were experiencing a dramatic rise in the number of immigrant children from Mexico, and the mostly European American, English monolingual staff was having a tough time providing for the educational needs of these children. Fortunately, they had a principal who was an expert in the area of second-language acquisition and bilingual education. She made it a high priority to provide professional development in these areas for her staff throughout the year. In addition, through a unique binational program with community and district support, teachers from Mexico were placed in the school to assist with classroom instruction. They provided a rich resource of cultural and linguistic knowledge for the local teachers. In the summers, many local teachers were acquiring firsthand knowledge of Mexican culture and the Spanish language through the district's summer program in Mexico. All these professional development efforts helped teachers better understand immigrant children's backgrounds, break away from stereotypes about Mexican or Hispanic people, develop empathy for how hard it is to learn a second language, and learn strategies for teaching students who are not yet proficient in English.

Teachers at Cornell Elementary School, frustrated by the lack of teacher dialogue at their school about equity and strategies for antiracist teaching, adopted for their own professional development the model of the SEED Project on Inclusive Curriculum (Seeking Educational Equity & Diversity).

The administration supported several teachers in getting trained in the SEED model. A teacher explained that the model consists of five stages of inclusion, from the first one, in which "the only relevant things that are taught are things that have been done by white men," to the fifth. Her dream of this phase, that doesn't really exist, is that everybody is in the center; where you don't have to have a women's month and you don't have to have an African American month because everybody's included all the time."

About 10 teachers voluntarily participated in SEED, meeting once a month to discuss different topics related to equity, diversity, and interethnic relations. Most teachers in this group reported that the SEED group dialogues had had a powerful impact on their teaching. They also recognized that if their work was to have any impact on other classrooms beyond their group, they needed to share their work on a schoolwide level.

Cornell not only provides a good example of professional development for a core group of teachers but also illustrates the power of teacher leadership. These teachers recognized a problem in their school that troubled them, and together they decided to do something about it. While the administration was supportive, it was the teachers who took the lead on this particular approach.

CURRICULUM AND INSTRUCTION

Many of the leaders in our study found curricular and instructional approaches to be especially powerful as a means of improving interethnic relations. These approaches can take several forms:

- Addressing ethnicity and ethnic relations as a regular part of the subject matter students study in school
- Using cooperative learning structures in the classroom
- Establishing learning outcomes and content standards that provide all students with access to all levels of the curriculum

We consider curricular and instructional approaches necessary, not optional, for schools that are serious about improving interethnic relations. If students are to acquire knowledge and skills to relate to one another across lines of difference, these must be taught as part of the regular curriculum, not only as add-on or special activities. The message to students and families needs to be clear—this knowledge and these skills are not "fluff" but a serious part of the learning experience in U.S. schools, alongside math, history, language arts, computer skills, and other areas considered essential for the educated person.

When ethnicity and ethnic relations are explicitly addressed as subject matter in classes, students have continuous and regular opportunities to acquire both knowledge and skills that will help them relate to others in a diverse world. Banks (1997) and Grant and Sleeter (1989), among others, have pointed out that multicultural education efforts lie along a continuum from the most superficial to the most embedded in the daily functions of the school.

Ohlone High School provides a good example of a school where ethnicity and interethnic relations were addressed explicitly through curriculum. Teacher leaders there had developed four different curricular strategies to address issues of ethnic relations:

1. Ethnic focus classes such as African American History and Filipino American Heritage engaged students in studying the history and culture of a specific ethnic group or ancestry.

2. Infusion courses integrated interethnic-relations topics in core English and social science courses.

3. An introductory course called Ethnic and Women's Studies provided a foundation for learning about the experiences of different ethnic groups in the United States, with a focus on groups represented in the student population.

4. Individual teachers also said that they addressed interethnic-relations issues as they came up in classes, on a more or less ad hoc basis.

The development of these four strategies, however, did not come about easily or quickly. The first ethnic focus course was instituted in 1974, and other ethnic focus courses were added gradually over the next three decades. What really spurred growth in Ohlone's curricular approach was the formation in 1996 of faculty collaboration groups which met every Wednesday morning for an hour and a half. Through this structure that fostered teacher collaboration and leadership, teachers became empowered to play a more active role in school change. For a more detailed description of the four strategies and the roles of teacher leaders and administrators in their development, see Henze (2001).

In addition to treating ethnicity and ethnic relations as content that is part of the courses students take, teachers can also address ethnic relations through the instructional process, and school leaders can support and encourage such efforts. Cooperative learning and other forms of instruction that encourage interaction and group projects among diverse students provide a structured opportunity for students to learn about each other while accomplishing collaborative tasks. In the process, they can also see the value of working together across ethnic lines. Of course, this assumes that the teacher is well prepared to use collaborative learning structures in a way that furthers, rather than undermines, students' appreciation of each other's diverse learning styles and contributions. School leaders may need to provide high quality professional development for teachers in this area and then sustain it by instituting a peer-coaching model or mentoring relationships among teachers. They can also call teachers' attention to resources such as *Jigsaw Classroom*, *Cooperative Learning: A Response to Cultural and Linguistic Diversity*, and *Community Building in the Classroom*, which are good tools for encouraging interactive learning processes in the classroom (see Resource B).

A third way for leaders to use curriculum and instruction as vehicles for improving interethnic relations is to establish learning outcomes and content standards that provide all students with access to all levels of the curriculum. This addresses the underlying, systemic problem of different expectations for different groups of students, a problem that is institutionalized in the practice of tracking. But it can also appear within classes where teachers hold high expectations for some students and lower expectations for other students. The establishment of high-level learning outcomes and content standards doesn't teach students explicitly about interethnic relations, but it gets at one of the root causes of interethnic conflict—"inequality, in which power, status, or access to desired goods and services are unequally distributed among groups" (Kreisberg, 1998, p. 44). It can take a long time to actually do away with a tracked system and raise teachers' expectations of minority and low-income students. In order to be truly effective, this approach must involve the entire school district from elementary through high school so that students with lower proficiency in particular areas can receive appropriate interventions while they are in elementary and middle school, rather than waiting until high school to find that students are way behind and have no hope of catching up.

The curricular strategies described earlier at Ohlone High School were effective in teaching students about their own ethnic histories and backgrounds (affirming identity) and teaching them to appreciate, respect, and communicate more openly with those of other backgrounds. However, such courses did not, in and of themselves, address the persistent problem of underachievement, primarily among lower-income students of color. To do that, other support programs were necessary, such as mentoring and tutoring programs (see Programs later in this chapter). Such programs, which often teach study skills and school coping skills, provide the scaffolding that enables poorly prepared students to meet high expectations and standards.

Curricular approaches that are appropriate for high school students will not, of course, always be appropriate for younger students. At the elementary level, for example, several schools incorporated the Tribes curriculum in their classes. Tribes is a nationally distributed curriculum designed for elementary school children to develop social skills and build positive relationships (see Resource B). According to Tribes CEO Judy Johnson, "It doesn't address racial conflict directly but changes the environment in the school so there isn't any" (personal communication, phone interview, March 16, 1997). While this may be too broad a claim, Tribes does create social norms that support good communication skills and a positive sense of community. In addition to Tribes, curricular and video series are available for the elementary level to teach children coping skills for dealing with prejudice and racism (see Resource B).

Teaching children a second language can also be a powerful way to encourage positive interethnic relations. Several elementary schools had instituted a second-language curriculum as a vehicle for not only teaching students a second language but also increasing their sensitivity toward, and respect for, cultural and ethnic differences. The principal of Ferguson Elementary School used his knowledge and skills as a former bilingual professional specializing in English as a second language (ESL) to develop a language-learning approach for all students at Ferguson. The school offered programs in four different languages, and students and the wider school community had come to think it was "cool" to speak two languages.

At the middle school level, consistent with the greater awareness students have of being "different" as they approach adolescence, a more focused approach to ethnic and social-justice themes becomes appropriate. Teacher leaders in several middle schools in the study had developed themes that certain classes all addressed—for example, a focus on social justice in all history classes, or a focus on civil rights and tolerance in all language arts and social studies core classes.

Allaneq Middle School, in which students were organized in grade level teams, had quarter-long, interdisciplinary projects they worked on in their teams. One of the seventh-grade teams was presenting their culminating projects on family heritage when we visited. Students had worked on their projects for weeks, and were being videotaped as they shared their hard work with the class and teachers. Each student project had the following components: A map showing their family's movement; a family tree going as far back as they could find information; a selection of the ethnicity or ethnicities they most identify with, and their reasons; a selection of the ancestor they most see as a role model, and their reasons; a written speech which was also delivered orally; and a graph showing the amount of time spent on the project.

SPECIAL EVENTS

The most common approach to helping school communities value their diversity is via special events such as assemblies, retreats, and other formats that depart from the day-to-day functioning of the school. Many schools, for example, hold special celebrations to honor the contributions of different ethnic groups—a Cinco de Mayo assembly, a Chinese New Year celebration, or an African American History month. In other schools, multicultural events, such as International Day, highlight contributions of several ethnic groups at once. Special events can also focus not on ethnic groups per se but on the relations among them, such as a human relations retreat or a day of respect.

Special events can perform a valuable function in schools to give visibility to all the different ethnic groups on campus. They can also provide a structure in which students become involved in planning and implementing the event and taking part in performances of various kinds. For some students, especially those who may not be receiving attention for their academic prowess, this is an opportunity to shine and gain self-confidence. However, if special events are the only way nonwhite ethnic groups are represented, it can have the effect of trivializing ethnicity or turning it into an exotic, once-a-year display. While most schools in the study celebrated diverse cultures through a variety of special events, they did not stop there. Special events supported, and were supported by, multiple approaches. Yet even with a more multifaceted plan, special events posed certain problems for school leaders.

In some schools, special events that focused on ethnicity tended to become competitive, with groups vying for time on the yearly calendar.

At Cornell Elementary School, the Cinco de Mayo celebration received a high level of attention. It was the first ethnic celebration to be commemorated at Cornell many years ago, and it had begun as an all-day event in which the whole community participated, with food booths, speeches, and performances by students. When the school began to institute events celebrating other ethnic heritages, they couldn't allocate whole days for each one, so the other groups each got a noontime assembly slot. Although the leadership team had decided to institute a more equitable system in which there would be one all-day multicultural event, and many shorter events throughout the year to honor each ethnicity, a group of Latino parents, upon hearing this decision, expressed to the principal that they were shocked to hear the school was considering "taking our festival away." Since the student body was approximately 70% Latino, the principal worried that Latino parents would feel she had disenfranchised them. She asked the faculty to vote on the issue, and the vote came out in favor of maintaining the all-day Cinco de Mayo event, but there was a large faculty minority who still opposed this.

As you may recall from Chapter 3, time and schedules are a precious resource in schools that can become a bone of contention between ethnic groups. The principal at Cornell had inherited the special-events calendar from previous principals, and it carried with it strong emotional associations. It was tied to the history of the community, which used to be primarily African American, but recent years had seen more and more immigrants moving in from Mexico and Latin America as well as Southeast Asia. It was a low-income community, and resources were often scarce. Some long-time African American residents were resentful that funding and services seemed to flow more easily toward immigrants than toward African Americans. Community-wide issues such as these are always a powerful backdrop that influences how ethnic groups interact within the school setting. The principal knew she had the right to change the Cinco de Mayo event, but she realized she didn't have the parental support to change it. She was faced with an either-or decision in which some people would be unhappy no matter what the outcome was. She compromised by staying with the status quo for the time being and doing the best she could to equalize the situation by developing more special events throughout the year for the other groups.

Another dilemma leaders faced with regard to special events was what to do about celebrating the ethnicities of white students. When schools first started to have ethnic celebrations, they were generally designed to provide visibility and appreciation for minority groups. It was assumed that white students already had plenty of recognition in everything else that was part of the school fabric—history books, literature, and so on. However, in schools where European American students are a minority, there is increasing pressure from students and parents to have special events focusing on their cultures, too. Several of the study schools had decided to honor this request. Wisely, the leadership teams decided not to call these events "white assemblies," as this could have perpetuated the notion that all white people are of the same ethnic group. It also would have left the door open for suspicions of racist organizing along the lines of white supremacists such as Aryan Nation. One school called their event a European American assembly and another called theirs a "Celtic assembly." However, these assemblies, like all the others, ran into the problem of lumping together many diverse groups under one assembly and giving more attention to some than others. The European American assembly we attended, for example, focused primarily on people of the British Isles and hardly mentioned Southern Europe or the Balkan or Slavic peoples, even though there were a number of students with these ancestries.

PROGRAMS

Programs, as we are defining them, are specific interventions that are added to the regular curriculum. They are usually optional, and they usually take place after school, during lunchtime, or in the summers. These programs vary in length, targeted audience, and focus, with some being geared specifically to addressing diversity issues and others designed for more general purposes. School leaders have a great deal of discretion when it comes to after-school and extracurricular programming, so this is an area where it is relatively easy to intervene to make human relations a higher priority in your school than it currently is. Common programmatic approaches that can help to improve interethnic relations include

- Conflict resolution programs
- Mentoring and tutoring programs
- After-school and extracurricular activities such as sports, arts, and student clubs

Many schools in the study had conflict resolution programs in which students were trained as conflict managers. This model, popularized in the 1970s, has many variations and can be used at any level of schooling from elementary through high school (see Resource B for specific programs). A major advantage of these programs is that they nurture a type of leadership among students that is different from the traditional student-council leadership role. They provide a forum for students who are skilled at social problem solving to shine and, thus, may open the door for more students with diverse talents and abilities to assume leadership in the school. All the conflict resolution programs in the study schools had a strong component that taught conflict managers the communication skills and steps involved in mediation—such as active listening, establishing ground rules, defining the problem according to different participants' perspectives, identifying what participants need in order to have the problem solved, and seeking solutions the parties can agree to.

Some conflict resolution programs include a component that explicitly examines race and ethnicity, as well as gender, religion, physical abilities, and so on, as a potential dimension in conflicts. Others assume that the skills for resolving conflicts do not require a deeper understanding of the root causes of those conflicts, so they focus on building communication skills without necessarily teaching participants to engage in critical reflection about the sources of conflict.

After observing and hearing about many conflict resolution programs in the schools we visited, we think it would be wise for school leaders to seek programs that do include a component that explicitly addresses racial and ethnic conflict. Coleman and Deutsch (1995) reported that there is a scarcity of research on the mediation of interethnic conflict. However, they conducted a survey of expert mediators of interethnic conflict in the New York area, and found that, "Issues unique to interethnic conflict emerge from cultural misunderstandings, ethnocentrism, long-held stereotypes, and the importance of ethnic identity to self identity" (p. 387). In addition to other processes that are common to conflict resolution in general, mediators of interethnic conflicts help disputants identify and clarify ethnic assumptions, intervene in ethnocentrism, and avoid stereotypes. The more generic conflict resolution programs do not teach these skills, which are increasingly important for students and adults to acquire as our schools become ever more diverse. Leaders can exercise their choice by opting for conflict resolution programs that do address these skills.

In addition to conflict resolution programs, almost every school in the study had mentoring or tutoring programs designed to raise the achievement of underachieving students.

Leaders at Forest Hills High School were, for example, working with the feeder middle schools to improve articulation so that students would enter high school with better preparation. One of the programs they created was called Compass, which provided an intensive summer program for incoming ninth-grade students from the lower-income feeder schools. The program helped students develop the skills and confidence to do well in high school and was coupled with ongoing, year-round support for those students. This district, like many others, recognized that if they were able to raise the academic achievement of low-income African American, Latino, and Pacific Islander students, they would not only address the institutional inequities that have contributed to the achievement gap but also begin to undo the racial stereotyping of these students as less prepared, unintelligent, and not college material.

A third type of programmatic approach was the many after-school and extracurricular activities that focused on areas such as the arts, sports, and ethnic clubs. Some extracurricular activities and clubs actually focused on human relations. Particularly in schools where students were ethnically segregated during a majority of the day (because of tracking or special language needs), after-school and extracurricular programs could provide a more integrated antidote.

> At Maya Lin High School, for example, students became leaders in interethnic relations through the Pioneer Outreach Network for Diversity (POND) program, a local component of the countywide Building Bridges program. A core group of teachers who were trained in Building Bridges, in turn, trained a group of students who then became facilitators for retreats involving faculty and students. Students were thus provided with a structure in which they were able to assume more responsibility and authority for teaching others about interethnic relations.

> Extracurricular and after-school programs were not always integrated. Gladiola Middle School, for example, had several after-school clubs which had an ethnic as well as a gender focus in some cases, such as Mariposas— a club developed to help Latina girls navigate the difficult terrain of puberty and adolescence, and especially to encourage them to develop self-esteem and excel academically. This was especially important given prevailing attitudes among some Latino families that encourage girls to place familial roles of wife and mother above their individual academic development.

> Clubs such as these engaged in a wide range of activities, including conducting assemblies, doing community service, going on field trips to colleges, discussing problems students were having in school, and learning more about their cultural heritage and family history. Staff felt ethnic clubs played an important role in socializing students; at times, clubs were a vehicle for students to discuss racial and ethnic issues they were confronting in school; they also played a valuable role in affirming identity, as discussed in Chapter 4.

BEHAVIORAL STANDARDS

Across all the schools in our study, student behavior was an important focal point for efforts at creating more harmonious environments, particularly in those schools which had identified safety and security as the immediate high-priority need. But even in schools where safety and security were already well enough established, behavioral standards had to be continually revised and revisited. Thus we consider this an essential area for any school plan to improve interethnic relations. Maintaining and improving behavioral standards includes the following components:

- Identifying areas where disciplinary consequences may be unevenly applied
- Developing agreement among staff members and parents about disciplinary standards and consequences
- Defining terms more clearly
- Including security staff in behavioral-policy development and providing training for them
- Creating incentives for positive student behavior

A major issue in many middle and high schools is the uneven application of disciplinary policies. An assistant principal in a high school explained that,

> Our frustration has been that we're asked to kind of hold this line or standard of discipline, but at any given time, above us it's given in to, and then nothing is done. And then our level feels like, "Why are we even arguing days upon days with parents when within a half hour of an appeal meeting, all of a sudden, that's not the case?" Every year we go over the philosophy of what's going on for behavior. And we have an idea of what we're going to do. We do that, but then, depending on who the parent is or what kind of complaint there is, that may change. And as a result, it's become real inconsistent for a lot of consequences and for discipline. Some parents still have the belief that whatever the school says is it—my kid, you know, do the punishment. Whereas for that same scenario, another parent may come and complain and get that suspension reduced only because they came and raised a little bit of havoc.

In this school, like many others, disparities in treatment of disciplinary referrals tend to be patterned along ethnic and class lines, because, according to the assistant principal above,

> Most parents of color have the type of jobs that don't give them the freedom to be involved in a lot of things, so they don't have a lot of voice in a lot of school activities. So that's a kind of disparity there. So, because of that I've kind of—given the reduction, rather than give them the five-day suspension.

The kinds of inconsistencies the assistant principal identified above can lead to an erosion of trust on several levels. Students, of course, quickly become aware that the consequences for behavior vary, depending on who you are or who your parents are. Teachers also see that the administration cannot be trusted to uphold fairness and does not follow through on teacher referrals. This then cycles back to the classroom, as students realize that a teacher referral to the office carries little weight. Therefore, they do not necessarily need to respect classroom rules of behavior.

A first step in addressing policy inconsistencies like these is to develop agreement among staff members and parents about behavioral standards and consequences. Often this means revisiting earlier policies to determine if they are reasonable and if they can be applied consistently—or if they give privilege to certain groups. It also can mean defining terms more clearly. For example, at one high school, staff members had widely divergent understandings of the term *threat*. This was one of the reasons teachers could give for sending a student to the office, yet there was no agreement on what threatening behavior looked like and, given cultural differences in communication style between Asian students, Latino students, and African American students, the African American students tended to be penalized more often for talking loudly and being assertive. The assistant principal explained,

> The African American students tend to speak loudly and in high tones and maybe sometimes animated. And some staff here take that literally as a threat. And so, as soon as they see that they write it down in a report—"I was threatened by this person." Whereas, when you talk to them and find out what the student was doing—look, it's just mannerisms and things like that. On paper, you can write anything and make it sound like something is real serious, whereas it turns out oftentimes to be nothing more than a verbal back and forth and nothing serious. But students have gotten into real serious trouble because a teacher insists on calling it a threat.

Security staff are especially important to include in these conversations since they are often the frontline staff who deal with student behavior issues outside classrooms. One school in the study made it a point to hire security personnel who shared similar cultural backgrounds to the students, in order to foster better communication with students and reduce the earlier perception of favoritism by security guards who were all of one ethnic group. All security staff should be provided with training that emphasizes not only agreed-on policies and practices but also the importance of implementing policies fairly, without regard to race, gender, ethnicity, and other aspects of student identity.

Many middle and high schools use security personnel only for purposes of containing violence and other behavior problems. While containment is important, it is also possible to enhance the role of security personnel so that they play an educational role as well. We have already mentioned Allaneq Middle School, where security staff were trained to work one-on-one with students who had violated school rules, guiding students in making better choices and talking problems out rather than reacting violently. Some schools have police officers assigned to the school who can play an educational role as well.

Another way for leaders to move beyond containment in the area of behavior is to initiate more incentives for positive behavior. Basically, the idea here is to give students positive outlets to express themselves and act out in helpful, creative ways rather than destructive, harmful ones. Providing positive, supervised activities for students during lunchtime and after school is a way to channel adolescent energy in more beneficial directions. Two of the middle schools in the study, Gladiola and Allaneq, found this to be an essential component that went hand in hand with a stricter, more consistent discipline policy (see case study of Gladiola in Chapter 11). At both schools, students themselves were involved in decisions about what activities would be offered.

At Rosa Parks, an accelerated alternative middle school for at-risk students, students assumed even greater leadership in the area of discipline. All students served on a rotating basis on the school's discipline committee. Any student or staff member could make a referral to the committee, which met once a week. Referred students were required to appear before the committee to explain their actions and receive disciplinary consequences. The students themselves often applied stricter consequences than the teachers.

In elementary schools, approaches to behavior must be in tune with the development level of the students. Instead of hiring security staff, Rainbow Elementary School hired "student advisors" to act as role models for students on the playground and before and after school, monitoring their behavior and reinforcing good behavior.

Blue Ridge Elementary, a pre-K-2 school, was fortunate to have a very knowledgeable counselor who had implemented a comprehensive approach to student behavior and counseling based on choice theory (Glasser, 1986). Included in this approach were periodic lessons in every classroom dealing with social relations and managing anger; a series of 30-second interventions that consisted of short phrases in English and Spanish, which teachers could use to intervene when children exhibited inappropriate behavior; a guide for teachers to use in developing classroom behavior policies with their students and their parents; a planning process to be used by a counselor with individual children who had been pulled out of a class because of behavioral problems; and a time-out room where students could work individually with a counselor or counselor's assistant.

PARENT INVOLVEMENT

It is often said that children are not racist; it is the adults who are racist who then socialize children to develop racist attitudes. Given that parents and other adults in the home play a major socializing role with children, it is reasonable to expect that involving parents and other caregivers in a school's efforts to improve race relations would pay off. In fact, we consider family involvement an essential area for schools that seek to improve interethnic relations because if they are not involved, it is unlikely that you will receive their support in your efforts. Also, by working closely with diverse parents, you have an opportunity to challenge some of the prevailing socialization that children receive in the home (e.g., racist attitudes toward people of other ethnic groups).

In order for leaders to make family involvement meaningful and beneficial for students, however, they also need to confront prevailing attitudes among school staff that depict low-income families and families of color in stereotypically negative ways. Perceptions of families and community members by school staff, who often do not live in the community themselves, are shaped by our own particular contexts, as we pointed out in Chapter 1. Statements such as the following make the assumption that the speaker's culture and life experience are the norm and that anything that diverges from it is somehow deficient:

"They're welfare mothers, taking advantage of the government and taxpayers."

"Those immigrant parents aren't interested in their children's education; they're too busy just making a living."

"They don't even read to their kids at night."

"These children are culturally deprived—they've never ridden on an escalator or been to a shopping mall."

"I told the kids, 'Tell your parents to speak English to you at home. That way you'll do better in school.'"

Proactive leaders who are working to create a positive interethnic community take a different view of parents and family members, seeing them as a valuable resource for children's education rather than a problem to be addressed. Of course, some children do go home to unhealthy or unsafe environments that include drug and alcohol abuse, physical abuse, abandonment, and homelessness. But the point is that most families, even those with the most egregious problems, also have some resources that can be recognized and channeled for the benefit of children. To do so, however, may require a significant shift of consciousness for some staff members, and school leaders can play a key role in encouraging this shift, possibly through a series of professional development workshops on family involvement, as well as by sharing positive models used in other schools.

The resources that families may have include such things as knowledge of different languages; job-related skills like carpentry, cooking, candy making, and car repair; cultural traditions and family stories; and knowledge of the local community and its resources (e.g., churches, pastors, business owners, community-based organizations) as well as its problems (e.g., local drug dealers, child pornography dealer) that the school should be aware of.

When leaders begin to see families as resources, this also tends to expand the potential formats through which the school interacts with parents. Thus instead of seeing parent involvement as a one-way street in which the school has all the resources and the parents need to get access to what the school offers, a family-as-resource view sees a two-way exchange in which parents can offer benefits to the school as well. The school can benefit by learning what family members know and can do, and then finding ways to integrate these areas in curriculum. The Funds of Knowledge project (González, 1995b) is based on this premise.

Proactive leaders can build on and expand existing family involvement efforts as yet another platform for developing positive interethnic relations. Possible formats for increasing parent involvement include

- Special events for parents and students, such as Literacy Night and Family Math
- Meaningful inclusion of diverse parents in decision-making bodies
- Informational meetings for parents
- Physical space or center set aside specifically for parents on campus
- Home visits
- Parent participation in classrooms

Events designed for parent involvement are probably the most common format schools use to draw parents in. Here, as with students, leaders must consider questions about how to group parents. For example, when family events are held, should family members be grouped together by ethnicity and language in order to more efficiently provide translation services? Should leaders make an effort to encourage mingling among diverse parents and, if so, how, given that they may not speak each other's languages? In addition to language issues, transportation, work schedules, and childcare often function as barriers to parent involvement, so if school leaders want parents to be able to come to events and meetings, they need to find creative solutions to enable them to do so (Katz, 2001). For example, some meetings can be held in the neighborhoods where families live, making it easier for parents to get there. The proactive leaders in the study schools tried to offer a variety of options for parent involvement, some of which took place in affinity groups based on language and ethnicity, and some of which were more diverse.

When parents need to have access to basic information about the school and about their children's progress, this need is usually best addressed through the native languages of the parents. Language-based groupings also allow parents with similar cultural backgrounds to get to know each other and share resources, in some cases becoming a support network for each other. Other family involvement events may be designed to showcase student accomplishments in academics, the arts, and performances, or to support children's learning in a particular subject, for example, a family math night. In these activities, there is no reason why family members cannot enjoy the event all together. Translation can be provided, but it doesn't need to be provided in separate groups. These events serve a community-building purpose since all the family members who come share similar goals of supporting student learning and celebrating student accomplishments.

While events tend to be the most common way for schools to involve parents, many other means exist for increasing the connection between families and school. Several elementary schools in the study had physical centers especially set up on campus where parents could come to meet with each other and with staff or just to have a cup of coffee or juice and chat informally with a staff member.

Cornell Elementary used some of their Title VII and Title I funds to create a parent center in a portable unit in the middle of the schoolyard. They staffed the center with two parents, one African American and one Latina who spoke Spanish. Their job was to organize informal gatherings of parents who were interested in talking about and learning about specific topics, such as positive discipline, gangs, what one's child should be learning in third grade, and other parent-nominated topics. The two staff members also modeled interethnic cooperation for other parents and showed how parents could exercise leadership within the school. Joshua Tree Intermediate took the parent center concept a step further and, when designing their new school building, invited parents to be part of the design team. The parents used their authority within the team to vote for a parent center to be built in the center of the school building.

In some schools, parents formed groups of their own for the purpose of exploring diversity and developing more positive interethnic relations. The Multicultural Parent Group at Fillmore Middle School formed after a talk given at the school by a speaker who highlighted the districtwide pattern of low achievement among low-income African American and Latino students. Concerned parents decided to form a reading and discussion group to follow up on the issues the speaker had raised.

School leaders can also encourage teachers to develop meaningful connections with families through home visits and through parent participation in the classroom. Unfortunately, many parents have come to dread home visits because they are typically about how their child is not doing well. However, home visits can be used for an entirely different purpose—to help the teacher understand the knowledge base and practices of particular families and then develop ways to bring these resources into the curriculum. To become skilled at doing this kind of home visit, teachers need ethnographic training that will familiarize them with the methods ethnographers use when they enter and begin to learn about an unfamiliar community. One teacher in the Funds of Knowledge project (González, 1995b) in Tucson found, upon visiting with a family of Mexican immigrants, that the mother was an expert candy maker and ran a small business out of her home. The teacher realized that to do so required measurement and estimation skills, as well as methods of calculating profit and loss in the business. She was then able to design a curriculum unit based on the candy-making practice. In this model, parents can be invited into class to collaborate with the teacher in showing children how certain tasks are done.

The process of home visits serves several important purposes. First, the ethnographic training helps teachers see unfamiliar communities with fresh eyes that are less judgmental and more open to recognizing family strengths that can be tapped for educational purposes. Second, tying family practices to school curriculum makes the learning process more meaningful and engaging for children. Third, family members who have been involved in such classrooms have an authentic and highly respected role, unlike the more common practice of asking parents to come and assist with menial tasks in the classroom.

EXPANDING THE SCHOOL COMMUNITY

Community in this age of electronics is a slippery concept. It can mean anything from the immediate physical neighborhood to ties with sister cities in other countries, international partnerships, and electronic, Web-based communities. Leaders who are interested in considering possibilities for expanding the school community would probably do well to sit down with their leadership team and map out what potential communities might mean in their context and, specifically, who would benefit from a connection with these communities, and how. Schools that expand their community also expand the function of schooling beyond the conventional purpose of providing education to children. The school and defined communities they connect with become resources for each other, enriching each other in the process.

Schools can become resources for the immediate physical community by offering services such as English as a second language (ESL) and general education diploma (GED) classes for adults in the evenings, or opening up the gym or the library for community use during certain hours. Some schools, through Healthy Start or other funding sources, have been able to open health clinics on campus. Efforts such as these create more personalized, positive ties between the school and the surrounding community while also maximizing use of the space and enhancing the employment skills and well-being of local community members.

In some schools, leaders encourage staff and students to go out into the local community. At Cornell Elementary, staff regularly attended meetings at several community-based organizations in the neighborhood (e.g., clinics, a neighborhood park association, Spanish Speaking Unity Council), both to learn what they were doing and to see how their work might tie in with what the school was doing. At Allaneq Middle School, some students participated after school in a community service program which distributed food and clothing to needy members of the community.

Joshua Tree Intermediate School was in the process of building a closer relationship with the Native American community that the school served. Students and staff frequently walked from the school to the reservation to participate in meetings and events there, and, on the way, they had constructed a pathway with native plants. Each plant had a story about its use and cultural meanings associated with it, and students were learning these aspects of culture from native community members.

The principal at Dolores Huerta Middle School worked together with local Vietnamese community groups to create linkages between the school and the community. One result of this collaboration was that the school offered weekend classes in Vietnamese language; another result was that the Vietnamese community worked with the school to organize a large Tet Festival each year.

The most ambitious expansion of community among the study schools took place at Blue Ridge Elementary. There, a local attorney had become very much involved in trying to address the language barrier facing the largely Anglo teaching population and their growing numbers of Spanish-speaking students from Mexico. Together with local industry executives and school district officials, he developed a collaboration that expanded community ties far beyond the school or the district. The cornerstone of this approach was a multifaceted partnership between the school district and a Mexican university. This partnership brought Mexican teachers to the school district to work with local teachers in making instruction accessible and providing many other services. It also sent groups of local teachers to Mexico for summer study of Spanish language and Mexican culture.

These strategies have in common the fact that they strengthened ties between the staff and students, on the one hand, and, on the other hand, people in different places or situations who either needed services the school could offer or who could themselves offer something to the school. In the process, the school became less insulated, and, in many cases, those involved became more appreciative and respectful of differences.

ACTIVITY 10: SELECTING APPROACHES

Think about your own school, or a school you are familiar with, and consider the following questions. Jot down your responses individually at first. Then discuss them with a colleague or colleagues.

1.   Which approaches do you see being implemented at this school? Do you think they are working as desired? Why or why not? How could they be improved?

2.   Which approaches are not being implemented at this school? Do you think they are needed? Why or why not? (Explain in terms of the context of this school and the high-priority needs you identified earlier.)

3.   Think about the approaches you identified in question #1. Do you see them more as a coherent body of practices or as a miscellaneous shopping list? Do they embody any larger theme that is related to positive interethnic relations? What could be done to make them more coherent?

7

Implementing and Refining the Plan

Visions can die because people become discouraged by the apparent difficulty in bringing the vision into reality. As clarity about the nature of the vision increases, so does awareness of the gap between the vision and current reality.

—Peter Senge (1990, pp. 228-229)

Anyone who has spent time in schools knows that the initial plan is never carried out exactly as it was originally envisioned. Schools are organic communities like living, breathing cells that both contain life within and also respond to, and interact with, life in the surrounding community and larger world. It is actually a good thing that school change plans do not remain static—if they did, they wouldn't be very relevant or useful.

What happens to plans that make them change? The realities of implementation set in. New constraints and opportunities appear on the horizon. Staff members leave or are transferred, and new staff members come in. A teacher strike seems likely, and staff cohesiveness is threatened. The state department of education institutes a new mandatory testing program. A new group of students from Bosnia enrolls at the school, and their language needs must be taken into consideration in the plan. The school is awarded a grant to develop parent involvement. You name it—change is inevitable. As one of the study principals said wryly, "It's like trying to change a tire while driving down the freeway."

LEADERSHIP AND COMMUNICATION STYLE

Key Questions for Leaders

- How do I continue to guide and facilitate implementation of the plan we so carefully developed only months ago?
- What roles am I going to play in implementing the plan?
- What roles do I expect others to play?
- How can I clearly communicate my perception of my own role and my expectations of staff and students?

Principals and other school administrators are the gatekeepers of change. By sanctioning and actively supporting changes such as a plan to improve interethnic relations, principals and other leaders affect the implementation and outcomes.

> The more supportive the principal was perceived to be, the higher was the percentage of project goals achieved, the greater the improvement in student performance, and the more extensive the continuation of project methods and materials. The principal's unique contribution to implementation lies not in "how to do it" . . . but in giving moral support to the staff and in creating an organizational climate that gives the project "legitimacy." (Berman & McLaughlin, 1978, p. 31)

In thinking about your role as a leader in the development of positive interethnic relations, it is important to be aware of your leadership style, as this can have a direct influence on how the plan is implemented. Are you a take-charge sort of person whom others tend to look up to and follow? Are you someone who listens a lot before you speak? Do you share your thoughts and feelings openly, or are you more reserved? Do you like to initiate change, or do you prefer to facilitate and provide support for others to take the lead? One of the things we noticed right away in the Leading for Diversity study was that a few of the principals fit the stereotype of the strong, charismatic leader. Most did not. The principals in the study varied a great deal in their communication and styles—some were assertive and forceful in their expression of what was needed for the school, and others had communication styles that elicited the involvement of others in decision making. Yet they were all able to guide the implementation of major changes in the way the schools addressed interethnic relations.

Mr. Sebastian and the other administrators at Ohlone High exemplified a facilitative form of leadership. A teacher commented that, "They [the administration] provide the arena for us and we [teachers] go and provide the thing. We have a lot of ethnic classes, ethnic diversity. We're talking about opening an ethnic studies department. They've given us the stage, the theater to work those things. Where I've seen big changes in the last 7 or 8 years is, you don't get 'no' right away. You get: 'Let's see.' Where, before, it was, 'No that will never work,' and that would be it. Yeah, that's been a big change. We used to live under a dictatorial experience here, and anyone who knows the history of the place will know that's true. The pendulum has gone the other way."

Many staff felt empowered by Sebastian's style. One teacher said, "I think in this environment, teachers are empowered. We do have freedom to create curricula and to propose certain things in our departments and schoolwide. So I think just the climate of [Ohlone] is conducive to teacher empowerment."

As a result of Sebastian's style, teacher leaders emerged as driving forces in diversity efforts at Ohlone. But being a facilitative or supportive leader can sometimes be confused with being a weak leader. There were staff members at Ohlone who thought Sebastian wasn't doing enough to implement the school's diversity vision —"Diversity is our strength; unity is our goal." Sebastian reflected on this:

> I never did think it was my role to do the work. My role was to help [teacher leaders] organize the work, give them time and opportunity to plan the work, give them resources and compensation for doing the work. I really believe that's my role. And maybe I need to advocate publicly better for them. I really see my role as kind of a fulcrum between the opposing views and trying to get a sense of how to reach some level of equilibrium so that change can move forward.

Leaders like Sebastian, who have reserved communication styles and who facilitate rather than take the lead on change, can be very effective. But when teachers or other staff expect the leader to be a take-charge type, there can be a clash of role expectations. Staff members may not realize that the principal genuinely intends for them to take a leadership role, or they may not understand what that role entails; each party waits for the other to take charge, and after a time, both become frustrated and start blaming each other for not doing their job. For this reason, it is important for administrators to first identify their own preferred style of communication and leadership and, then, having identified it, communicate this clearly to staff. Knowing how leaders define their own roles can be a great help to staff members, who can then see more clearly what kinds of roles they can fill given the kind of administrative leadership they have. Lambert (1998) suggests that principals need to acquire specific strategies for breaking codependent relationships. For example,

> When a staff group remains silent, waiting for the answer from the principal, the principal can say, "I've thought about this issue in three ways. . . . Help me analyze and critique these ideas," or "I don't know the answers. Let's think it through together." (p. 25)

Issues of communication style and leadership roles are particularly critical in schools with many diverse cultures, because culture can greatly influence communication style, and ideas about leadership also can differ cross-culturally. As more culturally and ethnically diverse people begin to fill leadership roles, it becomes even more important for leaders to clarify roles and expectations because the potential for miscommunication is greater.

ACTIVITY 11: COMMUNICATION STYLE

Use this activity to reflect on your own communication style, and then discuss what you've identified with a colleague.

1. In view of what you've read in this section, how would you describe your own communication style as a leader? How directly or indirectly do you communicate? Are you a take-charge type or more of a facilitator? Do you tend to be the first to speak up in a group, or do you listen for a while before you speak?

2. Given this communication style, what does this imply for those with whom you work?

3. Can you think of a time when you and your colleagues communicated poorly about your respective roles? What did you do about it then? What else could you have done about it?

THE DYNAMICS OF POWER

Key Questions for Leaders

- How do the dynamics of power influence my role in guiding and facilitating our plan to promote positive interethnic relations?
- How can I, as a school leader, use my institutional power and authority to further the development of a positive interethnic community?

It is rare to run across instances in which politics and power relations do not play a role in the major challenges school personnel face in their work. Many a good plan has fallen apart because, somehow, politics and power relations got in the way and undermined whatever was going well. Nonetheless, politics and power relations are seldom explicitly recognized or addressed as legitimate topics of inquiry and discussion, even when they are consistently raised by those who occupy positions of relatively little power, such as instructional assistants, students, and parents. Often the discussions of power relations in the literature on organizational theory (see, for example, Harchar & Hyle, 1996; Nahavandi, 1997) are too broad and general to be of much practical use to school leaders. Delpit (1996) argues that the rules of the "culture of power" must be explicitly taught in the classroom. What this means is that there are implicit rules in schools about how to talk, how to write, how to dress, how to interact, and, unless these are made visible to all students, the school culture tends to favor those students who come from the dominant class and culture. If we want poor and minority students to succeed in school, they need to know how to operate by the rules of the culture of power.

While Delpit took an important step in making power more visible in the classroom, scholars have yet to devote much attention to the uses and implications of power by school leaders. Given that school leaders assume positions of authority and dominance relative to staff, students, and parents, it is essential that they consider the implications of this dynamic. How should those in positions of authority in a school use their power to create and sustain institutional opportunities for positive interethnic relations? How should they redistribute their power and authority so that others can enhance their leadership capacity?

One theoretical framework that lends itself to everyday application by school-based practitioners is Willie's (1991) theory of complementarity, which has been adapted by Norte (2001b) for use by school-based practitioners. This working framework for understanding the dynamics of power incorporates five basic tenets (see Box 7.1).

It follows from this model that those in positions of authority in schools—such as principals and other administrators—have a responsibility to listen to those in subordinate positions (staff, students, and parents). In order to listen, however, leaders need to create structures, policies, and practices that will better allow them to hear and respond to the needs that staff, students, and parents express. It is important to bear in mind that many people are not easily able to give voice to their concerns, especially if they are accustomed to not being heard by those in positions of power, or if English is not their primary language. Creating forums where people feel more comfortable airing concerns is a way to ensure that the voices the leader hears are not only those of the most empowered parents, students, or staff members.

Those in subordinate positions relative to the principal or other administrators have a complementary responsibility to let the person in the more dominant role hear how things are going. How is the plan for promoting positive interethnic relations going? What seems to be working well? Am I noticing any problems that concern me? How can I make sure that those who are in positions of authority know about these problems so that we can do something to address them?

In addition to recognizing and acting upon the responsibilities described above, those with formal authority in schools can also actively encourage others to assume formal and informal leadership roles. This is part of what Lambert (1998) describes as "building leadership capacity."

> Leadership requires the redistribution of power and authority. Shared learning, purpose, action, and responsibility demand the realignment of power and authority. Districts and principals need to explicitly release authority, and staff need to learn how to enhance personal power and informal authority. (p. 9)

Box 7.1   Dynamics of Power Relations

In this model, there are five basic assumptions:

1.   Power, like energy, is neither good nor bad in and of itself, and it exists in some form in all people at all times.

2.   Asymmetrical power positions—that is, dominant and subordinate—always exist to greater and lesser extents in all relationships, but they are not static.

3.   We each occupy either dominant or subordinate positions of power relative to different individuals and relative to context.

4.   Inherent in being in the dominant position is that we are blind, to greater or lesser degrees, to the negative consequences of our power over others. In the subordinate position, on the other hand, we have insight into the negative consequences of the decisions and actions of those in the dominant role because we are the ones who most feel their impact.

5.   There are responsibilities that correspond to each position of power. Specifically, those in the subordinate position have a responsibility to give voice to how decisions and actions affect them, and those in the dominant position have a responsibility to listen and respond to those in the subordinate role. When we recognize and effectively act upon these responsibilities, a symbiotic relationship that is mutually beneficial can result.

SOURCE: Developed by Charles Vert Willie, 1987, and adapted by Norte (2001b).

Collaborative teacher groups, such as the ones created at Ohlone High School, where teachers met in groups of their own choice for 2 hours each week to work on projects to improve curriculum or schoolwide efforts, are a good example. Because the groups were explicitly not departmental, they broke away from the traditional departmental fiefdoms and gave rise to new teacher leaders.

At United Nations High School, the principal, Tom O'Reilly, was especially skilled at promoting the development of teachers as leaders. He would entice them to attend a professional development opportunity and, then, when they returned with excitement about what they had learned, would offer them resources and support to take the lead in implementing what they had learned and involving other teachers.

The case study of Greenlawn Elementary School in Part II provides a more extended example of how one leader used his position of authority to address a power issue involving diverse parents and the school secretary. This case also includes several activities.

PROBLEM SOLVING USING THE
ELEMENTS FOR EFFECTIVE INTERVENTION

Key Question for Leaders

- How can we address areas of the plan that aren't working well?

One of the key roles of school leaders is to be problem solvers. The leaders we got to know during the study were constantly working to resolve problems on many different levels, some of which were specifically related to diversity and the plans they had developed to improve interethnic relations. For example, one leader found that the new conflict resolution program they had begun to implement at their school had a number of problems, including the fact that it existed completely apart from the classroom curriculum, even though there were valuable lessons that could have been incorporated into the curriculum within classrooms. Implementing new plans is always like this to some degree—some parts work well enough, but others clearly need to be rethought. How can leaders sort out all the pieces to the puzzle that result in the forming of healthy, positive, multiethnic school environments without losing sight of the whole, the total that is greater than the sum of the parts? How can leaders identify the key elements that are essential to creating positive interethnic school climates?

A framework that we have found useful begins with elements which are commonly recognized as part and parcel to any educational program, that is, *content* and *process*. However, this framework goes further by also teasing out some less-obvious elements that can contribute to or hinder successful implementation. These are *structure, staffing,* and *infrastructure*. Table 7.1 displays these five Elements for Effective Intervention and some questions leaders can pose to help identify problem areas.

Content simply refers to the *what*—the subject matter, information, topic, material, or ideas—that are the focus of attention. At the classroom level, content refers to what gets included as the topic of study or inquiry. At the school level, it could include the school's vision, mission, or stated priorities. Sometimes, leaders find that although they thought they had been successful in gaining buy-in and building consensus about the plan, some aspects remain unclear. The principal and other leaders play essential roles in framing and clarifying, if not establishing, the content of the school's mission—the vision, priorities, and focus of activity, and the underlying analysis and assumptions that will shape the nature and character of schoolwide efforts and initiatives.

All the school leaders in the study, with some variation in degree and emphasis, held a vision of creating a school that was inclusive of all students and families, responsive to their needs, caring, and just. Indeed, some of the most dynamic and effective school leaders were those whose vision included a sense of being part of a larger project for social justice. Equity and social justice, then, along with high academic achievement, were part of the content, the basic subject matter on which the school's efforts were focused, and so dialogue and reflection on these topics were officially sanctioned and supported.

Table 7.1 Elements for Effective Intervention

Content	Process	Structure	Staffing	Infrastructure
The subject matter of focus	*How people engage the subject matter*	*How time, space, and people are organized*	*The roles to which school personnel are assigned*	*Physical setting and economic resources*
What is the vision or mission?	Is the process interactive?	To what extent do staff have regular and sufficient opportunities to collaborate?	Do staff hold assumptions and values that are in concert with the school vision?	Is the venue accessible, safe, and comfortable?
How clearly is it communicated?	Are all participants provided with opportunities for active, meaningful participation?	To what extent do staff and students of diverse backgrounds have regular opportunities to interact and develop personalized relationships?	How suitable and capable are the staff of implementing the vision and plan?	How suitable are the facilities for producing the desired results?
What is the prevailing analysis of the school's greatest challenges?	Are students, parents, and staff encouraged and supported to work collaboratively?	What formal and informal structures exist for families and students to be involved in setting the school's agenda?	How can the effect of resistant or unsuitable staff be most effectively addressed?	Will the people who are expected to use the facility actually use it?
To what extent are values such as equity, inclusion, and social justice evident in all domains of the school?				How can we acquire financial or in-kind resources to implement our plan more effectively?

SOURCE: Adapted from Norte (2001b).

For example, Greenlawn Elementary School for years had a white male principal and an overwhelmingly white teaching staff for whom issues of equity and inclusion were not even on the radar screen. Ms. Fujita, a Japanese American teacher, did not feel it was safe to offer her perspectives and concerns about things she saw going on at the school because she felt hers would be a lone voice with no support. She reported, "When I was in college at the University of California at Berkeley, I was very active in movements for social justice and equity. That was a big part of my life. But when I came to work here, I found myself among staff, you know, all white, who just didn't care about or understand these things. For years, I just retreated into my room and did what I felt was right in my own classroom, but I never talked about [my multicultural curriculum] with anyone. It wasn't an issue for anyone else even though our student population was becoming majority minority."

It was not until Mr. Murakawa, a very competent and experienced Japanese American principal, who is well versed at working on issues of equity and inclusion, came to the school and began to help set new priorities that Fujita felt safe to, as she put it, "come out of the closet."

At this particular school, it was not only the principal who created a climate conducive to bringing forth the views and talents of this teacher, which had been lying relatively dormant, but also the district superintendent who made the academic achievement of historically underachieving students the district's top priority. The district's educational leader used his authority to sanction this issue as a high-priority content area, the vision toward which district's resources would be used. This was particularly powerful and controversial, because it established and legitimized what is traditionally regarded as a nonacademic area as a high-priority content area. This was done by establishing a districtwide team diversity initiative that set up both school-site and districtwide diversity teams whose task was to find more effective ways of improving the academic performance of historically underserved, underachieving students. These district priorities, and the accompanying structures designed to accomplish them, provided Fujita with a context within which she not only felt safe to pursue her passion for equity and justice but also to emerge as a highly competent and well-regarded instructional leader among the faculty; that is, she knew how to do well what was now expected of all district faculty. In fact, one recommendation of a districtwide diversity review conducted by district personnel, as one component of the team diversity initiative, was that Fujita become a mentor for other district faculty and that other staff be given release time to observe her classroom as part of their professional development.

As this example shows, leaders can give weight and legitimacy to the content of diversity and equity by allocating time and resources to it as well as by encouraging members of the school community to clarify the vision, discuss it, and refine it.

Process, in this framework, refers to the nature and quality of the procedures used to engage the content. At the classroom level, for example, a teacher might use what Freire (1970) calls a "banking" process with students, in which the teacher lectures on a preselected topic, and students passively record and regurgitate the given information. Alternatively, the teacher could use a problem-posing process through which students generate and engage the themes and issues that directly impact their lives as they learn to read the word and read the world—that is, develop meaningful skills that serve the process of understanding and shaping their worlds. This classroom example illustrates the interrelatedness of process and content; that is, a process that engages, elicits, and includes student voices and experiences also generates much of the content.

At the school level, the example of Dolores Huerta Middle School is instructive. The principal, Ms. Reeves, faced a formidable challenge in working with teachers whom she described as the union dinosaurs—teachers who had taught in the district for more than 25 years and had watched the demographics shift dramatically from a white, middle-class majority to a majority of low-income Vietnamese and Latino students. However, they persisted in delivering the same instructional program, with increasingly poor results. Their resistance to change was affecting the school climate and creating tensions among the faculty.

A turning point came when Reeves sought assistance from an outside consultant, and together they adapted a process called the history walk. This process was the central piece in a daylong staff development event. Teachers were asked to indicate the year they first came to the school, to describe what the school and the community were like at that time, and to identify the major issues or challenges the school faced then. This was done chronologically, with successively newer staff members sharing their impressions and challenges last, while the more veteran staff members chimed in to compare, contrast, and fill in historical context as the school's history unfolded into the present.

This process served several functions. It provided newer staff members with a historical overview of the school context they had stepped into. It also served to honor the knowledge and experience of those staff members who were feeling threatened and defensive given the new demographics of the community, and it may have reminded them of their own potential for change. Staff members were able to locate themselves as part of an ongoing process of change. Last but not least, the process allowed staff members to get to know each other better as whole human beings engaged in a common project. This process is part of what Vargas (1985) called the "conocimiento principle," or the invaluable process of getting to know those with whom one will be working on a long-term, collective project. Leaders need to bear in mind that while the content of their vision may be laudable in terms of the equitable outcomes they seek for underserved students, the processes they use to achieve those outcomes are crucial for success. In other words, process matters deeply.

Structure refers to how time, space, and people are organized and configured. Different structures facilitate different processes. At the classroom level, cooperative group structures are the most well-known ways of configuring time, space, and people to facilitate their engagement in cooperative, interactive processes. Physically configuring the room in straight rows of desks will facilitate a process of teacher lecturing and students listening, while configuring clusters of table and chairs into stations around a room will facilitate a process of student teams working together.

At Allaneq, the middle school discussed in Chapter 5, Principal Chauncy was greatly influenced by Gardner's (1985) theory of multiple intelligences when she initiated the new team structure. She wanted to create a structure that would recognize and value different learning and teaching styles and, in this way, she thought some of the problems diverse learners were experiencing in classrooms might be alleviated. So she designed four teams to focus on different learning styles. The Red team emphasized student-centered, alternative forms of instruction and multiple modalities. The Blue team emphasized a more teacher-centered, direct instruction style. The Green team emphasized bilingualism and learning a second language, and the Fireweed team emphasized Native Alaskan ways of learning. Teachers chose the team they felt best fit their own teaching style or interests, and the idea was for students and families to be able to choose as well. Not surprisingly, however, the teams quickly became ethnically segregated, especially the Fireweed and Blue teams. Fireweed became mostly Native Alaskan, and the Blue team became mostly African American and Latino. Students even dubbed the hall where the Blue team was located "ghetto hall." Although the team idea was working in some senses—for example, it was helping to personalize relationships among students and between students and teachers—it clearly wasn't encouraging students to relate across ethnic lines.

When Ms. Turner became principal, she immediately heard complaints from the teachers about the team structure. Some teachers wanted to abandon the whole idea and go back to a more traditional structure. But Turner didn't want to throw out the baby with the bathwater. She recognized that there was a structural problem with the teams, but the basic idea was still a good one. So, after discussions with faculty and parents, the principal restructured the teams, and students were assigned at the beginning of the year to teams. Those who did the assigning paid close attention to making sure each team had a mix of ethnic groups, as well as honoring students' learning styles in cases where this was clearly known to the staff. If the initial assignment didn't work out, students could be reassigned within the first few weeks of school, so they still had a degree of choice. The simple change in structure resulted in a much more integrated school while still retaining the high degree of personalization afforded by the team structure.

Staffing has also emerged as a crucial element in implementing a plan to foster positive interethnic relations. Given that all the schools in our study were public schools, most school-site administrators could not be selective about which students and families were part of the school community. However, they did have the power to hire and assign school faculty and staff, and district superintendents had the power to hire and assign administrative staff. Leaders in the study had developed a strong sense of how to use this power to hire and assign staff in order to create a culture that had a shared vision of holding high standards, valuing diversity, working collaboratively, and meeting the needs of underserved, underachieving students. Sometimes, minor changes in how and where particular staff are assigned can maximize their effectiveness in realizing the school vision.

In schools where the climate begins to change from a traditional, monocultural school to one that embraces multiculturalism and holds equity and inclusion as strong values, it is not uncommon for faculty members who are uncomfortable with this kind of change to choose to leave. This seems to be a common part of the school change process. However, reconstituting staff in this way is not always likely or possible.

The veteran staff members at Dolores Huerta Middle School seemed to have no intention of leaving except for retirement. Given little choice but to work with the staff she had, Principal Reeves used a walk-a-mile-in-my-shoes approach to deal with certain veteran staff who were not going away. For example, she was constantly being subtly challenged and derided by one teacher who had no apparent respect for the role and function of administrators and who undermined her efforts to improve the school's climate whenever possible, claiming that the work administrators did was unnecessary to the smooth functioning of the school.

Seizing an opportunity to win this teacher over when her assistant principal (AP) went on leave for a semester, Reeves asked this teacher to assume the role of AP on an interim basis. While being very supportive and collaborative with this teacher as he confronted myriad tasks and responsibilities in his new role—dealing with discipline issues, working with parents and families in crisis, responding to teacher needs and requests, coordinating student activities, dealing with scheduling issues, preparing for and facilitating staff meetings and staff development—the principal made sure he had the opportunity to experience all facets of being a school administrator. After a difficult semester and a steep learning curve, the teacher came away with a deep appreciation for all that administrators have to contend with, and he became a staunch supporter of the principal.

While in this case, a temporary reassignment made a big difference in a staff member's attitude, shifting positions of existing staff members doesn't always help. Many of the principals in our study have had to take on the difficult task of getting rid of teachers who they felt were ineffectual or outright damaging to the physical, emotional, and intellectual well-being of students. This is a difficult and unenviable task, and it comes at a cost to the principal, both personally and in terms of relations with other staff who are sympathetic with the teachers who are removed. But when all else fails, leaders have to rely on their sense of values and their best judgment. Reeves engaged in a long struggle with one teacher who eventually filed a grievance against her, but she did not relent. She commented, "I have to weigh this man's retirement needs against the damage he's doing to all the kids he's not serving."

Infrastructure refers to the physical space that is available for carrying out the desired activities, and to the financial resources and in-kind contributions that support the desired activities. Ideally, the physical environment is conducive to the purposes for which it is used. A classic example of this, which we have already mentioned, is the pod school design in which classrooms are configured in pods that surround a large central area. Within each pod, classrooms that are adjacent to each other share a smaller communal space. Such physical settings can greatly enhance collaboration, but will not automatically produce high-quality interactions unless there are also corresponding organizational structures. At Gladiola Middle School, for example, the pod infrastructure was available, but it was not until the principal placed all teachers of a certain grade level in the same pod area that the infrastructure was put to its best use.

Another way that infrastructure affects the school culture is in its physical condition and appearance. While many schools in our study did not have architecture specifically designed to promote a sense of community, the maintenance and appearance of the sites demonstrated a standard of value for the school and those who occupied it. One huge high school in our study, located in a nearly 100-year-old brownstone building in the Bronx, was far from having this kind of design but was, nonetheless, always gleaming: walls and desks clean and uncluttered, bathrooms clean and stocked with soap and toilet paper, floors always shiny. Such physical conditions were typical of the schools in our study and spoke volumes to the high respect and regard students and school personnel alike had for themselves and others. The physical setting, then, is an element of the school environment that can shape the attitudes that school-community members have about their school and themselves.

Financial and in-kind contributions are another type of infrastructure that leaders often need to adjust as they move farther along in carrying out their plan. It is easy to underestimate the costs of implementing new activities. Leaders need to gauge when the funding simply isn't enough to do what was intended and how much additional funding or in-kind support (e.g., donations of food, materials, staff time) would be needed to make the plan work.

Clearly, the categories we have discussed here—content, process, structure, staffing, and infrastructure—are abstractions. Because a community is a complex, webbed system in which all elements dynamically interact and affect one another, there is much overlap and melding of the elements we have delineated here. The whole is greater than the sum of the parts. The purpose of the model is to make the complexity of a school community more comprehensible so that school leaders can assess their effectiveness in these areas and determine where best to intervene. Once again, the "necessary but not sufficient" principle is evident: that is, each of the elements described above is important or critical to the successful achievement of a given goal, but being successful in only one or a few of these areas may not be enough to achieve overall success. The schools in our study that were the most broadly successful were those that best addressed all the elements described in this model.

ACTIVITY 12: ELEMENTS FOR EFFECTIVE INTERVENTION

1. Think of a particular innovation that is running into some problems at a school you know well. Using the five Elements for Effective Intervention, analyze the problem (i.e., is it a problem of content, process, structure, staffing, infrastructure, or a combination of several?).

2. What could be done to intervene?

8

Documenting and Communicating Success in Interethnic Relations

Today, the information available on negative activities youth engage in vastly out-numbers that on the positive. We know how many youth use drugs, but do we know how many volunteer? How many have the skills to make sound decisions? How many know about and are working toward career goals? How many have been leaders?

—Karen Pittman (1991, p. 17)

When a school leadership team puts a great deal of effort into developing more positive interethnic relations in their school, they also have to consider how they will show others whether things have actually improved and, if so, how. Members of the school community and the public want to know and have a right to know how the changes you are implementing are working and whether they are bringing about the desired outcomes.

YOU ARE WHAT YOU MEASURE

Key Question for Leaders

- Where should we expect to see improvement if our plan is working well?

The aphorism, "You are what you measure," has become frighteningly true. Our school system in the United States focuses quite narrowly on defining school success as achievement levels on standardized tests. This is even more true now than in past decades, due to the increased emphasis on standards and accountability. We have used standardized tests to measure student performance for many years, but recently, these outcome measures have acquired far more weight and significance for children's futures, as well as for teachers and principals, as states begin to rate schools by how well their students perform from year to year.

Some schools in the study, especially those that had safety and security issues well under control, did show gains in academic achievement, but many had not yet arrived at the point where students were showing these gains. They were still building the foundation of safety and security and creating an environment where students could focus on learning. It is interesting to note that several schools which did not show academic gains during the time of the study have since reported to the authors that their standardized test scores have gone up, suggesting that the approaches put into place during the time of the study take 2 or more years to bear fruit in terms of academic gains.

But what can leaders say about schools that have not yet arrived at the point where results are evident in terms of academic achievement? Do we not value the other achievements that enable academic learning to take place? In every school in the study, there were other successes, such as improvements in interethnic relations among students, a drop in the level of conflict and violence, increased involvement of diverse parents, increased staff collaboration, more diverse student leadership, enhanced reputation of the school in the community, and improved school climate. If we truly value outcomes such as these, shouldn't schools be monitoring progress in these areas from year to year?

Unfortunately, because academic achievement and standardized testing dominate our efforts toward monitoring school improvement in the United States, most schools are poorly equipped to measure improvements in human relations. They do not have the staff expertise or systems in place to gather data that would demonstrate improvements from year to year. For example, many categories of disciplinary referrals, such as the term *defiant* in one school, are very subjective and do not lend themselves to valid monitoring of patterns even within the same school. An assistant principal explained,

> There's a range of what gets defined as defiant. *Fight* and *defiant* could be the same behavior labeled differently by different people. We have 150 people defining defiant. There is agreement at the center but not at the edges of the concept.

In addition, students told us that many racial conflicts are never reported to any school authority. Therefore measuring the number or frequency of racial conflicts on the basis of student reports would be like measuring only the tip of the iceberg. Only the most overt conflicts or the ones that students felt comfortable reporting would be included.

An even greater issue in measuring success in human relations is that the phenomenon to be measured needs to be defined. If a reduction in racial conflict is the only goal, then behavioral indicators, such as a drop in referrals for fighting, would suffice, assuming they could be consistently monitored. However, proactive leaders do much more than merely reduce racial conflict. As we have shown in the preceding chapters, they use a multitude of approaches that are designed to build more personalized relations and to address the root causes of racial and ethnic conflict, such as segregation, inequality, and negative socialization about other groups. The impact of such approaches, if they are working effectively, would not be captured by a single measure of decrease in racial conflict. Rather, they would be reflected in other indicators of a more positive school environment, such as less rigid segregation among student groups, more collaboration among faculty members, a better reputation of the school in the community, more diverse parental involvement, and other outcomes. Ultimately, these approaches should contribute to higher academic achievement as well.

Since educational policy at this time does not require school leaders to measure their schools' progress in human relations, those who consider this an important area of school functioning have to figure out ways to demonstrate their successes. It is important to do this for several reasons. First, documenting and reporting improvements in human relations sends a message to the school community that you are serious and committed to the vision and plan your school leadership team has developed. Second, it enables your school to get positive attention in the local media. Armed with evidence of improvement, you can call a journalist from the local newspaper or a reporter from a local TV or radio station and ask her or him to do a piece on your school's improvement in a particular area which you will name. Newspapers and TV tend to focus more often on what's wrong with schools because that is what gets reported to them. It is important for school leaders to provide balance by informing reporters of the positive things going on in schools. You can also use the media as an opportunity to educate the wider public about race relations and diversity, doing your part as an advocate to dispel negative stereotypes about ethnic groups and raise questions about inequities in the school system. A third reason to become more adept at communicating success is that it puts your school in a better position to receive additional funding. If you can show evidence that the strategies you are using are beginning to have a positive impact, funders are more likely to continue funding your efforts or to fund an expansion of your efforts.

ACTIVITY 13: DOCUMENTING IMPACT

This activity is designed to help you identify those areas of your plan that might lend themselves to measurement or documentation. This activity can be done individually or in groups. First, get a copy of your school's plan for developing positive interethnic relations. Review the vision, the approaches you have included, and the themes that tie the approaches together. Then try to answer the following questions:

1. If the plan is working well, where would we expect to see changes? Make a list of all the areas that you think might show changes. If you are working with a group, compare your lists, discussing what's different and what's the same.

2. Which of these areas are already being measured by the school or district, and which are currently not measured but could be? In other words, which areas can be monitored from year to year (or semester to semester, if you want a shorter time frame to show improvement)?

3. If you or your district has an evaluator with whom you work closely, make an appointment to discuss your ideas about documenting impact in the area of interethnic relations or, more generally, group relations. If your school or district is already evaluating certain programs, you may be able to extend the evaluation to include some or all your questions.

USING BOTH QUALITATIVE AND QUANTITATIVE EVIDENCE

Key Question for Leaders

- How can we measure or document the impact of the changes we are making?

Usually, terms like *measure, monitor,* and *evaluate* conjure up images of numbers and statistics. These are *quantitative* ways of documenting and showing evidence of change. Because they are believed by many to be more "objective" than words, most school districts rely heavily on quantifiable outcomes when they report to their constituencies about how they are doing. But *qualitative* accounts of change can also be very powerful as means to communicate about the impact of new or different practices. By combining both quantitative and qualitative measures of change, school leaders can have a wider palette of options to choose from and can present a more powerful case.

It would take another two books to adequately explain the philosophies and methods used in quantitative and qualitative research and evaluation. Fortunately, there are many already written, so we will simply refer you to some that we have found useful and readable. Patton (1990) provides a wealth of information on qualitative methods in language that is both humorous and accessible to school leaders. He focuses primarily on design issues and methods

Table 8.1 Sources of Evidence for Change in Interethnic Relations

Outcome Area	Specific Indicators	Possible Sources of Evidence That Can Be Compared Over Time
Improved interethnic relations among students	• Students are less likely to group exclusively by ethnicity on the playground • More friendships between students of different ethnicities • Students have a better understanding of other cultures and ethnic groups • Students have a better understanding of prejudice and racism • Reduction in overt conflicts related to race and ethnicity	• Observations • Interviews with students • Focus groups with students • Staff interviews • Interviews with students • Focus groups with students • Conflict management tallies • Referrals to main office for fighting • Suspensions for fighting • Student survey with specific questions about how many racial fights they have witnessed or been a part of in X amount of time

of gathering data. Miles and Huberman (1994) makes a good companion to Patton because it focuses more on the analysis and interpretation of qualitative data. Though the text is somewhat denser than Patton, this book has many examples of tables and charts that can be used to display qualitative data. Good data display can be a tremendous help if you are trying to communicate about change, impact, or improvements to your faculty or school board. For explanations of the key ideas in statistics, Fraenkel, Wallen, and Sawin (1999) provide a refreshing visual approach to statistical terms and methods.

In Table 8.1, we present a sample of how a school leader might go about gathering appropriate data to measure changes in one area of impact—improved interethnic relations among students.

However, as we have pointed out, there are many other areas that are related to this one that might also show improvement, depending on the approaches you have taken in your school. If your school team identified disproportionate discipline referrals as one of the root causes of ethnic conflict at your school, and if your plan includes attention to behavioral standards, then, over time, you should be able to see that the numbers of referrals and suspensions more closely match the demographics of the student population. Referral, suspension, and expulsion data can be disaggregated and compared over time to show whether the different ethnic groups in your school are proportionately represented in the discipline data.

Another area that might show changes, again depending on your plan, is the diversity of student leadership, for example, participation in the student council, conflict management, and after-school club leadership. It would be a simple matter to keep tallies of the number of student leadership opportunities, the students who participate in them, and the ethnicity of these students. Over time, you should be able to see whether more diverse students are participating in leadership at your school. Similarly, shifts in the diversity of parent involvement can be monitored on simple record-keeping sheets and analyzed at the end of each year.

SHARING GOOD NEWS

Key Question for Leaders

- How can we use positive outcome data to generate more momentum and sense of efficacy among staff and students?

When there is good news—that is, when efforts to improve human relations have paid off in some tangible way—school leaders need to share this with the rest of the school community. Teachers in schools where this was a common practice reported that they had high morale and felt their efforts were recognized by the leadership. They also said that knowing they had made a difference—even a small one—made them want to work even harder to make more of a difference. Several leaders in the study excelled at communicating the successes of the school to its teachers, students, and community. This included communicating improvements in the nonacademic areas mentioned above.

Robert Cohen, principal at Sojourner Truth High School, had turned this kind of positive reinforcement into an art form. He knew how to use public relations skills to the advantage of the students and the staff. He touted the smallest increments of change, and they grew exponentially each year. He explained, "As things start to improve, you need some quick wins. You need to target things that can be done, and you need to achieve them and then publicize them and share the credit. Then the momentum is inevitable. I think then we started to get a sense of excitement that things really could move. . . . Everybody said, 'See—what he's saying and what we're saying is true—we really can do this.'"

Cohen was constantly comparing outcomes so that he would be able to share positive news. Since Sojourner Truth High School was focused on raising academic achievement among its primarily low-income, black and

Table 8.2   Improvement in Performance Outcomes at Sojourner Truth High
School

Outcome Measure	Years	Percentage or Number	Years	Percentage or Number	Percentage Change
Attendance (average daily, excluding long-term absences)	1988-89	74.7%	1997-98	91.4%	+22%
Long-term Absentees	1992-93	10.0%	1996-97	3.9%	-61%
Drop-out Rate, Annual	1989-90	11.4%	1996-97	2.9%	-75%
Drop-out Rate, 4-Year Cohort	1989-90	23.0%	1996-97	9.1%	-60%
Graduation Rate, 4-Year Cohort	1986	11.8%	1997	59.6%	+405%
Regents Diplomas	1993	31	1998	113	+265%
Regents Exams Passed	1993	1,311	1998	3,228	+146%
Tested Out of Bilingual Classes	1992	14	1998	86	+514%
Advanced Placement Enrollments	Fall '93	131	Fall '98	553	+322%
College Admissions Rate	June '94	81.0%	June '97	95%	+17%
College Scholarships and Financial Aid Received	June '95	$898,761	June '98	$7,902,568	+779%
Met or Exceeded Chancellor's Standards	1991-92	6 out of 12 (50%)	1995-96	11 out of 11 (100%)	+100%

SOURCE: Table reprinted from Sather (2001, p. 516).

Latino students, Cohen kept tabs on many indicators of academic achievement (see Table 8.2). The table shows one way for positive results to be shared with the school community and beyond.

Along with publicizing "quick wins" and longer-term gains, such as the ones represented in the table, Cohen regularly and openly expressed his appreciation for people's contributions. He never took the credit by himself. "I try to spend as much time as I can thanking people, sharing the glory, sharing our pride. The improvement [in this school] wouldn't have happened if all the staff didn't work together." This generosity was noted by many staff members and students and contributed to a sense of shared ownership and pride in the school's improvement.

Part II

Cases in Interethnic Relations for School Leaders

In order to delve more deeply into the dilemmas and challenges faced by leaders, it is useful to consider extended cases of practice. When used in professional preparation programs or inservice professional development, cases have the advantage of leading participants to "grapple with a select number of authentic and significant educational problems" (Murphy, 1992, p. 152).

The six cases we present in Part II are organized by level—elementary, middle, and high school. They each present a particular conflict or set of challenges followed by a description of how the leaders at that particular school handled the conflict or challenges. Each case also includes a short summary that should enable you to decide quickly if it is relevant to your needs, and activities are embedded within the case. The activities often require participants to refer to material presented in Part I, thus providing opportunities to practice using some of the models and frameworks presented earlier.

9

The Ripple Effect of Conflict

Anne Katz

RAINBOW ELEMENTARY SCHOOL

The case at Rainbow Elementary School illustrates how conflict is not an isolated event but rather can spread beyond initial impact to wider and wider audiences, much like the rings a thrown pebble produces in a body of water. At Rainbow, student-generated conflict was a major problem addressed by school leadership. However, Rainbow's story includes an additional pattern of widening impact across other members of the school community. Conflict between parents and staff contributed to a lack of parental involvement, a decline in respect of students for teachers, and a disdain for parents on the part of staff. While parents are not the ostensible focus for schools, they are a critical element in the school community, especially at the elementary level. How can leadership build bridges between staff and parents to create a more harmonious community for educating children?

The Setting

Rainbow Elementary School was located in a relatively affluent and well-cared-for area of a San Francisco Bay Area community. The school was one block from the commercial center of this neighborhood. A city playground sat across the street from the school's entrance. A relatively small school with an enrollment of 217 students from kindergarten through fifth grade, it served a diverse student population. A little more than one third of the students were

Latino and one third were African American. About 12 percent were European American and the remainder were Chinese, Filipino, and American Indian. Most of the students came from low-income households; many were also immigrants. Because the district was under court-ordered desegregation at the time of this study, Rainbow was an assigned school. While a few students came from the immediate geographical area, 98 percent were bussed in from more distant neighborhoods. Thus the notion of community for Rainbow had multiple meanings: there was the physical community of the neighborhood around the school as well as the communities students left each day to attend the school.

Conflicts at Rainbow

For years, Rainbow operated as a traditional elementary school designed to deliver a basic curriculum. Student achievement, however, was low, and conflict and tension were rampant. Describing this era, one kindergarten teacher said,

> Out of the kindergarten class that I started with, only eight graduated from fifth grade. Twenty-four of them had gone to other schools—quite a lot of turnover. Partly the scores. Partly, it was very violent around here. People would get a rope around their neck or get kicked or get hurt.

Fighting on the playground every day was the norm. Instances of kicking, fighting, and swearing repeatedly interrupted playground games during recess. In telling me about this era, the principal characterized the situation as a "breakdown in management of child play and child conflict."

While analyses of school conflict tend to focus on students, it was clear at Rainbow that the adult relationships were also strained, particularly across racial and ethnic lines. Teachers, who were predominately white, were seen as showing a distinct lack of respect toward parents, particularly African American parents. Parents reciprocated, showing little respect to staff. Continuing in this vein, students picked up on this mutual lack of respect and viewed staff with little respect. Students' lack of respect led to a failure to heed teachers in the classroom. Thus inappropriate classroom behavior became even more of a problem. One teacher noted,

> There was a fair degree of violence, bullying, aggression towards teachers, a very minimal amount of support from families and community. Teachers were basically feeling as if they needed to move on for their health and well-being. It was just ridiculous.

ACTIVITY 14: POSSIBLE RESPONSES

Below are several ways a leader could respond to the situation that occurred at Rainbow.

- Ignore the situation and hope things will get better.
- Deal immediately with students when they break rules or show disrespect by sending them home and then suspending them.
- Set up a conflict resolution program for students; engage students as conflict managers.

- Ask parents to come in, and then provide them with rules for appropriate student behavior in school; explain that it is their responsibility to make sure that students exhibit appropriate behavior.
- Provide workshops for parents on topics such as anger management, helping students with homework, volunteering in the classroom, and participating in school management.
- Invite parents to school to talk about their children's behavior and how the school can work with the home to shape student behavior.

1. There may be more options than the ones listed above. What other possibilities can you think of? Remember to consider the school context.

2. Choose one or more options from either the list above or ones that you think might be better, and develop a plan for addressing the student, teacher, and parent issues. Consider implementation issues such as a timeline for undertaking different components of your plan.

3. Work with others in a small group to discuss your plan; compare and contrast the plans. Some plans may work better for one segment of the school community but not address the other members involved in the conflict. Make sure the plans get at the underlying issues among the adults as well as those issues concerning the students.

The Principal's Response

When Maria Snow picked up the reins at Rainbow, she was already known within the district as someone who could make change happen. While a one-year interim leader had begun the task of overhauling Rainbow and had replaced many of the teaching staff, it fell to Principal Snow to follow through. One staff member used the term "securing the perimeter" to describe the initial focus of efforts to create change at Rainbow. Specific strategies to create a safe, conflict-free school environment included training students in conflict resolution techniques, hiring student advisors to act as models for students while monitoring their behavior and reinforcing good behavior, and implementing consistent standards for behavior across classrooms and throughout the school.

However, a key initial step was creating a unifying vision that would act as the foundation for the developing school community. Rainbow's vision, as described in the 1996 to 1997 School Accountability Report Card, was "dedicated to teaching tolerance, celebrating diversity and achieving academic excellence in a nonviolent setting." Explaining this, one of the teachers said, "Our vision is if kids can get along, if the parents can get along, and the staff can get along, we will produce a group of kids that will not be matched anyplace."

Snow recognized that the adults at Rainbow needed to tackle racism while teaching kids to be antiracist. Thus she initiated staff development efforts focused on civil rights, race, ethnicity, class, and sexual orientation. Snow also wanted to recruit families who wanted to be at the school and who were enthusiastic. She felt that the key to the children's success was parental involvement. She reasoned that when parents had respect for education, when they chose to bring their children to a school, students had a greater chance to achieve. She also realized that implementing a vision took time. As she pointed out, "Our school will look different in 5 years than it does now and will look different in 10 years than it will in 5. We have a lot of promise to do some special things." And given the history of the relationship between parents and staff, she would have to build sturdy bridges to develop more parental involvement.

A central part of the principal's efforts to create change at Rainbow focused on shifting the dynamics of the relationships among members of the school community. To forge closer linkages across these constituent communities, she developed structures that would help them learn more about each other.

The principal instituted regular, frequent gatherings of the entire student body. Every morning, teachers, students, and the principal would gather in a giant circle, many holding hands, outside on the playground or, on poor weather days, in the auditorium. These brief gatherings provided a time for announcements, a short song, the pledge of allegiance in English or Spanish, or a pledge to the earth. Commenting on these opportunities for coming together, a student advisor noted,

> You know, it's like, you have all these kids here, and you can actually see that they all fit in one section of the yard. It's not scattered around. Kids won't get lost. You can look around and see kids from other grade levels and other classes, and you know, I think it's just the familiarity of the whole school that keeps a harmonious type of atmosphere.

Each member of the community participated in this connecting activity that opened the school day, sometimes merely by their presence, at other times, by singing or reciting. These informal assemblies reinforced the broader message that coming together as a community was a valued activity at Rainbow and that each adult and child was a valued member of that community.

Students also came together in another new way through a special structure called *families*. During family time, once a week, heterogeneous groupings of students came together under the guidance of an adult leader, either a classroom teacher or another adult at the site. Students across grade levels, from kindergarten to fifth grade, made up each family, and they remained in the same family for their entire time at Rainbow. The curriculum for families was fluid, varying not only over time but across groupings, depending, to some extent, on the adult leader.

In considering why families were so effective in creating closer connections within the school, one staff member suggested the key was familiarity:

You know, I think a lot of conflicts come because maybe this child doesn't know that child or, you know, some kids have a tendency to play with only kids in their classroom, and sometimes that's not the case here. We have kids of other classes interacting.

Families became a way for older and younger students to interact in a known environment; younger students looked up to older ones, and older students developed a new respect for younger ones.

Families also provided a way for adults throughout the building to develop relationships with children they might not have gotten to know. Teachers in self-contained classrooms often feel isolated from the rest of the school community, not only from other teachers, but also from children at different grade levels and from classrooms in other parts of the building. Through families, kindergarten teachers got to know fifth graders and fifth-grade teachers got to know the little ones.

One outcome from this increased awareness of one another was teachers' heightened sense of communal responsibility for maintaining behavior standards with all students they encountered, not only those in their class. Students in the hallways and on the playground knew they would be held to the same expectations by other teachers as well as their own. Structures like families breed these connections that undergird the creation of a real community.

When Snow began at Rainbow, parent involvement was practically nonexistent. As at many schools serving poor and diverse communities, few parents attended evening events like Back to School Night or Parents Club meetings. Rather than attribute this low involvement to parental lack of interest, the blame game played by so many school staff members, Snow and her staff realized that other factors stood in the way of parents turning up for events. Many lacked transportation or worked daunting schedules that conflicted with evening meetings; still others had childcare responsibilities. These issues were compounded by distance, since many parents lived several miles from the school.

One way to get parents to school was to pick them up and bring them there. And that's exactly what Snow and some of her staff would do. While a few carloads didn't make a large dent in the transportation needs of the school, it was both a symbolic and practical effort. It showed parents that the school was committed to involving them to a greater degree in school events, and some parents actually got to school. It also revealed the school's understanding of the real issues parents faced—a lack of economic resources.

While this daunting economic reality continued to shadow many of Rainbow's efforts, progress was made in enticing more and more parents to school. Teachers designed a variety of school events centered around children or their work. In addition to traditional events such as Back to School Night and Parents Club meetings, Rainbow held monthly meetings for parents and their children tied to specific curriculum areas. For example, one month there was a family science night; another time there was a family math night; other examples included a literature fair and an art show, each featuring student work.

Given the difficulties parents faced getting to school, teachers were encouraged to go to parents. Although not all teachers adopted this strategy, those teachers who did gained the opportunity to see families in their own settings and to connect with them in more personal ways than possible in the classroom during parent-teacher conferences or at back-to-school nights.

The principal felt that parents should play a crucial role in the leadership of the school. The existing structure for this leadership was the site council, a governing body designed to include a range of stakeholders at the site—the principal, teachers, other staff, and parents. One of the site council's primary functions was to make decisions about the school budget. Another key task might include overseeing the development and implementation of the school site plan. At the beginning of her tenure at Rainbow, the principal realized that she had to not only recruit parents for this council but also develop their expertise in a variety of tasks, from understanding the range of educational acronyms connected with schooling to learning how to create a budget. This distinction between recruitment and professional development is critical, for it illuminated the level of commitment at Rainbow to respecting and nurturing the expertise of the parents in the community.

ACTIVITY 15: EXTENDED REFLECTION

1. As you read about how Principal Snow addressed the many issues facing Rainbow, did her responses spark any ideas for changes you would like to make to your action plan?

2. Rainbow is a small school, and so several of the strategies for connecting the members of the community may be dependent on this. How do you think these strategies would work at a larger school? Would they be appropriate at a secondary school? Why or why not?

3. Snow was an experienced leader with the backing of the school district to make change. What other contextual features do you think may have helped her resolve conflict at this site? What contextual features worked against her?

Author's Reflections

Many of the strategies developed and implemented at Rainbow illustrate the adage, "It takes a village to raise a child." This case centers on the notion of building a web of relationships as a means to nurture children's development as responsible members of a community, and it does so in several ways.

First, at a school with a mostly bussed-in population of students, the principal invested time and energy in creating connections with the surrounding neighborhood of the school. Local merchants were enlisted in fundraising campaigns; school facilities were made available for local community meetings and events; children paraded up and down area sidewalks as part of seasonal activities; and their artwork appeared in merchants' windows. These efforts forged a positive identity for Rainbow within the community, which helped to open up avenues for fundraising and business partnerships within the neighborhood.

Second, the principal worked hard at strengthening parental connections, extending the school into the sending communities by encouraging home visits and scheduling evening meetings at community facilities in children's neighborhoods. She also encouraged and welcomed families to visit the school by instituting a variety of activities centered on their children. Families were viewed as assets who could contribute to the school's efforts instead of social liabilities to be overcome or, at best, ignored.

Lastly, the principal created structures that nurtured the development of relationships within the school. Through heterogeneous "families" and frequent assemblies, for example, the children and adult members of the Rainbow community had a variety of opportunities to get to know each other beyond individual classroom boundaries. Through these relationships, each member of the community was expected to shoulder the responsibility for maintaining expected norms of behavior.

10

The Power of the School Secretary

Edmundo Norte

GREENLAWN ELEMENTARY SCHOOL

This case concerns underlying tension that surfaced in the form of a school secretary's unwelcoming behavior toward minority parents. The school already had a reputation as a racist school among some of the parents, and the principal realized that the secretary's behavior was part of the problem. In resolving the issue, he drew on his understanding of power relations and did some individualized staff development with her, with positive results.

The Setting

Greenlawn Elementary and its surrounding community had changed in recent years, from being largely middle class and white to having more low-income children and more ethnic diversity. The student population now numbered 480, of whom 38% were white, 25% were Asian, 14% were African American, 11% were Latino, and 8% were Filipino. The Asian and African American populations in particular had seen large increases recently. There was still some resentment of these changes in the community, manifested most recently in the broadcasting of racist comments by police over the police radio.

Underlying Tensions in the Front Office

David Murakawa had been the principal of Greenlawn for only a few months when he realized with dismay that the school secretary, a European American woman, treated people differently depending on her perception of their ethnic background. She tended to interact warmly with European American parents, but was less friendly with members of minority groups, especially those who spoke little English. She would often act as if they weren't there until they tried to say something to her. Once they finally caught her attention, she would often be brusque, leaving an impression that they were a nuisance. Murakawa was especially concerned because she was the first person parents and visitors to the school encountered, and in that role she was largely responsible for people's first impressions of the school.

Murakawa, a Japanese American who was raised in the community, had been hired by the district to play a key role in a new diversity initiative that the superintendent was undertaking. He knew that the school mirrored some of the simmering resentment against immigrants and African Americans that existed in the surrounding community, and he was concerned about the secretary's behavior because her unequal treatment of parents and visitors had given her a reputation as a racist.

ACTIVITY 16: POSSIBLE RESPONSES

Individual Reflection

Picture yourself in Murakawa's role. Below are some possible ways for a principal to address a situation like this. What do you think the consequences of these responses might be? What assumptions do they make about the human capacity for behavioral and attitudinal change?

1. Speak to the secretary and simply tell her that you have observed her treating people differently and that it seems to be based on her perception of their race or ethnicity. You want her to treat every parent coming into the office the same way.

2. Ignore the problem for the time being and look for a way to move the secretary to a different position where she will have less contact with the community. Then you can bring in a secretary who is more sensitive to the diversity of the community.

3. Use this as an opportunity to do some individualized staff development with the secretary. What kind of staff development might be useful in a case like this?

Group Discussion

4. Share your reflections with members of your group. Are there other possibilities besides the ones listed?

Murakawa's Response

Murakawa believed firmly that people *can* change their behavior if they see a positive reason to do so. He decided to do some informal staff development to see if he could influence the secretary to see things another way. He waited until a convenient time when both he and the secretary would not be interrupted, and then he met with her and explained a model of interaction that addressed what he saw as the essential problem in her relationships with the parents—the issue of power dynamics (see Chapter 7).

He explained that in his own role as a leader, he has to do a lot of listening and responding because he doesn't always know the impact of his decisions and actions until he hears about it from the people who are affected. Similarly, he explained, the school secretary's role is a dominant one in relation to the community members who enter the school. In the eyes of visitors and parents, the secretary is the gatekeeper who holds the key to unlock the services and information the school can provide. She can turn them away without giving them the assistance they seek, or she can respond in a welcoming way and actively point them in the right direction to get what they came for. In the case of immigrant, non-English speaking parents, it is particularly important for the school secretary to make sure that someone who speaks their language is located to talk with them. Her responsibility in the dominant power position is to listen actively and respond to those in the subordinate position.

Several weeks after this meeting, Murakawa reported that the secretary's manner of interacting with diverse parents, as well as how parents perceived her, had improved markedly. She displayed more welcoming behavior when parents walked in, greeting them warmly and asking how she could help them. If they did not understand English well enough, she would politely gesture to them to sit down and wait while she tried to find someone who would translate.

ACTIVITY 17: EXTENDED REFLECTION

Individual Reflection

1.   Do you think that Principal Murakawa's ethnicity played any role in the way he responded to this issue? Why or why not?

2.   Having read the actual response, is there anything you would do differently?

3.   Turn to Box 7.1 (Dynamics of Power Relations). Can you think of a situation you've experienced where this model might have been helpful? How would you use it?

Group Discussion

4.   Share your reflections with others in your group.

Group Project

5.   Together, develop a plan for sharing the dynamics of a power model with your staff during a staff development day. How would you introduce it?

6.   What activities would you design so that people would gain some hands-on experience with the model?

7.   How would you hope they would use it in the future?

Author's Reflections

While this was only one of many efforts this principal made to improve the school's relations with parents and the community, it illustrates several important points. First, many people make the assumption that racial and ethnic conflicts are primarily a problem among students. But as this case indicates, adults, as much as or perhaps more than students, also need to improve in cross-cultural communication skills and ways to combat racism. Second, Murakawa realized that a direct confrontation about the secretary's racial attitudes would probably only make her defensive. He would probably be forced to provide examples to back up his point, and this might only make things worse. If she did become defensive, the discussion could devolve into an argument over what she did or did not say. It is unlikely that this approach would help him accomplish his goal of making the front office a more welcoming place. He knew that if he was to have any hope of influencing her behavior, he had to approach her in a positive way. By recognizing her power in the front office and sharing the model with her, he created a context that enabled her to listen to his suggestions and use them.

Murakawa also knew that if things didn't improve, he might have to resort to moving the secretary to another position. But his willingness to try to work with her indicated his faith in the possibility of individual change. Fortunately for all concerned, his faith was justified.

It is unclear whether Murakawa's ethnicity as a Japanese American man played any role in this particular issue and its resolution. In other aspects of his work within the school, however, it did. He was a leader who was not particularly flashy and who tended to let others talk until he really had something to say. This may have been part of a cultural style of communication common in Japan, in which it is considered impolite to draw attention to oneself. This is not to say that all people of Japanese ancestry will shun drawing attention to themselves—it depends on how one was raised, and is certainly not a given at birth. Murakawa was also a leader who was particularly well attuned to the more subtle tensions in his school. He noticed, for example, that while there was little overt conflict among students, there were patterns of exclusion and lack of participation based on race or ethnicity. He told us that oftentimes the Asian students, rather than confronting a tense situation directly, would simply withdraw from participation. Other faculty members didn't perceive this as problematic, but Murakawa recognized—perhaps based on his own experiences growing up in the community—that withdrawal was a common response to conflict among Asian students.

11

Challenging Attitudes

Edmundo Norte

GLADIOLA MIDDLE SCHOOL

This case involves the challenge of a new administrative team addressing old and rather negative and dysfunctional attitudes among both students and staff. Gladiola, a suburban middle school, was characterized as a school fraught with student discipline problems and staff alienation and disaffection. The case illustrates how different, identifiable elements at a school come together to shape the school's climate—for better or worse. It provides an opportunity to examine how the new principal and administrative team approached the challenge of reshaping the school's climate and culture.

The Challenging Attitudes

Even with 1,400 students, there were many reasons that life at Gladiola Middle School should have been idyllic: It was a well-funded school in an ethnically diverse, predominantly upper-middle-class suburb; the majority of the staff were veteran or experienced teachers, and there were four administrators (three full-time and one half-time) to run the school; the school facility was well maintained, clean, bright and attractive. In fact, the physical setting of the school was park like, and the grassy knolls and fields of the grounds merged with an adjacent park without demarcation. Designed to foster a sense of community, the main school building was built around a central hub consisting of an open forum space next to the administrative offices, around which extended

143

building wings (or pods), each of which housed six classrooms around a common meeting space. The structural design of this main building lent itself to community building by facilitating the frequency and accessibility of contact among both students and teachers.

Yet the climate at Gladiola was neither idyllic nor cohesive. In fact, the single most glaring consequence of its systemic ills was the school's tremendous problem with discipline and behavior. Gladiola had an extraordinarily high rate of suspensions and expulsions, higher in fact than the local high school that was nearly three times larger. The bulk of these student disciplinary actions were for fighting, although students leaving campus and cutting class, along with drugs being brought on campus, were also reasons for action. There were tensions and fights between different ethnic groups, some gang related, and also between immigrants and second-plus generation student groups. Some staff members believed that many of these problems were due to outsiders coming in and causing problems.

However, outsiders had little to do with the related problem of staff alienation and disaffection. Many faculty members did not feel connected with the school beyond the four walls of their classrooms. This was partly because teachers felt their efforts to address student behavior were undermined by the previous administration's inconsistent application and follow-through on the school's disciplinary policy. A majority of the staff felt that, in addition to the student behavior issue, inconsistent application of policies and procedures also affected them directly; that is, they felt that only a small group of staff members had an in with the principal, and they seemed to be the ones who had the most influence in acquiring resources, privileges, and recognition. This had left many of these staff members frustrated and cynical toward the administration and their own involvement in the school. As one teacher explained,

> A lot of us just checked out. We used to be a lot more involved and energetic, but after years of being unappreciated, if they weren't going to recognize the discipline efforts we were making and weren't going to follow through when we referred them, then why bother? That only undermined our credibility with the students. So they shouldn't complain later about student behavior if they're not holding up their end. I mean, why should I worry about how so-and-so is behaving again if I know that no matter what I do, the administrators are only going to give them a slap on the wrist and send them back to me—and then we're the ones who have to deal with them. It's not fair for them to expect us to do our part when they're not doing theirs.

Another factor that made matters worse was that faculty and staff did not reflect the student population. Gladiola, like many other schools, had a faculty that was predominantly European American even though the student population was very diverse. Although the district personnel office had reportedly been making efforts to recruit teachers from diverse backgrounds, this continued to be a challenge. Cultural and socioeconomic class differences between the students and school staff may have also contributed significantly to the disproportionate number of students of color who were suspended or expelled.

Another contributing factor to student behavior problems was the fact that there were relatively few venues for positive, meaningful involvement for students at the school. In fact, throughout the city, there were relatively few recreational facilities for youth, particularly for students from lower-socioeconomic backgrounds. There were no movie theaters, and the library was open for only a limited amount of hours per week; while the city did have a number of parks, they offered few structured activities to which youth were drawn. Similarly, under the old administration at Gladiola, there was comparatively little support for extracurricular activities for students, particularly activities that affirmed and highlighted the cultural dimension of students' lives. Previously, the issues, activities, and concerns that were the most salient to students' lives were beyond the scope of the broader school curriculum. Where students were involved at school, it was largely relegated to student government and a few clubs that were primarily composed of upper-socioeconomic and European American students. The activities director at the school, a veteran of over 20 years, was pleasant and well meaning but no longer as energetic and responsive to students as she had once been.

A parallel situation existed with parental involvement at the school. As mentioned earlier, parents and teachers perceived that a few select parents received preferential treatment under the previous administration. Perhaps, due in part to this perception, there was very little involvement by parents generally, and ethnically and linguistically diverse parents were particularly absent from school involvement. The only formal venues for parent involvement were the Parent Teacher Club (PTC) and the School Site Council (SSC). The SSC had only a few token parents, who were chummy with the principal and were basically his rubber stamp, and the PTC was small and predominantly composed of more-affluent, European American, stay-at-home mothers whose functions were primarily fundraising for the band—which was disproportionately European American—and organizing faculty appreciation teas and breakfasts. Participation by parents of color was limited to those rare times when their children were involved in student performances or, more often, when they had to come to school regarding disciplinary issues.

ACTIVITY 18: POSSIBLE RESPONSES

Below are several ways a leader might respond to the situation at Gladiola:

- Simply ignore the situation, hoping it will go away.
- Request additional resources from the district office for security personnel.
- Institute a zero-tolerance policy for violations of behavioral standards.
- Meet with the PTC and the SSC to solicit ideas for increasing parental involvement and building a stronger sense of community.
- At a staff meeting, raise the issue of the need for more opportunities for positive student involvement.
- Meet with students and faculty in focus groups to seek their input on the greatest needs at the school and to hear any suggestions they have.

Individual Reflection

1. Imagine that you are have been assigned as the new principal at Gladiola Middle School. As the new principal, you have been given the opportunity to select two of the three assistant principals (APs) who will be joining your administrative team. What qualities and attributes should you consider in making your selections? To what extent, if any, will your own ethnicity shape your decisions?

2. Next, consider the list of possible responses above and critically reflect on the pros and cons of each one.

3. In addition to the options listed above, what other possibilities can you envision? What about these other possibilities is important?

4. Decide which response, or combination of responses, you would use, and develop a plan for addressing the issues of student discipline, the climate of alienation and disaffection, and the lack of meaningful involvement by parents of color.

Group Discussion

5. Now work together in small groups to discuss your plans and the advantages and disadvantages of each. What are the underlying assumptions about students, parents, and staff in each of the plans you are discussing? Try to come to a consensus in how to approach the problems at Gladiola or, if necessary, simply agree to disagree, before you read ahead to what was actually done at the school.

Actual Responses: Challenging the Attitudes of Students and Staff

In several ways, it made a significant difference that, in addition to being experienced, effective leaders, the new administrative team at Gladiola was also diverse: The principal was Latina, and the three APs were Filipina, African American, and European American. The new administrative team at Gladiola was able to infuse multicultural perspectives and information, and raise awareness in both formal and informal ways among the predominantly European American staff. The administration's diversity also helped considerably in facilitating communication with the previously alienated students and parents from diverse backgrounds.

However, although Alicia Ramírez, the principal, knew that the administration's diversity was a strength they brought to the school, she also knew that this alone would not turn the school around. From her experience in the district, along with discussions she had with the superintendent who assigned her to the school, Ramírez already had a general sense of the problems at Gladiola. She knew she would have to gain the trust and buy-in of her staff as a first step in making long-term changes in the school culture. Given the history of rather arbitrary and inconsistent decision making by the previous principal, Ramírez understood that it was all the more important that the newly constituted administration act consistently and as a team. Good communication within the administrative team was essential and, to this end, she established a weekly, 7 a.m., Monday meeting to review the previous week and to go over all the issues and tasks that needed to be addressed in the week ahead. A central principle was that they act fairly and consistently with students and staff and that they support each other's decisions. Thus coming to consensus on policy and practices for the coming weeks was a key purpose for these meetings. However, this structural opportunity for communication went beyond simply addressing tasks; early on, it helped them know each other, develop a common vision, and establish their working relationship as a team.

Because of the student behavior problems underlying the high suspension and expulsion rate, Ramírez felt that getting a handle on student discipline was the top priority because it affected all aspects of the school enterprise, including academic achievement, teacher morale, and student interethnic relations. Thus a major undertaking for Ramírez during her first semester at the school was to very tangibly make the school more secure, which included putting up a fence around the school grounds to have better control of who came in and who left. In the judgment of many staff members, the ability of students to easily get in and out of the school was a major factor in both truancy and fights. While the fence construction met with some resistance by the community and staff, who objected that it ruined the aesthetics of the school grounds, she managed to get the buy-in of both the staff and community by framing it as part of a concerted effort to create a safe and secure school environment.

As this was being done, the administration spearheaded a campaign of developing schoolwide consistency in communicating and following through on behavioral standards and consequences. The four administrators invested a good deal of time and energy discussing with both teachers and students the expectations that teachers should have for students and that students should have for themselves. The principal let the staff know that she was expecting them to follow through consistently on the behavioral standards that were being communicated to the students, and that the administrative staff would also follow through.

Initially, particularly with the seventh- and eighth-grade students who had spent more time under the previous administration's comparatively lax and inconsistently applied set of standards, the discipline referrals increased, but suspensions and expulsions dramatically decreased. In the previous year, there had been 342 suspensions. Under the new administration and with the implementation of a more consistent discipline policy, suspensions dropped by 13% the first year and by 24% the following year.

From the students' perspective, the response to the new behavior standards was generally positive. While there were still some inconsistencies in enforcement, students perceived the new policy to be stricter but fairer. As one Afghani student put it,

> They're more strict. Most people don't tend to be tardy on purpose. Now the teachers are standing at the door, and if you're tardy, they mark it. It depends on the teacher. Some are fair, but sometimes they can be stubborn when you know you didn't do it, but they say you did. Then it goes up to the AP. They accuse you even though they're not sure, but most of the time, they're fair. They're reasonable about what the consequence should be.

The stricter discipline policy was balanced by a new ethos of listening to and respecting students' needs and experiences. The principal discussed and negotiated with students on a variety of topics of student interest, such as dances, field trips, and performances. Her tone was one of respect and problem solving. She treated students as members of the school community who had equal value and deserved equal consideration within the limits and responsibilities of their different roles. With students as with staff, she operated with the same high standards and consistently demonstrated caring and open communication. While each administrator had different strengths, Ramírez had developed a strong set of shared values that she encouraged among all administrative team members. The following statement reflected a common sentiment held among the students about the APs:

> I like [AP#1] the best cause she likes and understands me the best. I like [AP#2] because she was my teacher last year and she's really nice. To me, they're all OK. When I was in the seventh grade, I didn't care. [AP#1] was the first AP I liked. She understands, and if you admit you messed up, she sort of understands. They are all the same on the rules, but you could tell her, "I didn't do this," or "I didn't mean to do this." I don't know if it would change the consequences, but she would understand.

This combination of being caring and showing understanding, while still holding to standards and following through on consequences, garnered respect rather than contempt from both students and staff.

While disciplinary referrals reportedly increased the first semester of the new administration's tenure, this did not continue. There was an adjustment period during which students tested and learned that the standards were real and would be enforced and supported by the administration. Over the course of the academic year, however, they increasingly learned to adhere to the new standards, and the number of referrals dropped. By mid fall of the subsequent year, Ms. Ramírez reported to the faculty the following decreases in disciplinary referrals compared to the previous year: fifth grade, 18%; sixth grade, 34%; seventh grade, 61%; eighth grade, 59%. The very fact that the new principal began keeping referral data demonstrated a structural support to making discipline issues a priority. It is important to note that these data included the gender and ethnicity of the students, and could, therefore, be disaggregated and looked at according to these categories. While initially she did not make the disproportionate number of students of color who were being referred a major focus of discussion, but merely reported it, it was important to her to be able to monitor and measure progress in this area. This collecting and comparing of referral data was an example of Ramírez walking the talk, responding, or acting proactively to make real her espoused values and vision. It demonstrated to the faculty that she did in fact care about the discipline issue, which was a major concern of theirs, and by disaggregating the data by gender and ethnicity, she raised the issue of bias and equity in a way that did not appear heavy handed or unnatural.

Once the faculty began to see that the new principal and administrative team were in fact supporting them by making a difference in student behavior, they slowly began to be more receptive to requests for their assistance. Both at faculty meetings and individually with particular teachers, Ramírez let the faculty know that to fundamentally change the school climate rather than just control student behavior, the school would have to offer more activities and opportunities for positive student involvement. This meant that teachers would have to be willing to invest more time and energy in these areas. Staff members responded in a number of ways. Some were willing to become involved, while others, mostly veteran teachers, were unwilling to commit to anything until the administration had more fully proved themselves. Over time, however, a momentum developed toward creating a more-positive, engaged, student-centered climate.

The activities involved in creating this climate included asking teachers to volunteer as sponsors for more student clubs, particularly those that were ethnically based; to bring in diverse authors and speakers to make presentations to students and staff; providing noontime music and dances as rewards for good clean-campus or testing weeks; and to produce schoolwide assemblies that featured the histories, contributions, and current challenges of all the major ethnic groups represented on campus, including European Americans. These multicultural assemblies were initially developed primarily by Ramírez and required a substantial investment of time and energy. While a few teachers were irritated that the administration invested so much time and energy in producing them, over time these assemblies came to be seen as the highlight of the school year, and students, staff members, and parents looked forward to them.

It is important to note that the administrators made a point of communicating to faculty and student leaders that they should strongly encourage participants from all ethnic groups to join in the club activities and assemblies of each of the different ethnic groups—that there should be lots of "cross-fertilization." This effort, particularly with regard to planning, practicing, and performing in the multicultural assemblies, was highly successful in building crosscultural bonds among students, as they necessarily had to spend time working together in a project of common interest and came to develop close relationships with each other. These new opportunities for positive student involvement were the carrot that complemented the stick of more consistent discipline.

In terms of faculty cohesion, having more faculty involvement provided an opportunity for greater collaboration in both formal and informal ways. While the school had had a wonderful structural opportunity for collaboration in the form of a weekly, 90-minute collaboration time, this opportunity had not always been used appropriately or effectively. Ramírez and her team now made sure that this time was being used productively by groups of teachers who were working on substantive tasks in which they had an interest or stake, including different aspects of a shared decision-making model they were moving toward as a school. Other structural changes that helped build greater cohesion included Ramírez's decision to move all the sixth-grade teachers into the same wing so that they could have greater opportunities to collaborate. While this was initially difficult for a couple of the more veteran teachers who did not want to change rooms, this structural change, in combination with the opportunity to spend a number of days together off campus in staff development training, helped create a more cohesive team among the sixth-grade teachers.

Another change, this time in staff assignments, was to team a new, energetic teacher with the veteran activities director and give them coresponsibility for working with the student government and for schoolwide activities development. This combination of new energy and veteran wisdom and experience created a new synergy that was quite successful in spawning a number of engaging events and opportunities for students. Another less-formal, yet significant intervention toward building greater staff cohesion was that the principal made a point of bringing in goodies to celebrate staff birthdays and other notable personal events, as well as sponsoring, encouraging, and attending TGIF, after-work get-togethers. This demonstrated to her staff that the administrative team had an interest in them beyond their work and helped build relationships and team spirit. All of these efforts helped, slowly but steadily, to create a more cooperative, collaborative climate at the school, which made it a more attractive and appealing place to be.

For parents, particularly those who were culturally and linguistically diverse, having someone they could call upon at the school, and with whom they could comfortably communicate, made a significant difference in developing greater contact and interaction. Ramírez and the Filipina AP, who also spoke Tagalog, established a multilingual parent committee to discuss the issues of linguistically diverse students and families. This monthly meeting created a common meeting place at the school for the different-language communities and gave them an opportunity to network with each other, as well as learn about their issues and characteristics as distinct cultures. Translators, often teachers' aides, were available for the major linguistic groups, and childcare was provided. Snacks were provided and occasionally potluck dinners were coordinated. This became the most institutionalized way of accessing and communicating with these members of the community.

Parents were also regularly involved at the school through attending the regular multicultural assemblies that were performed not only for the student body but also for the community in the evening. These assemblies were the culmination to weeklong activities and events on the featured culture (door decorations, lunchtime music and food, guest speakers, thematic writing assignments in many classes, etc.) and built momentum and interest in the student performances and community-sponsored booths that were part of the year-end multicultural fair that became a tradition at Gladiola.

ACTIVITY 19: EXTENDED REFLECTION

1. Now that you know the principal's actual response to this situation, are there changes you would make to your action plan?

2. Review Figure 4.1 (Progression of School Needs). How does the model help you think about the way Principal Ramírez approached addressing the multiple challenges at Gladiola?

3. In what aspects of this case can you see the operation of the necessary-but-not-sufficient principle (see Chapter 4). What things do you consider to have been necessary to building a more-collaborative, more-equitable environment? In what ways do you think they would not have been sufficient by themselves?

4. If you are or were European American and monolingual, how would this affect your decisions, priorities, and approaches to dealing with the challenges at Gladiola? How would you ensure that diverse voices and perspectives were heard and included in all aspects of the school?

Author's Reflections

Several elements are worth noting in the Gladiola case. First, the approaches used at this school addressed the continuum of school priorities, as described in Figure 4.1. The problems of safety and security of the students, of which the discipline problems were one symptom, were initially addressed through Ramírez's focus on providing clear, fair, and high standards of behavior for all students. The challenge of developing a stronger sense of community and belonging was addressed by building on these efforts and creating structural opportunities for students to develop relationships with students from different cultural backgrounds as they participated in clubs and programs that involved positive, collective projects. At the same time, by encouraging and enabling staff members to create such opportunities for students, Ramírez paved the way for staff members themselves to develop a greater sense of community, belonging, and investment in the school. Ramírez and her leadership team fostered this by providing the staff with structural opportunities to come together to both work on school-improvement projects and site-based management as well as by hosting events aimed simply at developing social relationships.

However, these community-building efforts for the staff were effective only after administrators won the staff's trust by supporting their needs in substantive ways. This support included following through on disciplinary policies with students and establishing procedures that dealt with all staff members in ways that were fair and were consistent with the stated vision of the school leadership and the mission statement of the school.

While the Progression of School Needs (Figure 4.1) provides a general framework for assessing context, needs, and priorities, in reality, the needs and issues at Gladiola were much more complex, interwoven, and dynamic. For example, while initially, it could be said that the needs of students generally revolved around issues of safety and security, for the teaching staff—a different subset of the overall school community—the need for developing a sense of community and belonging was the dominant issue. Different constituencies within the school community have different collective needs. No school is monolithic in its needs. Even so, here the response of the administrative leaders was one which simultaneously addressed the needs of both of these constituencies in a largely integrated way. By providing a clear vision that the behavior problems of students would be remedied by the consistent application of high expectations (behavioral as well as academic) and high support (both in terms of discipline follow-through for the teachers and increased opportunities for positive engagement and involvement for students), the administrative leadership initiated the process of addressing the safety and security needs of students through a process which involved creating greater community and belonging among the teaching staff members.

Two other important principles were also in play here. One is that the administrative leadership used their inherent power and authority in developmentally responsible ways: that is, in their positions of power relative to the staff and students, they were attentive to the voices and expressed needs of these groups and used their power and authority to respond to these needs. For example, the school leadership—administrators and faculty—drew on their knowledge of the developmental needs of middle-school-age children (their need for social interaction and identity development) and exercised their power and authority in developmentally responsible ways by creating a variety of opportunities for students to address these needs in prosocial ways. The administrative team also used their power and authority to create policies, structures, and procedures that addressed the needs of the teaching staff for substantive support. By recognizing and addressing the needs of faculty, the administrative leadership demonstrated that they respected and appreciated the work and challenges of faculty members and. thereby. fostered a relationship between administrators and faculty where the faculty members were more willing to participate in developing community in a context where they could maintain their sense of self-respect.

Another principle evident in this case is that of the administrators, particularly the principal, walking the talk. The principal consistently applied the vision she espoused of open communication, collaboration, fairness, and consistency in her practice with all members of the school community, from her own administrative team, to the faculty, to the students, and with parents. This consistency of practice in pursuit of the highest standards of the vision and mission of the school brought coherence to the multiple projects undertaken to improve the culture of the school. This practice, systemically consistent with the clearly articulated, coconstructed vision for the school, was the glue that brought the community together and gave meaning and direction to the organizational structures and resources that were necessary, but not sufficient, to achieve the school's goals. Conversely, it was essential that the administrators provide the structures and resources that were necessary to move from vision to reality.

This case provides a striking example of how a clear vision for the school, sustained by structural supports (time, space, and resources) and consistent follow through, was successful at addressing the developmental needs of various constituencies within the school community in a systemic, integrated, and coherent way that resulted in greater health and cohesion for the entire school community.

12

What's Data Got to Do With It?

Susan Sather

FILLMORE MIDDLE SCHOOL

An in-depth look at student outcome data served as a wake-up call to school staff to take a hard look at the unrecognized disparities that existed among students. This case profiles a school already doing great work with students, both in terms of human relations and academics. Yet an examination of disaggregated data revealed variance by ethnicity and social class in student achievement and disciplinary actions as well as participation in sports and other extracurricular activities. This occurred despite the fact that this school had an ongoing dialogue about race and ethnicity and an ongoing and significant diversity focus led by the history department. In the hands of competent and caring administrators and teachers like those at Fillmore Middle School, disaggregated data can be used to track equity efforts and further refine an outstanding mission.

The Wake-Up Call

In 1998, Fillmore received a planning grant to develop a Healthy Start Collaborative. Significant personnel, time, and money were allotted to the process, which involved teachers, support staff, parents, students, and community members. They collected several types of data and examined them carefully to help them develop a program to address the real needs of their students. Prior to this process, teachers had already recognized that they were challenged by the economic disparity of the student body. Fillmore drew almost half its students from the flatlands of the city and the other half from the more affluent hills. Nevertheless, teachers felt that the socioeconomic and ethnic diversity of the city's population brought richness to the school along with some serious challenges. But until they wrestled with the actual data, they did not quite realize the enormity of these challenges.

The Healthy Start coordinator and planning committee collected and examined multiple types of data. When teachers had their first chance to look at these data, they were alarmed. They already knew the suspension and detention rate was much higher for African American and Latino boys, mostly the same 40 students. However, when achievement scores were disaggregated by ethnicity, they revealed that, despite the commitment of staff to teach all students, significant numbers of Latino and African American children were falling farther and farther behind academically. In fact, the longer these students attended Fillmore, the greater the spread became between high and low grade point averages. It seemed that instead of narrowing the achievement gap, the school was somehow making it grow.

The recognition of this widening achievement gap forced the staff members to question themselves. Despite their long record of heterogeneous grouping, were they still (unintentionally) practicing de facto tracking by race or ethnicity? They began to look into the numbers of students of color who were scheduled into computer or art classes rather than foreign language and algebra, which are required for college entrance. One teacher described this as a class problem:

> You have kids that took algebra here, and they are taking community college and university classes when they're juniors and seniors. These difficulties have to do with diversity. These things become, for sure, class segregated and often racially segregated, too. So it affects the diversity of the school. These kids in my classes know the story. They know who is in those foreign language classes and who's not. They look around the room and the kids say, "Oh my god." This is not a good thing—the kids who take algebra and those who don't—it affects the whole school.

Echoing the frustration of others, another teacher asked,

> Why is this happening? How should we intervene? Algebra is a huge dilemma, a huge gatekeeper for college admission, and we don't have a clear-cut commitment to making that work for every kid. So what are we going to do? Are we going to make it available to all kids? What about the kids who don't know enough to know they should make a choice.

In addition to encouraging teachers to discuss their responses to the data, the Healthy Start committee also listened to the voices of students and parents by holding a series of focus groups. Teachers who regularly worked overtime to reach students and personalize education were stunned to hear that many students did not perceive the school or their teachers as caring, committed individuals.

The committee also reproduced a zip code study done by a university professor at the district high school. The data showed that students in lower-socioeconomic-status (SES) neighborhoods not only had lower achievement scores but they also participated in sports less than their more affluent peers. In both the high school and Fillmore, it was apparent that, for the most part, poor students lived in certain zip code areas separate from other students. When this information was combined with achievement and enrollment in the school's rich extracurricular sports program, which required a C average for participation, teachers learned that,

> It's the same kids doing the same sports over and over. If after-school sports are restricted to certain zip codes [based on achievement, and achievement correlates with zip codes], then we are spending our sports budget on people who have money.

One teacher's response was, "That's something that we, as a staff, need to address. We should be sure that everybody is participating in a sport rather than the same kids being subsidized to do each sport."

ACTIVITY 20: ISSUES TO GRAPPLE WITH—SAFE ENVIRONMENT AND DETENTION

Creating a Safe Environment for Discussion of Race and the Achievement Gap

1. Think of the staff at your school or a school you are familiar with. Do you think it would be difficult for the staff to view and discuss disaggregated student outcomes? Why or why not?

2. As a leader, what could you do to create a safe environment for the examination and discussion of race and the achievement gap?

3. What kinds of professional development do you think might help staff discuss student outcome data constructively?

Detention

4. One Fillmore teacher said, "It certainly looks racist, because it is the same kids, and mostly black kids, who get detention the most." Think of your school or a school you are familiar with. Is there a certain racial or ethnic group that is overrepresented in detention? If so, why do you think this is occurring? Do you agree with this teacher that it looks racist?

5. At Fillmore, detention itself was the subject of much debate. Some teachers felt that it did not solve the problem; it kept students out of classes at times and thereby withheld core instruction, which, given the preponderance of black students in detention, was indeed racist. They argued that the school should eliminate detention all together. Other teachers argued vociferously that detention was necessary. Without it, the school would end up in chaos.

In your small group, discuss both sides of the detention issue. Come up with several workable alternatives to detention. You do not have to come to consensus on this issue.

Leveling the Playing Field at Fillmore

In the aftermath of the 1992 Rodney King decision (Mydans, 1992), when there were strong feelings, marches, and, in some cases, rioting, Fillmore Middle School pulled together. Veteran teacher Arlene Sanders described this event, a defining moment for the school:

When we really knew we were on the right track—I'll never forget this moment, you know one of those defining moments—the day after the Rodney King decision, and all hell broke loose. The kids were universally upset, so we knew that we couldn't just do business as usual. Overnight we put together a plan for dividing the students into four parts. One fourth of them went to a series of rooms, monitored by teachers, to write letters of protest, to vent their objections to what seemed to them, at the time, so unfair and so outrageous. And one fourth went to the gym, where we laid out butcher paper in a snake pattern, maybe 400 feet of snaked butcher paper, where they drew and wrote whatever came into their heads, whatever message they wanted. We sent that to our congressman, and he put it up in Washington, took pictures of it, and talked about it in his publication. One quarter went to the cafeteria where they had a discussion session about it. There was a fourth component, and I can't think what that was. We took all the letters, and Ying Kelly, who volunteers for the congressman, flew them to Washington and delivered them to him. And the defining moment was, here were these kids and this wonderful black woman named Amy Smith. She took me under her wing 30 years ago, and we've been through a lot together. We were sitting in the room (she begins to cry) and these kids of all races, pushed shoulder to shoulder, writing frantically, and you could feel in the room, it was one voice. And so we turned to each other and commented on that—that what we wanted in the school had worked. That was the defining moment.

Faculty and administrative leaders had been focusing for several years on creating opportunities for dialogue and developing a harmonious environment among ethnic groups. The principal, Jan Cho, came into the school with a vision of equity and had clearly articulated a program that addressed racial conflicts. She felt that a "major part of the journey is looking in the classroom to see what's happening to students there." In addition, Fillmore drew teachers from a nearby university, known for its liberal atmosphere, which may have contributed to the level of open discussion about race and ethnicity at the school. Several of these teachers articulated a strong social vision that permeated the school. They also told us that diversity was central to the principal's vision:

> I think diversity has always been a really high priority for her. That's why we tackle those kinds of things at retreats—what to do about the honor roll, what to do about detention, and these various problems. She's always been a person who has been an advocate of equal access for all, and appreciation of diversity, understanding, and learning to get along. She sets a great example. She's always been the first one to try to organize and get things going. No moss ever grew under her feet when it came to that.

> She has made a climate and has a fairness that is recognized. She has encouraged parents who are really into creating a diverse committee and pursuing diversity, not just recognizing and supporting and honoring diversity but cultivating diversity. Recognizing that issues need to be confronted head on.

Cho recognized issues of race and ethnicity and was candid about existing problems, not allowing them to be swept under the rug. She encouraged debate, airing all sides of issues. As a former teacher, she understood curriculum and instruction and recognized the need to infuse diversity into teaching and learning. In this quest, she worked to create conditions that empowered teachers, and, as a result, teachers told us that they were highly involved in working with students, parents, and the community. She was also forthright about the need for teachers to be inclusive. Staff retreats always included support people as well as teaching staff, and she brought the campus supervisors into the administrative team as equals.

Cho's style was to confront issues as they happened. At one staff retreat, a presentation by two teachers was attended by only a handful of people. During the next session, she called the group to task about not supporting their colleagues. One teacher reflected, "She might criticize, but she will never abandon." Another said, "She gives you her undivided attention and makes you feel like you count. She makes us deal openly with problems and does not support backbiting." She also made sure that teachers were recognized and financially rewarded. When necessary, she took the heat from parents. She encouraged "innovation, creative ideas and, at the same time, was good with paperwork and follow-up." Staff members could "scream and yell over issues in her office and still walk out as a team." Above all, she not only had an open-door policy but also was highly visible in the school, always seen out in the hallways and among teachers. As a result of her leadership, teachers worked overtime and were involved in multiple school activities and committees.

At one point in her quest for equity, Cho went to the history department regarding diversity:

> I kind of chewed them out and said, "I look to you for leadership in this area. This is, after all, what history is about. Then help me do something more, schoolwide, that makes Fillmore put its stamp on diversity—making clear this is what we will tolerate or not tolerate!" That's when we came up with this action plan that the history department will adopt a diversity focus every year and lead discussions with students. They now work to make it a schoolwide effort to do more integration in the curriculum, rather than use a pure history book. They initiate more discussion among students about what's going on—the put-downs, the stereotypes, the intimidation, all the things that go on.

Fillmore also had a parent diversity group that raised money and purchased films and materials to support the development of early adolescents in their search for identity and healthy ways of relating to others across lines of difference. Teachers used films like *The Color of Fear* and *Skin Deep* (see Resource B) dealing with race issues as well as other resources focused on sexual orientation issues. In one of the parent meetings, Cho brought the committee to task, saying, "You need to come up with one goal, one idea, a theme. Then we can figure out where it fits into the curriculum. What is the goal of this committee?" One parent's response was, "We'd like to integrate issues of diversity into the whole school, if we can find ways to introduce and include diversity in all curricula." A teacher added, "We need to incorporate the attitudes into all classes."

Fillmore was among the first schools in the state to pioneer detracking in the early 1980s. All of the core classes were heterogeneous, and much time and effort had been poured into professional development to help teachers teach in multilevel classes. Many teachers asserted that heterogeneous grouping made a difference, and several reported that there were indeed more African American and Latino students in the middle and high groups than there had been before detracking. Fillmore students as a whole scored *above* the national average in reading comprehension, total reading, total language, math problem solving, and total mathematics. According to one teacher,

> The most important thing is our heterogeneous classes. In 1980, we were a model school for a state demonstration-school grant and we used the money to have smaller class sizes and to hire tutors for all the English classes, and we made the English classes heterogeneous. And later, we were a state demonstration-school grant for math, and they made math more heterogeneous. And that was a signal to the students that we viewed them as being equal. And that's an important message. I've devoted my life to untracked classes. Absolutely, it makes a difference in achievement of the students of color. What has happened is that it's about the same around the top. It's better in the middle and astoundingly better on the bottom. And that is heterogeneity research that's well documented everywhere. However, it isn't truly heterogeneous, because we have algebra.

Despite the school's history of detracking, and the many ways that school leaders and teachers worked to grapple with issues surrounding diversity and creating a climate of fairness, Fillmore staff discovered they had not entirely achieved their equity goals. We completed our study just as the school submitted the Healthy Start grant proposal. However, they used this planning process to advantage in addressing the achievement issue head on. A central piece of this grant was creating after-school programs like tutoring, homework club, and mentoring of at-risk students as well as working to ensure equitable inclusion in extracurricular activities. Wrestling with the hard, cold facts brought to the surface while examining data prevented this staff from resting on their laurels and status as a Distinguished School (1995). A real support in this effort was the climate and spirit of camaraderie in a school that many called "family" as well as the established norm that valued open discussion and debate around thorny issues.

ACTIVITY 21: ISSUES TO GRAPPLE WITH—DETRACKING

Detracking

1. Imagine that you are a leader at a middle school. How could you take into account the need for foreign language and algebra as college requirements while still keeping classes heterogeneous? How could you ensure the equitable inclusion of lower-SES and diverse students in these classes?

2. If you have the time and enough people in your group or class, organize a debate about detracking—one side will be pro and the other con. You don't have to agree with your role. Each team should have time to read some material about tracking and detracking and to formulate their argument. (For good sources, see Fine, Weis, & Powell, 1997; Lipman, 1998; Mehan, 1996.)

Author's Reflections

Fillmore Middle School was chosen specifically for this study because the school had a notably higher level of open conversation around issues of race, ethnicity, culture, and class than most schools. This made it all the more remarkable during the last year of this study, when the school looked critically at their disaggregated data and discovered that their self-perceived notions about heterogeneous grouping and equity, as well as creating a caring environment, were not working the way most staff members believed they were. This eye-opener came about only because of the Healthy Start data collection, analysis, and grant-writing process.

This illustrates the need for schools to set up a systematic way to collect and disaggregate several types of data and to use this information to influence policies about discipline and participation in extracurricular activities as well as to inform instruction. Examining standardized test scores is a necessary, but not sufficient, step in gathering a complete picture of conditions for all students in a school. By all counts, most visitors would agree with the staff's perception that they worked very hard to meet both the social and academic needs of students. The results of the efforts made by the principal, staff, and parents to create and sustain the diversity initiative were evident in classrooms, curriculum, and casual conversations. The most striking outcome was the school's climate of unity after the Rodney King decision. While many staff members valued the detracking efforts of the school, it took that hard look at the data to underscore the need for additional attention and interventions to ensure equitable access along with equitable outcomes for all students. While this kind of data collection and analysis is time consuming and takes a concerted and sustained effort, it is a tremendously important component for educators hoping to truly level the playing field for all students.

13

Dilemmas of Pluralism and Unity

Rosemary Henze

OHLONE HIGH SCHOOL

This case begins by describing a direct confrontation between two groups of high school students—African American and Latino—over the issue of whether the Latino students should go ahead with their plans for a Cinco de Mayo assembly given the fact that there had been a recent death in the African American student community. Underlying this incident, however, is a complicated history of ethnic assemblies at the school and different people's perspectives about the value of these assemblies. The case provides a springboard for discussion of the twin goals of pluralism and unity: to what extent do the pluralistic goals of ethnic assemblies undermine the goals of unity? How can schools integrate events that focus on certain groups in a way that supports both ethnic identity and positive intergroup relations?

The Setting

Ohlone was a very large comprehensive high school (approximately 4,100 students) on the West Coast. The student body was extremely diverse, consisting of Latinos (25%), Asians (21%), whites (17%), African Americans (14%), as well as small numbers of Pacific Islanders and American Indians. The faculty, though growing in ethnic diversity, was still about 80% white. Although in the 1980s, the school had been considered extremely tough, with a lot of gang problems, it was now considered relatively peaceful, and many staff members and students were proud of how well such a diverse student body got along. Two of the school's strongest points, where diversity is concerned, were its rich array of ethnic-studies courses as well as its efforts to infuse multicultural perspectives in the required English and social studies courses. There were also many after-school ethnic clubs, which were responsible for planning and carrying out the many ethnic assemblies. The principal, Rick Sebastian, had recently coined a motto for the school: "Diversity is our strength; unity is our goal." However, as the following case suggests, the school continued to struggle over how to achieve this unity.

The Conflict

In the spring of 1995, Ohlone High School experienced a near confrontation between African American and Latino students that almost turned violent. It was a tense situation in which leaders had to decide quickly on a strategy before serious harm was done. For many weeks, the Latino students had been planning a large assembly to commemorate Cinco de Mayo. This was a regular yearly event on campus, along with other ethnic assemblies at various times during the year. On the day of the assembly, however, some African American students confronted the Latino students with a serious complaint: They felt it was disrespectful to go ahead with the planned assembly given the recent death of a young African American man whom many of them were close to. According to Sherry Nickle, a teacher who witnessed the death, the police had killed the young man in a car chase. He was the father of one of the student's babies, and thus,

> It was a real tough time on campus for the kids that were associated with the girl, who had lost the father to her baby, and, of course, the friends of this boy. He was no longer a student at the time he was killed, but he had been very closely associated with our black community here on campus.

The tension of the moment was evident in Nickle's description:

> All of a sudden, a bunch of African American kids were confronting the Latinos because they had not canceled their assembly; they were going ahead with it. And it was a total emotional reaction; they hadn't really talked to anybody calmly or rationally about it, and the Latino kids were like, "We worked really hard on this, we're not canceling our assembly." And here come 400 kids—200 Latinos and 200 blacks [she makes noises like swords crossing] in the court over here.

Perspectives

LeAnne Ferris, a European American faculty member who does a lot of work with peer support groups, said she thought a lot of the problem in that particular conflict was due to a lack of cross-cultural understanding. She had seen similar misunderstandings at other times when death struck the African American student population:

Frankly, the white people did not understand how black people do death, how they grieve. The grief processes are very different. Northern Europeans grieve very differently from Southern Europeans and African Americans. And so, there are a lot of judgments that are based on a lack of understanding. Here's this group that is expressive of their emotion, and they want to do it together. They don't want to go into a single room with a counselor and talk about it. And the white teachers and counselors are getting afraid of this, because there were groups of folks gathering to grieve, and this was kind of a frightening thing, because they didn't know what this is going to lead to. So a lot of the response tends to be, "Well, they certainly are milking it."

Apparently, this was not the first time Ohlone had experienced tensions around the time of ethnic assemblies, though people agreed that this incident was probably the "scariest" in that it came the closest to an out-and-out race "war."

There had been ethnic assemblies here for years. In fact, Frances Lyons, science department chair and an African American teacher, said that the idea of ethnic assemblies as an educational event had started many years ago with the African American Student Alliance on campus. The idea was to use assemblies as a vehicle for celebrating the diverse cultures and histories of students on campus and also to educate people about things that are left out of the history books. Assemblies were intended as a vehicle for promoting greater awareness of diversity and improving cross-cultural understanding. Over the years, many more groups began to put on ethnic assemblies. Lyons was the faculty advisor to the African American Student Alliance at one time, and she recalled that there was often tension around the assemblies:

> Students and teachers would go and look at the assemblies, and when it was African American students, there was always something wrong. One time, we were giving different aspects of the African American community and how these different groups had contributed to present day African American communities. And one of our choices was the Black Panthers. Some people just see the Black Panthers as a violent group, and others see them as helping people in the community or whatever. But others would think that we were boasting about our culture instead of just trying to understand and share the history. We had to go in for conferences with the principal about it.

Principal Sebastian recalled this same history and remembered that the African American students felt the audience's response had been racist. From his perspective, the student presentation about the Black Panthers had been "too subtle, and they failed to make their point about the Black Panthers as a part of history that we should know about." He said he sat down with the students later to discuss this, and by the time the discussion was over, they understood that it wasn't a matter of racism but rather that the message of the assembly had not come through clearly to the audience.

Daniel Pérez, a teacher who had been involved with the several Latino clubs on campus, also felt that the Cinco de Mayo incident was probably the outcome of a growing sense of tension that had been building for some time. "Emotions were just running rampant on that day. And it might have been based on a lot of deep-seated things that had never been resolved before, and this gave them a place to vent those concerns."

One of the things that was not resolved centered on different styles of dance during the assemblies. Another African American teacher said, "You get a sense that the African American teachers are kind of wading in the criticism of dances that go on, that they're too sexually suggestive, but yet, when another culture might do it, they're just being cultural." Lyons echoed this observation: "When the Hispanics were doing theirs, and they had suggestive dances, the response was, 'Oh, that was beautiful.'"

Jorge Galindo, a counselor and one of the Latino club's sponsors, added that the "immature, teenage mentality comes into it, too, and creates problems. There are a few kids who extend it beyond pride and tend to boast; they say, 'We are the best,' even knowing that this causes friction."

Although all of these people agreed that ethnic assemblies had a problematic side, they and many others also recognized that the assemblies and the planning that led up to them were important parts of the school's efforts to affirm the diverse ethnic groups on campus. About the benefits, an administrator commented, "I've learned a lot about the different cultures from listening to the assemblies."

A European American parent said she liked the fact that the assemblies helped make people aware of the diversity within supposedly uniform racial groups:

> It was great that Ohlone did a European American assembly because sometimes European American students feel bad—like it's about white power—but it helps to recognize Dutch, German, Portuguese—they're not just white. Some people wouldn't know that unless there were assemblies.

Many students felt the assemblies were "one way to combat racism" because "they teach you the truth about different groups, not the stereotypes":

> For the longest time we had a lot of ethnic assemblies, but what my friends and other students said was, "What about the white assemblies?" I was like, "What else is behind just white? There's Polish, there's Swedish, there's Irish. There's so much more than just white. And I'm like, "If you categorize just a white assembly, it does sort of sound, like, stupid. I mean, why are you going to put on a white assembly? I mean, my shirt is white; therefore, I am in a white assembly. But no, there's, like, so much heritage behind just white.

However, there were also many students who felt the assemblies generated a kind of competition among ethnic groups. They pointed out that many students behaved rudely when another ethnic group was on stage, booing them and making derogatory comments to other students sitting nearby. Furthermore, the way time was allocated for different groups was constantly being revisited. A group of East Indian students, for example, went to the principal to protest the fact that Indian students were lumped in as part of the Asian assembly, which gave them little time to explain their complex culture to others.

Principal Sebastian, in reflecting on the school's pluralistic strengths, felt that they still had some work to do: "That's always been our own criticism of our school; equally important to showing the importance of an ethnicity is to show how we're all the same as well. And we don't do that."

ACTIVITY 22: MULTIPLE PERSPECTIVES

Individual Reflection

1. What explanations for the conflict do the different speakers offer?

2. Are there any perspectives that seem to be missing?

3. Drawing on these perspectives and your own sense of the situation, write down a short (one to two sentences) definition of the central problem in the Cinco de Mayo incident.

Group Discussion

4. Share these problem definitions with others in a small group. How are your definitions different or similar?

5. Together, look at the list of trigger issues in Chapter 3. Do any of these seem to fit the situation described in this case?

6. Do certain definitions of the problem lead toward certain resolutions?

ACTIVITY 23: POSSIBLE RESPONSES

Imagining Responses

1. In small groups, imagine that you are members of the leadership team at Ohlone, and you must decide how to respond to the confrontation. What are

your choices? What are the potential advantages or disadvantages of each? (You may want to review Table 7.1.)

2. Given your limited knowledge of the context, what seems to be the best response and why? Does your group agree on a best response? If not, what is the difference in your outlooks?

3. Share your group's list of responses, advantages, and disadvantages with the whole group. Someone should record on chart paper or a large board all the different responses that are mentioned. Is there a best response that the whole group can agree on? Why or why not?

Alternative Responses

Obviously, maintaining the safety and security of all students and staff is paramount. One possible course of action is to use security guards to separate the students in conflict, keep them apart until they have calmed down, and then go ahead with the assembly as planned. Disciplinary consequences can be given to those students who violated the school's behavioral standards. Another course of action, building on the first, would be to reconsider the value of having separate assemblies for the different ethnic groups at the school, and, perhaps, shift future assembly programming to more multicultural events. A third course of action, given that this situation has not yet become physically violent, is to try mediation.

The first course of action—separating the students in conflict and proceeding with the assembly as planned—might contain the immediate problem; essentially, it protects the physical safety of the students and staff for the time being, but it does nothing to prevent a similar or worse problem from occurring later. If this is the only response to the incident, none of the hurt and angry feelings will have been resolved, and the students in conflict will have not learned anything from the experience—except that no one expects them to be able to resolve their conflict. For that matter, the adults will not have learned anything either, except, perhaps, to reinforce existing stereotypes about the potential for violence among minority communities.

The second course of action—omitting future ethnic-specific assemblies and replacing them with events that are more multicultural—is one that some schools have adopted based on the belief that ethnic assemblies encourage greater separation among groups. While the multicultural approach seems to work well in some schools, its success depends greatly on the context and the degree to which different stakeholders—students, faculty members, parents of different ethnic groups—feel a sense of ownership and commitment to the decision. When a school has a long history of celebrating ethnic-specific events, removing them from the yearly calendar can be seen as punitive. Furthermore, a growing body of evidence suggests that young people whose cultural identity is nurtured, both in school and at home, have a stronger self-esteem and are more capable of appreciating other cultural patterns and relating across lines of difference (see Chapter 2).

A third course of action—mediation of some kind—represents a fundamentally different approach in which conflict is viewed as a normal part of human social life and as a springboard for learning. While it is unfortunate that the incident occurred at all, it represents an opportunity for education—a teachable moment, as it were. Mediation can take many forms, from peer conflict resolution to various forms of adult intervention. However, many schools with peer conflict resolution programs establish policies that an adult must mediate certain kinds of conflicts, such as racial issues and sexual assaults, or, at least, there must be an adult present during the mediation.

4.   What do you think of these alternative responses? After reading them, do you want to change anything about your earlier decisions?

The Response From Ohlone's Leaders

In the actual case from which this scenario was drawn, the principal, a European American man, realized he could not handle this confrontation by himself. He knew he needed to call in additional people whom the students in conflict would relate to and respect. Ohlone High School was so large that there was no way Sebastian could have a relationship with every student. Fortunately, he had several teachers in mind who he knew related well to the students involved in the conflict, and it wasn't by chance that they included both African American and Latino teachers. For many years, the school and the district had worked to recruit more teachers of color, with some degree of success. These teachers, once they arrived on the scene, quickly identified a few of the involved students, who were seen as leaders among their peers, and then took them to a quiet place to talk—first separately, to give each group a chance to air their concerns to a calm and willing listener, and to consider what kinds of resolutions might assuage their concerns. After this first step, the two groups met together, again with adult facilitation, and in this structured setting, the African American students were able to explain why they were so hurt and angry and why the celebratory nature of the Cinco de Mayo assembly seemed so disrespectful, given the context of a recent death. The Latino students were able to explain how hard they had worked to prepare for this day and that they couldn't simply hold it on another day because it was already nearly the end of the school year.

They were able to reach a compromise in which the Latino students began the assembly by recognizing the sad loss that had occurred just days before and stating that they meant no disrespect in carrying out the Cinco de Mayo event; this was followed by a moment of quiet reflection. The more celebratory parts of the Cinco de Mayo assembly, such as the dancing, were placed later in the program, and the more solemn parts, such as the speech about César Chávez, were placed closer to the beginning so that the juxtaposition of parts would flow smoothly. With leaders from both groups of students having agreed to this plan, the assembly proceeded peacefully.

Interestingly, in the years that followed, Ohlone's leadership did not change the basic structure of having ethnic assemblies throughout the year. However, a few years later, they did institute an annual event called Days of Respect, which focused specifically on intergroup relations. Teacher leaders also pressed for and won district approval for a graduation requirement in multicultural studies. And peer support and conflict mediation programs were established as structures for addressing student concerns and conflicts prior to adult intervention.

ACTIVITY 24: EXTENDED REFLECTION

Questions for Discussion

1. Review the iceberg model of racial or ethnic conflict (Figure 3.1). How does this model help you explain the case you have just read?

2. Having read how the principal and teacher leaders at Ohlone responded to the confrontation, is there anything you would change about your response?

3. In this case, people other than the principal are seen exercising leadership. What forms of leadership do you see, and why are they important in the development of positive interethnic relations?

Author's Reflections

There are several points worth noticing about this resolution. First, as noted earlier, the principal took a proactive stance, viewing this conflict as an opportunity for both students and staff to learn more about human relations and, specifically, how to improve relations between culturally different groups. Second, whereas in many schools the norm is to pretend that we live in a color-blind world, in this case, mediation created a free space in which issues of cultural differences and tensions related to race could be openly addressed, rather than avoided. Third, the peaceful outcome can be seen not only as the result of a successful mediation but also as the natural outgrowth of a whole series of earlier shifts in the school's approach to diversity that had created a strong foundation for intergroup relations. Clearly, the mediation served as the immediate resolution to the problem. However, the mediation itself rested on a foundation that included

1. Diverse staff members who understand students' backgrounds and cultures

2. Curricular opportunities for students to learn about their own ethnic group's history and culture as well as to delve into the cultures of others and to examine the dynamics of intergroup relations

3. Leadership that was distributed among many staff members rather than a few administrators, allowing the principal to feel confident that he could step back and let others carry out the resolution

The fact that the school continued to develop more approaches to promote positive interethnic relations (e.g., the graduation requirement in multicultural studies; peer support and conflict mediation programs; Days of Respect as an annual event) illustrates how the leadership at Ohlone viewed interethnic relations as an ongoing concern, always in need of attention due to the continually changing context.

14

Maintaining Confidentiality

Susan Sather and Ernest Walker

METROPOLITAN HIGH SCHOOL

This case concerns a racial conflict between an African American teacher and a European American student in an alternative high school. Both the teacher and student were inappropriate in their use of racial slurs against each other. In handling this issue, the principal was confronted with her own ethical obligation to respect confidentiality while working for a satisfactory solution to the problem.

The Setting

Metropolitan High School, a small alternative high school within a large urban school system, was designed to meet the needs of students who were failing in the comprehensive high schools. The majority racial and ethnic groups at the school were African American, Latino, and European American; 90% of the students came from low-income households. The intent was to build a social and intellectual community for those students. From the beginning, the staff had a propensity to talk about issues like race with each other. This was underscored when they adopted the curriculum, Facing History and Ourselves. Each year, they also adopted a humanities theme with a focus on social issues, such as "What is justice?" or "What does it mean to be human?"

In the mid-1990s, the school became a pilot charter school, enabling the doubling of its staff. Principal Laura Frye took this unique opportunity and used it to hire more staff of different ethnic backgrounds. The ethnic composition went from 12% staff members of color to over 50%. This move not only allowed the staff to better reflect and relate to the students' background cultures but also, according to Frye, "it enriched and inspired the community." School leaders sometimes say, "We can't find qualified staff of color." However, Metropolitan was conscious and deliberate in their recruitment and hiring practices; they called, wrote, posted e-mails, and made it clear that they were committed to finding, placing, and supporting teachers and administrators of color. The school had a strong public profile, and many candidates came through their network of friends and associates. This helped them gain access to qualified candidates, one of whom was an African American man who was hired as codirector of the school and who became a trusted confidant of the principal, helping expand her awareness in many areas, including diversity-related issues.

However, despite the atmosphere of openness encouraged by the principal and codirector, some tension related to race remained among faculty members. One staff member said that during the first 3 years of her tenure there, diversity issues were raised but not dealt with until there was an incident that happened that brought the issue from a simmer to a boil.

The Conflict

At one point, Frye was faced with an administrative dilemma. In relating this incident, she delineated the complexity of dealing with issues around race in schools while also maintaining administrative confidentiality:

> A young black teacher got into a mix with a pretty tough white girl who was using profanity around him. They ended up having a long, difficult history together. He was inappropriate in his dealings with her, and he cursed back at her. It got very complicated. Some people came to me and asked me to tell the story to staff. But I could never say that he had cursed that girl out, called her white trash, and hung up the phone on her. That's the burden of administration; there are confidentiality rules.

The conflict began to have damaging effects on staff relations as different people took sides. Some of the teachers of color would stop talking in the hallway when Frye, a European American woman, came by. They felt she was not adequately supporting the teacher, though, as Frye noted, they didn't know the whole story, only the part about the girl's behavior. Other staff members took the side of the girl, pointing out that, "We have a responsibility to teach her how to live with people of color and with people who disagree with her philosophy."

ACTIVITY 25: POSSIBLE RESPONSES

Among the possible ways to address the situation that occurred at Metropolitan are the following:

- Simply ignore the situation, hoping it will go away.
- Fire the teacher, expel the student, or both.

- Work with both parties individually or together (through conflict mediation) in an effort to get them to take greater responsibility for their actions and to modify their behavior.
- Address the larger staff issues around the underlying tensions.
- Ignore confidentiality and explain both sides of the situation at a staff meeting.

Individual Reflection

1. Imagine that you are the principal at Metropolitan High School. As a principal, you may not be able to discuss this issue with your leadership team. Consider the above possible responses and weigh the pros and cons of each one.

2. There may be more options than those listed here. Can you come up with other possibilities?

3. Decide which response or combination of responses you would use, and develop a plan for addressing the student, teacher, and staff issues.

Group Discussion

4. Now work together in small groups to discuss your plans and the advantages and disadvantages of each. Keep in mind the issue of confidentiality and how you work with that.

Principal Frye's Course of Action

Ignoring the issue was not an option for Principal Frye. It was already fairly clear that the hostility between the teacher and student was accelerating and that as more and more individuals chose sides, the whole school community would become fractured. Furthermore, ignoring the incident would certainly not lead to any learning on the part of staff or students, except, perhaps, learning that racial incidents are not discussed. This went against the mission and values of the school.

Frye neither fired the teacher nor expelled the student. While either one of these actions would have addressed the immediate issue of the student-teacher conflict, it still would leave other staff members disaffected and would not result in any learning about how to resolve a racially tinged conflict such as this one.

Moreover, removing either the teacher or the student from the school would suggest that the individuals were not responsible human beings who are capable of changing their behavior.

Frye did attempt to work with both parties individually in an effort to get them to take greater responsibility for their actions and to modify their behavior. This response had the potential of providing some learning for both participants while maintaining their confidentiality. However, the teacher and student both refused to sit down together in conflict mediation. The situation was apparently too volatile for the disputants to sit down together and work toward a mutually agreed-upon resolution.

Frye noted, "We were really committed to keeping the teacher with us. We really thought we could work it out with him." As for the student, Frye suspended her for a few days and met with her and her mother.

> I got the mom in, and the girl admitted she was swearing near him but not at him. She was cursing in general, and he felt disrespected. I said, "I don't care if you thought he heard it or not, he heard it, and it was offensive. You are not going to talk that way to anyone here. You have to be aware that this is a young black teacher and you are a white student." To have been able to get this particular mother and student in and make those impressions was a powerful thing. That's a side that most people did not know. But this continued over 2½ years. She continued to push his buttons and he did things that were very unteacherly.

In addition, it was important to address the larger staff issues that came about as people began to take sides. Conflicts between two individuals of different ethnic groups can quickly spread and affect a whole school community as other observers tend to interpret such conflicts in even more strongly racial terms. Those in leadership roles need to recognize that any resolution will have to attend to the larger school community as well as the individuals involved. Thus Frye and the leadership team chose to bring in diversity consultants to work with the staff on the underlying racial tensions that had surfaced in this series of incidents. As a result, some staff members felt they made headway in recognizing that there were some racial issues in the school and developing a formal language to talk about the issues. Others suggested that they only worked with surface issues, not getting to the "nitty gritty of the situation."

The principal also sought guidance from her supervisor, an administrator in the district office. "Thank God he was an African-American and very wise man. He guided me through it and helped me counsel that young teacher in a way that preserved his dignity." In the end, the teacher went to another school, and the girl decided to take the general education diploma (GED) and leave high school early.

Frye chose to respect confidentiality throughout this situation. Despite the intensity, she did not take the easy way out and reveal to staff members that the teacher was as much at fault as the student was in using reciprocal racial slurs. The fact that this conflict stretched out for over two years increased the pressure on Frye, who nevertheless refused to affix blame and instead worked to craft a satisfactory solution.

While people often assume that racial conflict only happens between students in schools, it is not unusual for adults to be active participants in acts of racial and ethnic dissonance, as happened at Metropolitan High School. Those in leadership roles need to stay tuned to the possibility of conflicts between students, staff, and students—and parents and staff.

ACTIVITY 26: EXTENDED REFLECTION

1. Now that you know the principal's actual response to this situation, would you make changes to your action plan?

2. Can you think of other ways to respect confidentiality and continue to work with the staff on this issue?

3. Does the fact that half the staff members in this school were teachers of color affect your role as principal? If so, how? If not, why not? How do you ensure that all voices are heard and listened to?

4. The principal brought in diversity consultants to work with staff on racial issues. The results were mixed. In reflecting on your own experiences with diversity training, can you offer any explanation for these mixed reactions from staff?

Authors' Reflections

The principal in this case exhibited several attitudes and behaviors that made her work exemplary. First, she was willing to acknowledge her own limitations when it came to knowledge and practices about diversity issues in general, and she was willing to be open about her own learning process. This awareness of her own limitations led her to actively seek out people whom she trusted who had the ability to teach her what she didn't know, and she particularly reached out to others as she wrestled with the conflict between the student and the teacher. She also respected confidentiality while seeking multiple solutions for this problem. In addition, her ability to counsel the teacher to leave the school, while preserving his dignity, was unusual and remarkable. The principal modeled respect and care in a difficult situation that persisted for over 2 years. It required great self-control, maturity, and professionalism not to give in and share details of the entire situation with staff.

This way of dealing with the dilemma did bring to the surface underlying racial tensions among staff members in the school. At the time of our study, teachers had worked with diversity consultants to address some of the issues that emerged as a result of this overt conflict. Especially notable were the disparate opinions about the success of this work or intervention. Some white teachers saw the work with diversity consultants as having varying degrees of success, while one black teacher felt they had barely scratched the surface in terms of underlying feelings, tensions, and racist attitudes. It was apparent to many that the consultants had their own limitations in working with these issues.

The case illustrates that it is not enough to uncover tender feelings and unexplored, perhaps even unconscious, stereotypes and attitudes. School leaders and staff members need to be prepared to commit to an ongoing process of self-examination that leads to a healthier climate around diversity issues. They also need to be aware that this process takes time and can sometimes be painful as they explore unexamined attitudes and related behavior.

Methodology

OVERVIEW

The study employed a qualitative, multiple-case study design. This design was appropriate for a project in which the primary aim was to describe approaches and processes used by school leaders in different contexts. In developing our methods, we drew on the work of qualitative researchers such as Erickson (1986), Goetz and LeCompte (1984), Glesne and Peshkin (1992), Patton (1990), and Miles and Huberman (1994). The study was designed to address the following two research questions:

1. How do school leaders or leadership teams address tensions and conflict that may be related to race or ethnicity?

2. How do school leaders or leadership teams bring about unity rather than division among different ethnic groups on campus?

The study was structured around two yearlong cycles of data collection. The first cycle involved nine San Francisco Bay Area school sites; the second cycle added 12 sites throughout the United States for a total of 21 sites.

In qualitative research, those who conduct the study are considered an integral part of the design because of the significant role they play in interacting with study participants and interpreting the data they collect. Thus it is important to note that the five members of this research team were ethnically diverse and brought a wide range of relevant experiences and perspectives to the study, including educational anthropology, sociolinguistics, developmental psychology, critical pedagogy, school administration, teaching, counseling, and conflict resolution.

180 HOW SCHOOL
LEADERS
PROMOTE
POSITIVE
INTERETHNIC
RELATIONS

SITE SELECTION

Sites were selected through a nomination, screening, and selection process that took place in 1996 for local sites and in 1997 for national sites. Although this was a very time-consuming process, the results were well worth it, as we were ultimately able to generate a wide range of nominations and were thus able to be quite selective. In order to meet the initial selection criteria, schools had to have (a) a diverse population including at least three major ethnic groups; (b) a history of racial or ethnic conflict or tension in the school or surrounding community; and (c) leadership that employs a proactive approach to addressing these conflicts and building positive relations among ethnic groups.

Altogether, we received 90 nominations, from which we selected 21 sites. Outreach for nominations was done by contacting school site and district administrators, university professors, graduate students, community members, state departments of education, and by calling for nominations in *Education Week* in the autumn of 1996 and in various newsletters and listservs.

A screening process was used to gather more information from nominated sites. Local sites were screened through an initial telephone interview with the principal followed by screening visits to eligible sites. National sites were screened through a more-structured telephone interview with the principal. Researchers met to make the final site selections, keeping in mind that we wanted the schools to vary in certain aspects such as size, demographics, and organizational structure.

DATA COLLECTION

To collect data at local sites, teams of two researchers made visits at least monthly over the course of three semesters. At the national sites, one or two researchers visited each school in 1998, once in the spring and once in the fall, with the exception of one school which we were able to visit only once. Each visit was approximately 3 days long. Sources of data at each school were semistructured interviews with a range of stakeholders (including administrators, counselors, teachers, students, parents, and community members); observations of key events and activities, such as classes, leadership meetings, and student activities; and documents and records provided by the schools. We interviewed a total of 1,009 individuals and did 441 observations across the 21 sites. Almost all interviews were tape-recorded, and about half were transcribed.

FEEDBACK SESSIONS

At the midpoint in data collection, we gave each school the option of participating in a feedback session. Nineteen of the 21 schools participated in these sessions. The purposes of feedback sessions were to share preliminary findings for the individual site, as well as emerging patterns across all 21 sites, and to elicit input from staff members as to the validity of our findings thus far. These sessions also provided a structure within which staff members could reflect on the positive approaches they were using and generate ideas for further enhancement of their efforts in interethnic relations. Final feedback was provided to all schools in the form of a case report, and, in a few instances, schools have planned additional follow-up involving the research team.

DATA ANALYSIS

As we analyzed and reviewed data from each site, we developed a coding scheme for use across all the sites. The coding scheme included the following broad categories:

A. *The school context*, for example, demographic information, relevant characteristics of the community, physical layout, funding and resources, student achievement
B. *Leadership*, including the formal governance structure, history of leadership, vision or ideology, style, dilemmas the leadership has faced, contributions they have made, and other sources of leadership
C. *The history of tensions or conflicts* around race or ethnicity as well as other conflict
D. *Current issues* the school is facing regarding diversity, race, ethnicity, or language
E. *Approaches* the school is using to address racial or ethnic conflicts or tensions to build positive intergroup relations
F. *The impact* these approaches have had on students, staff, parents, or community

We used a qualitative software package, QSR NUD.IST, to assist us in the coding process. Based on this coding, then, we were able to retrieve all the data about a particular category. Case reports for each school, organized in accordance with the coding scheme, framed the data we had collected. These individual case reports then provided a basis for systematic cross-site analysis in which we looked at the same categories across all 21 sites to discover differences, similarities, and patterns that helped us address the research questions.

Resources for Schools

This resource list addresses issues of race and ethnic relations. It was updated in July 2001. We plan to update it periodically, at least as long as our project continues (currently, through 2002). At this point, we are not recommending any particular resources over others. Resources appear on this list because (a) they have been used by one or more of the 21 schools that participated in the Leading for Diversity Project, or (b) members of the research team were familiar with the resource. We expect that you (interested users) will review materials yourself and decide whether they are appropriate for a particular context. We have focused this list on resources that specifically address interethnic relations, with a few exceptions for materials or programs that are widely used to address intergroup relations more broadly. For an updated copy of this list, please visit our Web site: www.arcassociates.org/leading.

Videos and Films (Note that many of these require a facilitator.)

Color of Fear. Lee Mun-Wah holds a dialogue with six men, including Asian, African American, European American, and Latino men about race and racism in their lives. To find out how this video can be used in your context and for information on local facilitators contact StirFry Consulting; 470 3rd Street; Oakland CA. Tel: 510/419-3930. Web site: www.stirfryseminars.com.

Skin Deep. A group of multicultural college students dialogue on issues of race and racism. Originally filmed in 1994; includes an update filmed with four of the students in 1997. Discussion guide included. Iris Films Web site: www.irisfilms.org. Skin Deep; 105 Terry Drive, Suite 120; Newton, PA 18940-3425.

Peace Talks: Stepping Up to Peace. Series of videos shows multiethnic groups of teenagers in three cities—Bronx, NY; Tallahassee, FL; and Pinole, CA—talking

184 HOW SCHOOL
LEADERS
PROMOTE
POSITIVE
INTERETHNIC
RELATIONS

about violence, race relations, and building community. Michael Pritchard is the facilitator. Distributed by Bureau for At-Risk Youth; 135 Dupont Street; Plainview, NY 11803.

Fear and Learning at Hoover Elementary. An award-winning documentary on the conflicts and tensions created by the current anti-immigrant, antibilingual climate and the impact on teachers and children. Good for raising awareness but does not provide strategies or solutions. Video Finders, 800/842-2298.

Off Track: Classroom Privilege for All. M. Fine, et al. Publicity notice: "This [30-minute] video takes the viewer into a World Literatures classroom where all the students in the room—lower income, middle class, and affluent: white, African American, Asian-American and Latino; girls and boys; those automatically 'advanced' and those who have been labeled in need of 'special education'—receive and produce high quality education. Ideal for staff development." NECA/Teaching for Change; PO Box 73038; Washington, DC 20056-3038. Tel: 202/238-2379. Fax: 202/238-2378. E-mail: necadc@aol.com. Web site: www.teachingforchange.org.

Magazines

Rethinking Schools (An Urban Educational Journal). Regularly contains features addressing issues of ethnic, racial, and linguistic diversity from critical perspectives. Rethinking Schools; 1001 E. Keefe Avenue; Milwaukee, WI 53212. Tel: 414/964-9646. Fax: 414/964-7220. Current subscription rate $12.50 for one year.

Teaching Tolerance. Designed for teachers. Published by the Southern Poverty Law Center; 400 Washington Avenue; Montgomery, AL 36104. Tel: 334/264-0268. Order fax: 334/264-3121. Free to educators whose request for a subscription is on school letterhead.

Curricula

Making the Peace: A 15-Session Violence Prevention Curriculum for Young People. P. Kivel and A. Creighton. (1997). Designed for high school students. Distributed by Hunter House; PO Box 2914; Alameda, CA 94501-0914. Tel: 510/865-5282. Fax: 510/865-4295.

Open Minds to Equality: A Sourcebook of Learning Activities to Promote Race, Sex, Class and Age Equity. N. Schniedewind and E. Davidson. (1998). Publicity notice: "Grades K-12. Useful for teachers and parents. Ready-to-use classroom lessons to build trust, communication and cooperation; challenge stereotypes; analyze the impact of discrimination; and learn how to create change." Boston: Allyn & Bacon. NECA/Teaching for Change; PO Box 73038; Washington, DC 20056-3038. Tel: 202/238-2379. Fax: 202/238-2378. E-mail: necadc@aol.com. Web site: www.teachingforchange.org.

Project REACH: Ethnic Perspectives Series. Published in 1991, this series of books covers Hispanic/Latino, African American, American Indian, Asian American, and European American perspectives on U.S. history. It is appropriate for middle and high school level students. REACH Center; 180 Nickerson Street, #212; Seattle, WA 98109. Tel: 206/284-8584.

Cooperative Learning: A Response to Linguistic and Cultural Diversity. D. D. Holt, editor. Publicity notice: "This book provides teacher trainers with the theoretical rationale and practical strategies for creating successful group activities for students from diverse language backgrounds. It brings together two fields, cooperative learning and applied linguistics, to create optimal schooling experiences for all students." Delta Systems; 1400 Miller Parkway; McHenry, IL 60050. Tel: 800/323-8270 (9 a.m. to 5 p.m. EST). Current cost is $18.95 plus shipping and handling.

Community Building in the Classroom (1992). V. Shaw. Provides structures and processes for team building and conflict resolution, focusing on different issues involved in group development—inclusion, influence, openness, and community. Kagan Cooperative Learning; San Juan Capistrano, CA. Tel: 800/933-2667.

Conflict Resolution: An Elementary School Curriculum, and *Conflict Resolution: A Secondary School Curriculum*. These curricula are widely used in the greater San Francisco Bay Area. They seem to be popular due to their human relations and how-to-get-along orientation as well as their teacher friendly lesson plan format. The elementary curriculum does not, however, deal explicitly with conflicts about ethnicity, race, and racism. The Community Board Program; Conflict Resolution Resources for Schools and Youth; 1540 Market Street, #490; San Francisco, CA 94102. Tel: 415/552-1250.

Conflict Resolution Unlimited. Publicity notice: "Student Mediation Programs for students at elementary, middle, and high school levels can help create more productive lives. The program is an effective way to teach anger management, conflict resolution, and basic communication skills to young people. It is preventative as it targets high-risk students and helps them develop self-esteem as well as new strategies for dealing with conflict including cultural diversity issues . . . [and it also provides] a team of trainers who practice mediation and who also reflect ethnic, cultural and gender diversity." CRU; 845 106th Avenue NE, Suite 109; Bellevue, WA 98004. Tel: 206/451-4015. Fax: 206/451-1477. Email: cru@cruinstitute. org. Web Site: eric-web.tc.columbia.edu/directories/anti-bias/cru.html.

Conflict Resolution in the High School: 36 Lessons. C. M. Lieber, L. Lantieri, and T Roderick. Includes a focus on diversity and intergroup relations, and ideas for infusing conflict resolution throughout the standard curriculum. Educators for Social Responsibility: Tel: 800/370-2515.

Jigsaw Classroom: A Cooperative Learning Technique (2000). Jigsawing is a classroom cooperative-learning technique developed in the 1970s by Eliot Aronson. It is said to improve race relations, promote learning, and improve student motivation. Web site: www.jigsaw.org.

Tribes: A New Way of Learning and Being Together. (1995). J. Gibbs. Also available in Spanish. Elementary curriculum designed to teach social skills such as collaboration, appreciation of others, and use of "I" messages. Although Tribes does not address race and ethnicity explicitly, some educators say the curriculum lays a foundation for respectful relations, leading to less intergroup conflict. Center Source Systems, LLC; 85 Liberty Ship Way, Suite 104; Sausalito, CA 94965. Tel: 415/289-1700. Fax: 415/289-1702. Web site: www.tribes.com.

Anti-Bias Curriculum: Tools for Empowering Young Children (1989). L. D. Sparks. Curriculum developed with premise that very young children absorb societal

186 HOW SCHOOL
LEADERS
PROMOTE
POSITIVE
INTERETHNIC
RELATIONS

biases. National Association for the Education of Young Children; 1834 Connecticut Avenue, NW; Washington, DC 20009-5786.

Different and the Same: Helping Children Identify and Prevent Prejudice (1995; Family Communications). Units include name calling, being excluded from mainstream culture, speaking a different language, stereotyping, standing up against prejudice, interracial friendships, cultural identity and assimilation, definitions of being American, and hate crimes. GPN; Box 80669; Lincoln, NE 68501-0669. Tel: 800/228-4630. Fax: 402/472-4076.

Organizations That Provide Assistance and Materials

A World of Difference. Developed by the Anti-Defamation League of B'Nai B'rith, this program offers teachers and community groups free workshops in such areas as designing extracurricular activities for youth, teaching conflict resolution techniques, and involving immigrant parents in their children's activities. Tel: 212/885-7700. Web site: www.adl.org/awod/awod_institute.html.

Bridges: A School Inter-Ethnic Relations Program. Orange County Human Relations; 1300 S. Grand Avenue, Building B; Santa Ana, CA 92705. Tel: 714/567-7470.

Educators for Social Responsibility. Books, videos, and professional development workshops. Tel: 800/370-2515. Fax: 617/864-5164. E-mail: esrmain@ igc.apc.org. Web site: www.esrnational.org/.

Facing History and Ourselves. This organization promotes an approach, rather than a curriculum package, that teaches students to critically examine historical events, most intensely the Holocaust, to help them understand the roots of racism and hatred and to promote a more humane and informed citizenry. Facing History and Ourselves; 16 Hurd Road. Brookline, MA 02146. Tel: 617/232-1595. Fax: 617/232-0281.

National Conference for Community and Justice. Founded in 1927 as the National Conference of Christians and Jews, NCCJ is a nonprofit organization dedicated to fighting bias, bigotry, and racism in America. NCCJ promotes understanding and respect among all races, religions, and cultures through advocacy, conflict resolution, and education. Tel: 212/545-1300. Web site: www.nccj.org.

Network of Educators on the Americas (NECA). From their catalogue: "NECA's goal is to promote peace, justice and human rights through critical, anti-racist, multicultural education. NECA creates opportunities for the development of equitable relationships among families, students, school staff and community members. We believe that these relationships are essential to transform schools so that they are academically rigorous, participatory, culturally affirming, equitable, liberating, connected to the community, and respectful of the strengths that people bring. NECA offers speakers, seminars, and staff development workshops." NECA/Teaching for Change; PO Box 73038; Washington, DC 20056-3038. Tel: 202/238-2379. Fax: 202/238-2378. E-mail: necadc@aol.com. Web site: www.teachingforchange.org.

Teaching for Change was launched to provide resources for school staff and parents who seek to transform schools. Going beyond the traditional heroes-and-holidays approach, the materials in the Teaching for Change catalog help educators integrate the experiences of the peoples who have been left in the margins of the curriculum: African Americans, Latinos, Native Americans, Asians, women, and working-class people of all races.

STAR (Students Talking about Racism). Designed by the People for the American Way to help middle and high school students confront feelings about prejudice and diversity through discussions facilitated by college students and peer mentors. Used in the San Francisco schools, the Los Angeles Unified School District, and elsewhere. Dr. Joe McKenna, STAR Managing Director; 2852 S. Barrington Avenue; Los Angeles, CA 90064-3613. Tel: 310/478-5857.

People's Institute for Survival and Beyond. This cadre of very experienced and knowledgeable multicultural trainers provides workshops in leadership, community empowerment, and unlearning racism. They regularly conduct training workshops throughout the country. 1444 N. Johnson Street; New Orleans, LA 70116. Tel: 504/944-2354.

TODOS Institute. A coproducer of the Making the Peace curriculum, the institute conducts training on conflict resolution that explicitly address issues of ethnicity, culture, race, and racism. 1203 Preservation Way; Oakland, CA 94612. Tel: 510/835-2433.

West Oakland Health Council Conflict Resolution Program. Trains students in crosscultural conciliation skills to help resolve conflicts among peers. WOHC; 2730 Adeline Street; Oakland, CA 94607. Tel: 510/430-1771.

SEED Project on Inclusive Curriculum (Seeking Educational Equity and Diversity). Provides information and materials for K-12 teacher groups on five-stage model of inclusion developed by Peggy McIntosh. Web site: www.wcwonlinc.org/seed/.

Youth Together: Multicultural Student Teams Leading for Cross Cultural Understanding, Respect, and Justice. A youth program in five high schools in Oakland, Richmond, and Berkeley, CA. Margaretta Lin; ARC Associates; 1212 Broadway, #400; Oakland, CA 94612. Tel: 510/834-9455. Fax: 510/763-1490. Web site: www.arcassociates.org.

Regarding Race. This project is a collaboration between the Center for Documentary Studies and the North Carolina Teaching Fellows Program at the University of North Carolina, Chapel Hill. The project uses photography and writing as catalysts for tapping into teachers' perspectives on race and engaging them in an exploration of race and ethnicity in their own lives and in their work with children. For information, contact Alexandra Lightfoot at 919/660-3694 or at aligh@duke.edu.

Books and Manuals

Alameda County Office of Education. (1997). *Hate Motivated Behavior in Schools: Response Strategies for School Boards, Administrators, Law Enforcement, and Communities.* Hayward, CA: Author.

Banks, J. (1997). *Teaching Strategies for Ethnic Studies.* Boston: Allyn & Bacon.

Bigelow, B., et al. (1994). *Rethinking Our Classrooms: Teaching for Equity and Justice.* Publicity notice: "This 216 page booklet includes creative teaching, ideas, compelling narratives, and hands-on examples of ways teachers can promote values of community, justice and equality—and build academic skills." (Currently $6). Rethinking Schools; 1001 E. Keefe Avenue; Milwaukee, WI 53212. Tel: 414/964-9646. Fax: 414/964-7220.

188 HOW SCHOOL
LEADERS
PROMOTE
POSITIVE
INTERETHNIC
RELATIONS

Cantor, R., et al. *Days of Respect: Organizing a School-Wide Violence Prevention Program*. Publicity notice: "Step-by-step instructions for putting together an event that brings together students, parents, teachers and community leaders for a common goal: preventing violence and creating an atmosphere of respect in school." Hunter House; PO Box 2914; Alameda, CA 94501-0914. Tel: 510/865-5282. Fax: 510/865-4295. (Currently $15). Also available from NECA/Teaching for Change; PO Box 73038; Washington, DC 20056-3038. Tel: 202/238-2379. Fax: 202/238-2378. E-mail: necadc@aol.com. Web site: www.teachingforchange.org.

Delpit, L. (1995). *Other People's Children: Cultural Conflict in the Classroom*. New York: New Press.

Lee, E. (1998). *Beyond Heroes and Holidays: A Practical Guide to K-12 Anti-Racist, Multicultural Education and Staff Development*. Publicity notice: "... offers classroom lesson plans, staff development activities, reflections on teaching and an extensive resource guide for any educator who wants to go beyond the 'heroes and holidays' approach as they address multicultural education in their school." (Currently $27). NECA/Teaching for Change; PO Box 73038; Washington, DC 20056-3038. Tel: 202/238-2379. Fax: 202/238-2378. E-mail: necadc@aol.com. Web site: www.teachingforchange.org.

Grant, C., and Sleeter, C. (1991). *Turning on Learning: Five Approaches to Race, Class, Gender, and Disability*. Englewood Cliffs, NJ: Merrill Press/Prentice Hall.

Kivel, P. (1999). *Uprooting Racism: How White People Can Work for Racial Justice*. A guide for white people struggling to understand and end racism. Gabriola Island, BC, Canada: New Society Publishers. Tel: 800/567-6772.

Oakes, J., Quartz, K. H., Ryna, S., and Lipton, M. (2000). *Becoming Good American Schools: The Struggle for Civic Virtue in Education Reform*. San Francisco: Jossey-Bass.

Tatum, B. (1997). *Why Are All the Black Kids Sitting Together in the Cafeteria? And Other Conversations About Race*. Scranton, PA: Harper Collins. Tel: 800/331-3761.

Zinn, H. (1995). *A People's History of the United States*. New York: Harper Collins.

President's Initiative on Race. *Pathways to One America in the 21st Century: Promising Practices for Racial Reconciliation*. Describes and gives contact information for approximately 125 programs nationwide. Web site: clinton3.nara.gov/initiatives/OneAmerica/america.html.

U.S. Department of Education, Office for Civil Rights. (1999). *Protecting Students from Harassment and Hate Crime: A Guide for Schools*. Web site: www.ed.gov/pubs/Harassment.

Short Articles for Staff Development

McIntosh, P. (1989, July/August). White Privilege: Unpacking the Invisible Knapsack. In *Peace and Freedom*, 10-12.

Lee, E. (1994). Taking Multicultural, Anti-Racist Education Seriously. In B. Bigelow, L. Christensen, S. Karp, B. Miner, & B. Peterson (Eds.), *Rethinking Our Classrooms: Teaching for Equity and Justice*. Milwaukee, WI: Rethinking Schools.

Assessment Materials

School Diversity Inventory. Provides surveys of faculty, staff, and students to assess such areas as diversity policies and practices, race and ethnic relations, and inclusion, perceived fairness, and equity. The organization analyzes the surveys and generates a school report. Behavioral Science Research and Development; 3239 B Corporate Court; Ellicott City, MD 21042. Tel: 401/461-5530 and 888/733-9805. Web site: www.gottfredson.com/school.htm.

Alignment With Standards for School Leadership

The Interstate School Leaders Licensure Consortium (ISLLC) (1996) adopted standards for school leaders which are intended to "help stakeholders across the education landscape (e.g., state agencies, professional associations, institutions of higher education) enhance the quality of educational leadership throughout the nation's schools" (p. iii). There are six standards, each of which is specified in terms of certain knowledge, dispositions, and performance.

Since the Leading for Diversity Project has a similar, though more specific goal—to enhance the ability of leaders to develop positive, interethnic school communities—we decided it would be valuable to align aspects of this book with the ISLLC standards. In this way, readers will be able to see how the material in this book addresses the ISLLC standards.

192 HOW SCHOOL
LEADERS
PROMOTE
POSITIVE
INTERETHNIC
RELATIONS

Table C.1   Alignment of Leading for Diversity Project With ISLCC Standards

ISLLC Standards	*Leading for Diversity Materials*
Standard 1: A school administrator is an educational leader who promotes the success of all students by **facilitating the development, articulation, implementation, and stewardship of a vision of learning that is shared and supported by the school community.**	• Engage leaders in a process of inquiry that informs development of a school vision. • Provide a process for developing a shared vision of diversity, interethnic relations, and equity. • Include strategies for leaders to develop authentic participation by diverse stakeholders. • Explicitly connect vision with practical approaches for improving interethnic relations in schools.
Standard 2: A school administrator is an educational leader who promotes the success of all students by **advocating, nurturing, and sustaining a school culture and instructional program conducive to student learning and staff professional growth.**	• Provide a model for leaders to understand the development of racial identity and student needs at different stages of growth. • Provide a model for leaders to identify high-priority needs among different school constituencies, recognizing that students need to be safe and secure in order for academic learning to occur. • View both students and adults as continuous learners about diversity, interethnic relations, equity, and social justice. • Explain how these topics can be included both within and alongside more traditional content areas such as math and language arts. • Show how professional development for staff can contribute to the development of positive, interethnic school community.

Table C.1 Continued

ISLLC Standards	*Leading for Diversity Materials*
Standard 3: A school administrator is an educational leader who promotes the success of all students by **ensuring management of the organization, operations, and resources for a safe, efficient, and effective learning environment.**	• Show how proactive school leaders deal with violence, harassment, name calling, and other conflicts that have a racial or ethnic dimension. • Describe organizational structures that promote collaboration among staff and greater personalization of the learning environment for students. • Explain what a diverse staff can contribute to a school. • Describe how proactive leaders recruit and retain diverse staff members.
Standard 4: A school administrator is an educational leader who promotes the success of all students by **collaborating with families and community members, responding to diverse community interests and needs, and mobilizing community resources.**	• Provide guidance for leaders to identify and assess constraints and supports outside the school. • Show how proactive leaders reach out beyond the school to create partnerships and collaborations with local, regional, and international resources to improve learning and enhance relationships among diverse students.
Standard 5: A school administrator is an educational leader who promotes the success of all students by **acting with integrity, fairness, and in an ethical manner.**	• Describe how proactive leaders deal with ethical dilemmas involving race or ethnicity. • Guide leaders in clarifying their own values regarding diversity, equity, and social justice so they can act from a strong base. • Show how the recognition of multiple perspectives can shape the ways we define and resolve problems.
Standard 6: A school administrator is an educational leader who promotes the success of all students by **understanding, responding**	• Show how larger forces in education, such as the standards and accountability movement, can be used to

194 HOW SCHOOL
LEADERS
PROMOTE
POSITIVE
INTERETHNIC
RELATIONS

Table C.1   Continued

ISLLC Standards	Leading for Diversity Materials
to, and influencing the larger political, social, economic, legal, and cultural context.	promote greater attention to diversity, interethnic relations, and equity.
	• View economic trends such as globalization as contributing to a homogenizing trend that devalues diversity and ethnic identity and, at the same time, requires increased understanding and cooperation among diverse individuals and groups.

SOURCE: Interstate School Leaders Licensure Consortium (1996).

References

Allport, G. (1954). *The nature of prejudice.* Cambridge, MA: Addison-Wesley.

American Anthropological Association. (1998, September). AAA statement on race. *Anthropology Newsletter* (p. 3). Retrieved March 22, 2002 from www.aaanet.org/stmts/racepp.htm

Anderson, Gary. (1998). Toward authentic participation: Deconstructing the discourses of participatory reforms in education. *American Educational Research Journal, 35*(4), 571-603.

Aronson, E. (2000). *The jigsaw classroom: A cooperative learning technique.* Retrieved March 22, 2002 from http://www.jigsaw.org.

Asian and Pacific Islander Task Force. (2001). *2000-2001 year-end report.* Retrieved March 22, 2002 from www.apitaskforce.org.

Banks, J. (1989). Multicultural education: Characteristics and goals. In J. Banks & C. M. Banks (Eds.), *Multicultural education: Issues and perspectives* (pp. 2-26). Boston: Allyn & Bacon.

Banks, J. (1997). *Teaching strategies for ethnic studies* (6th ed.). Boston: Allyn & Bacon.

Bartolomé, L., & Maccdo, D. (1997). Dancing with bigotry: The poisoning of racial and ethnic identities. *Harvard Educational Review, 67*(2), 222-244.

Bay Area Coalition of Essential Schools. (1999). Data-based inquiry and decision making. *On principles, 5*(1), 1, 8-10.

Bell, L. A. (1997). Theoretical foundations for social justice education. In M. Adams, L. A. Bell, & P. Griffin (Eds.), *Teaching for diversity and social justice: A sourcebook* (pp. 3-15). New York: Routledge.

Berman, P., & McLaughlin, M. W. (1978). *Federal programs supporting educational change (Vol. VII: Implementing and sustaining innovations).* Santa Monica, CA: Rand Corporation.

Bigelow, B., & Miner, B. (1994). Creating classrooms for equity and social justice. In B. Bigelow & M. Miner (Eds.), *Rethinking our classrooms: Teaching for equity and social justice* (pp. 4-5). Milwaukee, WI: Rethinking Schools.

Bowles, S., & Gintis, H. (1976). *Schooling in capitalist America: Educational reform and the contradictions of economic life.* New York: Basis Books.

Brehm, S. S., & Kassim, S. M. (1996). *Social psychology* (3rd ed.). Boston: Houghton Mifflin.

Brisk, M. E. (1998). *Bilingual education: From compensatory to quality schooling.* Mahwah, NJ: Lawrence Erlbaum.

Brown v. Board of Education of Topeka, 347 U.S. 483 (1954).

196
HOW SCHOOL
LEADERS
PROMOTE
POSITIVE
INTERETHNIC
RELATIONS

Coleman, P., & Deutsch, M. (1995). The mediation of interethnic conflict in schools. In W. Hawley & A. Jackson (Eds.), *Toward a common destiny: Improving race and ethnic relations in America* (pp. 371-396). San Francisco: Jossey-Bass.

Cross, W. E. (1991). *Shades of Black: Diversity in African American identity.* Philadelphia: Temple University Press.

Delpit, L. (1996). *Other people's children: Cultural conflict in the classroom.* New York: New Press.

Erickson, F. (1986). Qualitative methods in research on teaching. In M. Wittrock (Ed.), *Handbook of research on teaching* (3rd ed.). New York: Collier Macmillan.

Erickson, F. (1987). Transformation and school success: The politics and culture of educational achievement. *Anthropology and Education Quarterly, 18*(4), 335-356.

Fine, M., Weis, L., and Powell, L. (1997). Communities of difference: A critical look at desegregated spaces created for and by youth. *Harvard Educational Review, 67*(2), 247-284.

Fraenkel, J., Wallen, N., & Sawin, E. (1999). *Visual statistics: A conceptual primer.* Boston: Allyn & Bacon.

Freire, P. (1970). *Pedagogy of the oppressed.* New York: Continuum.

Fullan, M. (1999). *Change forces: The sequel.* Philadelphia: Falmer.

Gardner, H. (1985). *Frames of mind: The theory of multiple intelligences.* New York: Basic Books.

Genesee, F. (Ed.). (1999). *Program alternatives for linguistically diverse students (CREDE educational practice report #1).* Washington, DC: Center for Applied Linguistics.

Glasser, W. (1986). *Choice theory in the classroom.* New York: Harper Perennial.

Glesne, C., & Peshkin, A. (1992). *Becoming qualitative researchers: An introduction.* Plains, NY: Longman.

Goetz, J., & LeCompte, M. (1984). *Ethnography and qualitative design in educational research.* Orlando, FL: Academic Press.

González, N. (1995a). Processual approaches to multicultural education. *Journal of Applied Behavioral Science, 31*(3), 234-244.

González, N. (Ed.) (1995b). Educational innovation: Learning from households (Special Issue on the Funds of Knowledge Project). *Practicing Anthropology, 17*(3), 3-6.

Grant, C., & Sleeter, C. (1989). Race, class, gender, exceptionality, and educational reform. In J. Banks & C. Banks (Eds.), *Multicultural education: Issues and perspectives* (pp. 46-66). Boston: Allyn & Bacon.

Harchar, R. L., & Hyle, A. E. (1996). Collaborative power: A grounded theory of administrative instructional leadership in the elementary school. *Journal of Education, 34*(3), 28-40.

Haury, D., & Milbourne, L. (1999). Should children be tracked in math or science? *ERIC Review, 6*(2), 13-15.

Helms, J. E. (Ed.). (1990). *Black and white racial identity: Theory, research, and practice.* Westport, CT: Greenwood.

Hensel, C. (1996). *Telling our selves: Ethnicity and discourse in Southwestern Alaska.* New York: Oxford University Press.

Henze, R. C. (2001). Curricular approaches to developing positive interethnic relations. *Journal of Negro Education, 68*(4), 529-549.

Henze, R. C., & Hauser, M. E. (1999). *Personalizing culture through anthropological and educational perspectives (CREDE educational practice report #4).*

Washington, DC: Center for Applied Linguistics. Retrieved March 22, 2002 from www.cal.org/ crede/pubs/#epr1.

Henze, R., Katz, A., Norte, N., Sather, S., and Walker, E. (1999). *Leading for diversity: A study of how school leaders develop positive interethnic relations.* Oakland, CA: ARC Associates. Retrieved March 24, 2002, from www.arcassociates.org/leading.

Holt, D. (Ed.). (1993). *Cooperative learning: A response to cultural and linguistic diversity.* McHenry, IL: Delta Systems.

Interstate School Leaders Licensure Consortium (Ed.). (1996). Standards for school leaders. In *Educational leadership* (pp. 97-113). San Francisco: Jossey-Bass.

Katz, A. M. (2001). Keeping it real: Personalizing school experiences for diverse learners to create harmony and minimize interethnic conflict. *Journal of Negro Education, 68*(4), 496-510.

Kluckhohn, C. (1949). *Mirror for man.* New York: McGraw-Hill.

Kreisberg, L. (1998). *Constructive conflicts: From escalation to resolution.* New York: Rowman & Littlefield.

Krovetz, M. L. (1999). *Fostering resiliency: Expecting all students to use their minds and hearts well.* Thousand Oaks, CA: Corwin.

Lambert, L. (1998). *Building leadership capacity in schools.* Alexandria, VA: Association for Supervision and Curriculum Development.

Lau v. Nichols, 414 U.S. 563-572 (1974).

Lindsey, R., Robins, K. N., and Terrell, R. (1999). *Cultural proficiency: A manual for school leaders.* Thousand Oaks, CA: Corwin.

Lipman, P. (1998). *Race, class and power in school restructuring.* Albany: State University of New York Press.

Lucas, T. (1997). *Into, through, and beyond secondary schools: Critical transitions for immigrant youths.* McHenry, IL: Delta Systems and Center for Applied Linguistics.

Lustig, D. F. (1994, November). *"Sometimes you just have to fight:" Honor, status, and violence among teen mothers.* Paper presented at the American Anthropological Association Annual Meeting, Atlanta, Georgia.

Maslow, A. H. (1968). *Toward a psychology of being.* New York: Van Nostrand Reinhold.

McCall, J. (1994). *The principal's edge.* Larchmont, NY: Eye on Education.

McIntosh, P. (1989, July/August). White privilege: Unpacking the invisible knapsack. *Peace and Freedom Magazine,* pp. 10-12.

Mehan, H. (1996). *Constructing school success: The consequences of untracking low achieving students.* Cambridge, UK: Cambridge University Press.

Miles, M., & Huberman, M. (1994). *Qualitative data analysis* (2nd ed.). Thousand Oaks, CA: Sage.

Montagu, A. (1997). *Man's most dangerous myth: The fallacy of race* (6th ed.). Walnut Creek, CA: Altamira Press. (Original work published in 1942.)

Murphy, J. (1992). *The landscape of leadership preparation: Reframing the education of school administrators.* Thousand Oaks, CA: Corwin.

Mydans, S. (1992, April 29). Los Angeles policemen acquitted in taped beating. *New York Times.* Retrieved April 11, 2002, from www.nytimes.com/learning/general/onthisday/990429onthisday_big.html#article.

Nahavandi, A. (1997). *The art and science of leadership.* Upper Saddle River, NJ: Prentice Hall.

198 HOW SCHOOL
LEADERS
PROMOTE
POSITIVE
INTERETHNIC
RELATIONS

Nelson, J. (1996). *Positive discipline.* New York: Ballantine.

Nieto, S. (1996). *Affirming diversity: The sociopolitical context of multicultural education.* White Plains, NY: Longman.

Noguera, P. (1995). Preventing and producing violence: A critical analysis of responses to school violence. *Harvard Educational Review, 65*(2), 189-212.

Norte, E. (2001a, January 30). *Power and perception in schools.* Workshop presented at Lodi Unified School District, Lodi, California.

Norte, E. (2001b). "Structures beneath the skin:" How school leaders use their power and authority to create institutional opportunities for developing positive interethnic communities. *Journal of Negro Education, 68*(4), 466-485.

Oakes, J. (1985). *Keeping track.* New Haven, CT: Yale University Press.

Olsen, L., & Jaramillo, A. (1999). *Turning the tides of exclusion: A guide for educators and advocates for immigrant students.* Oakland, CA: California Tomorrow.

Omi, M. (2000, March 14). *Transforming race relations: The state of Asian Pacific America.* Paper presented at LEAP Roundtable, San Francisco.

Park, E. (2000, March 14). *Transforming race relations: The state of Asian Pacific America.* Paper presented at LEAP Roundtable, San Francisco.

Patton, M. (1990). *Qualitative evaluation and research methods* (2nd ed.). Newbury Park, CA: Sage.

Pittman, K. (1991, September 30). *A new vision: Promoting youth development* (commissioned paper #3). Testimony presented before the House Select Committee on Children, Youth, and Families. Washington, DC: Academy for Educational Development. Retrieved April 5, 2002, from www.aed.org/index.html.

Rosaldo, R. (1989). *Culture and truth: The remaking of social analysis.* Boston: Beacon.

Sather, S. (2001). Leading, lauding, and learning: Leadership in secondary schools serving diverse populations. *Journal of Negro Education, 68*(4), 511-528.

Senge, P. M. (1990). *The fifth discipline: The art and practice of the learning organization.* New York: Currency Doubleday.

Shaw, V. (1992). *Community building in the classroom.* San Juan Capistrano, CA: Kagan Cooperative Learning.

Simon, J. (1999). *The economic consequences of immigration.* Ann Arbor: University of Michigan Press.

Sleeter, C. (1996). *Multicultural education as social activism.* Albany: SUNY Press.

Spindler, G. (1996, November). Keynote address at the Exploring Culture Institute, San Francisco, California.

Spindler, G., & Spindler, L. (1982). Roger Harker and Schönhausen: From familiar to strange and back again. In G. Spindler (Ed.), *Doing the ethnography of schooling: Educational anthropology in action* (pp. 14-20). New York: Holt, Rinehart & Winston.

Tatum, B. D. (1997). *Why are all the black kids sitting together in the cafeteria? And other conversations about race.* New York: Basic Books.

Tatum, B. D. (1998, December). What do you do when they call you a racist? *National Association of Secondary School Principals Bulletin,* pp. 43-48.

Tatum, B. D. (2001). Which way do we go? Leading for diversity in the new frontier. *Journal of Negro Education, 68*(4), 550-554.

Taylor, K. (2000, October). Equal treatment for student clubs: Do you have the answers? *Principal Leadership*, pp. 68-71.

U.S. Census Bureau. (2001). *Racial and ethnic classifications used in Census 2000 and beyond*. Retrieved March 22, 2002, from www.census.gov/population/www/socdemo/race/racefactcb.html.

Vargas, R. (1985). *Provida leadership: A guide to human/social transformation*. Castro Valley, CA: Author.

Walker, E. (2001). Conflict in the house: Interethnic conflict as change agent, change as conflict instigator. *Journal of Negro Education, 68*(4), 486-495.

Wasley, P. A., Fine, M., Gladden, M., Holldan, E., King, S. P., Mosak, E., & Powell, L. C. (2000). *Small schools: Great strides*. New York: Bank Street College of Education.

Wijeyesinghe, C., Griffin, P., & Love, B. (1997). Racism curriculum design. In M. Adams, L. A. Bell, & P. Griffin (Eds.), *Teaching for diversity and social justice: A sourcebook* (pp. 82-109). New York: Routledge.

Willie, C. V. (1991). *Black and white families: A study in complementarity*. Dix Hills, NJ: General Hall.

Wolcott, H. (1991). Propriospect and the acquisition of culture. *Anthropology and Education Quarterly, 22*(3), 251-273.

Index

202 HOW SCHOOL
LEADERS
PROMOTE
POSITIVE
INTERETHNIC
RELATIONS

108571

204 HOW SCHOOL
LEADERS
PROMOTE
POSITIVE
INTERETHNIC
RELATIONS